World Scientific Series in Computer Science — Vol. 27

# ADVANCES IN ARTIFICIAL INTELLIGENCE

## APPLICATIONS and THEORY

Editor
**James C. Bezdek**
Division of Computer Science
University of West Florida
Pensacola, Florida

World Scientific
*Singapore • New Jersey • London • Hong Kong*

*Published by*

World Scientific Publishing Co. Pte. Ltd.
P O Box 128, Farrer Road, Singapore 9128
*USA office:* 687 Hartwell Street, Teaneck, NJ 07666
*UK office:* 73 Lynton Mead, Totteridge, London N20 8DH

**ADVANCES IN ARTIFICIAL INTELLIGENCE – APPLICATIONS AND THEORY**



ISBN 981-02-0525-2

Printed in Singapore by JBW Printers and Binders Pte. Ltd.

# PREFACE

This note introduces you to our special issue consisting of papers which are, in the main, extensions of preliminary work reported in the *Proceedings of the 1989 SPIE Symposium—Applications of Artificial Intelligence VII*, edited by Mohan Trivedi.

I chose six papers each in the applications and theory areas. The applications papers were chosen because each discusses a system that is (or is close to being) a fielded system that solves real problems using one or more AI techniques. The six theory papers included in this issue were selected as representatives of recent advances in various theoretical aspects of AI technology; that is, these articles concern themselves with one or more components of next generation AI systems. My overall plan for the issue was to strike a genuine balance between applications and theory; and I believe the contents of this issue reflect that objective.

Rather than provide a detailed synopsis of the twelve papers, I will be content to indicate their general scope. In the applications group, the set of articles describes the use of expert systems in six richly varied problem domains: computer-aided education, hydrocarbon (oil) exploration, satellite image analysis for oceanography, particle beam accelerator tuning, assessment of predilection to bleeding in tonsillectomy patients, and the design of internal combustion engines. Note especially the *general* areas covered by these contributions: education, energy, physics, control, medicine, and mechanical engineering. This breadth seems to corroborate early beliefs that AI-based technologies will eventually provide a means for representing and solving difficult problems in every domain dominated by human experts.

Papers in the theory group cover a wide spectrum of more basic issues. These papers are devoted to topics that I call "building-block" issues; theories, algorithms, architectures, and software tools that can or will be used for modules within future systems. Areas included in this group: conceptual clustering for non-numerical data, natural language interfaces to object-oriented databases, adaptive planning for air combat maneuvers, a distributed problem-solving paradigm for cooperative computation, and two papers about AI tools—CAUSA for knowledge acquisition, and PRIOPS for knowledge-based system programming. As in the applications group, this set of papers covers a nice range of topics related to theoretical issues in AI: clustering, natural language, adaptive algorithms, distributed processing, knowledge acquisition, and systems programming.

Collectively, then, this issue amounts to a sampler that illustrates: (i) that AI theory continues to advance, just as applications in many domains are beginning to mature; and (ii) the varied and various nature of the aforementioned SPIE conference, which is held annually in Orlando, Florida, USA. The papers were carefully selected, all being first rate, and should satisfy the appetite of almost all readers. I enjoyed preparing the special issue; I certainly encourage you to enjoy reading it.

James C. Bezdek
*University of West Florida, Pensacola*

# CONTENTS

# AN INTELLIGENT IMAGE-BASED COMPUTER-AIDED EDUCATION SYSTEM: THE PROTOTYPE BIRDS

AMOS ABAYOMI DAVID, ODILE THIERY
and MARION CREHANGE

*Centre de Recherche en Informatique de Nancy (CRIN)*
*Campus Scientifique, B P 239*
*54506 Vandoeuvre-Les-Nancy, France*

Received 1 April 1990
Revised 2 August 1990

The authors have studied how to integrate concepts from other fields such as psychology and imagery into Computer-Aided Education (CAE) using Artificial Intelligence (AI).

It is believed that images (graphic or real) may play an important role in learning. However, if images are not to be used only for illustration, it is necessary to employ concepts like those of AI. In this paper, the application of AI concepts in an image-based CAE system is developed and the prototype BIRDS is briefly presented.

The concepts presented here include the pedagogical and psychological aspects of learning, and the importance of images in learning, both as pedagogical objects, and as means for obtaining psychological information about a learner. A student model, defined by the authors, is developed, and its components, construction and use are explained.

*Keywords:* Evocative habit; Learning strategies; Knowledge representation; Student model.

## 1. INTRODUCTION

The aim of inspiring interest, attention and curiosity in schoolchildren has been a great concern of educationalists for many years. One of the good reviews on this subject in particular is that of V. J. Bassan.[1] Among the recent propositions to further this aim, two areas have arisen which are not always in agreement: the use of computers, and the use of images.

The use of computers in education is termed Computer-Aided Education (CAE). Early CAE systems were rigid and employed simple and repetitive teaching methods. Their construction was complex. The introduction of AI brought greater flexibility and facilitated the designing of tools capable of retaining the student's attention. CAE systems that integrate AI concepts are called intelligent tutoring systems.[2,3]

The use of images has proved its efficiency in developing curiosity. Initially, images were used as simple illustrations in the form of cards, maps, photographs, films, or slides. They are now used more and more as the basis for teaching because of the ease with which their sequence can be controlled with the computer. For example, due to its ease of use and ability to provide rapid access to data, the videodisc has become a privileged medium for storing images.

Our work is at the intersection of AI, CAE, and image search. We propose a flexible system, mainly based on images. It is capable of making deductions, and of understanding and helping the student. This is why we call it an Intelligent Image-Based Computer-Aided Education (IICAE) system.

This work originated from a project called EXPRIM (''système EXPert pour la Recherche d'IMage'': Expert system for image retrieval).[4,5] The objective of the project was to develop an expert environment for image retrieval, with the images stored on a videodisc. The process adopted for the project was to divide a search session into steps, each of which was divided into the following three stages:

— the stage of demand formulation by the user, which can be followed by the reformulation of that request by the system, using heuristics and a knowledge base;
— the stage where the user observes and makes choices on presented images that resulted from the previous stage;
— the stage of analysis of the user's choice for a better understanding of the characteristics of desired images.

Our objective was the study of how this process could be used in CAE.

In Sec. 2, we present four principles that are indispensable in a CAE system. We present in Sec. 3 some concepts that are necessary for building an IICAE. These concern how learning can be viewed and how knowledge can be represented. In Sec. 4 we give the architecture of an IICAE system that is highly based on the use of images, and the integration of a student model. The student model, defined and implemented in the prototype BIRDS, is then presented in Sec. 5. We conclude with future developments.

## 2. THE FOUR PRINCIPLES

The study of existing systems led us to define four principal parameters (or principles). These parameters condition teaching. They are defined by the following questions, and illustrated in Fig. 1:

(1) What are the activities or processes involved within a teaching system?
(2) What are the pedagogical objectives?
(3) What is the predominant pedagogical strategy for a given objective?
(4) Given the answers to earlier questions, what are the implementation methods to choose?

### 2.1. Teaching Actions

The actions involved in teaching are to be considered from the learner's point of view as well as from the teacher's. For a learner, the sub-actions involved are principally observation, association of knowledge, and expression of the acquired knowledge. Though the teacher must take into account in his conception the transfer of knowledge and its control, he must also take into account the learner's motivation.

| | |
|---|---|
| **Processes in Education**<br>E.g.<br>Observation<br>Motivation<br>Association of knowledge<br>Transfer of knowledge<br>Expression<br>Control<br>**1** | **Pedagogical Objectives**<br>E.g.<br>Counting from 0–9<br>Gothic architectural structures<br>Recognition of birds<br>**2** |
| **Pedagogical Strategies**<br>E.g.<br>Memorization<br>Discovery<br>Examples<br>Analogy<br>**3** | **Pedagogical Methods**<br>E.g.<br>Simulation<br>Page turning<br>EXPRIM process<br>Multiple-choice questions (MCQ)<br>**4** |

Fig. 1. The four principles to explore.

### 2.2. The Pedagogical Objectives

The definition of the pedagogical objective is an important preliminary point. It must take into account the learner's level. The principal objective may be decomposed so as to elaborate the desired IICAE scenario. For example, if the principal objective is the capacity of counting from 0 to 9, then sub-objectives could be

(a) the ability to recognize the 10 symbols and

(b) the capacity to pronounce them.

### 2.3. Pedagogical Strategies

Learning strategies can be considered from either a pedagogical point of view, or a psychological point of view.

#### 2.3.1. Pedagogical point of view

These are learning strategies (of the learner) that are rather classic. The strategies range from the very simple, like memorization, to the very complex, like "learning by reasoning", including the one that is of most interest to us, that is, "learning by discovery", which can be either simulation or recognition. It should be noted that these strategies are closely linked.

#### 2.3.2. Psychological point of view

We can also consider learning from the psychological point of view.[1,6,7] The first stage in learning and probably the most simple is *observation*. The second stage is the simplest form of *abstraction* as a result of observation; for example, associating words with observed objects. The third stage, *symbolization and reasoning*, is another form of abstraction, but here the learner constructs his own symbols or figures to represent what is observed. The fourth stage is the extension of acquired knowledge for constructing objects which have never been observed. This can be termed *creativity*. These stages are considered as levels of evocative habits by de La Garanderie.[7]

Our interest is centered on how to create a learning environment by implementing these two approaches.

### 2.4. Implementation Methods

The following methods are in common use in CAE: games, multiple-choice questions (MCQ), simulation, etc. Progression within the system can be more or less complicated. In our IICAE system, we allow this progression to be as flexible as possible while keeping to the defined objective and strategy.

## 3. BASIC CONCEPTS FOR CONSTRUCTING AN IICAE SYSTEM

We present briefly in this section, the types of concepts required for constructing an IICAE system and their application.

### 3.1. How Learning Can Be Viewed

Learning can be considered as the activity of acquiring ability or information. What is to be acquired (or more precisely what somebody wants to make part of himself) can be a mental activity or habit. The starting point of all forms of learning consists in transforming concrete elements into their abstract form. The concrete objects are in general visible and when they are not, they can be transformed into their visible form. It is on this observation that we based our approach for the design of an IICAE system.

When the concrete elements are put into images, the learner can then observe them and construct an abstraction of what is observed. It is during the process of observation that learning starts.[1,7] The result of observation depends on the individual observer, because observation is in fact a process of image interpretation. The intellectual activity during the period of observation consists in the association of already acquired knowledge with new knowledge. If the knowledge already acquired is considered as elementary concepts with associations, then one can interpret the intellectual activity as finding new associations of elementary concepts or deriving other concepts from those already acquired.

### 3.2. From the Pedagogical Objective to Knowledge Representation

The pedagogical objective chosen for the prototype BIRDS is to allow the students to cultivate the ability to associate the morphological characteristics of birds with their different types of nutrition. In order to build our knowledge base, we established links between the types of nutrition and the characteristics. In Fig. 2, we give an example of our knowledge in the form of a semantic network.[8] The network is a graph.

In our knowledge representation,we distinguish two types of elementary knowledge: objects and concepts. Objects represent elements that can be seen as images, such as trees, insects, grains, fruits, long leg. Concepts represent abstract elements. They are

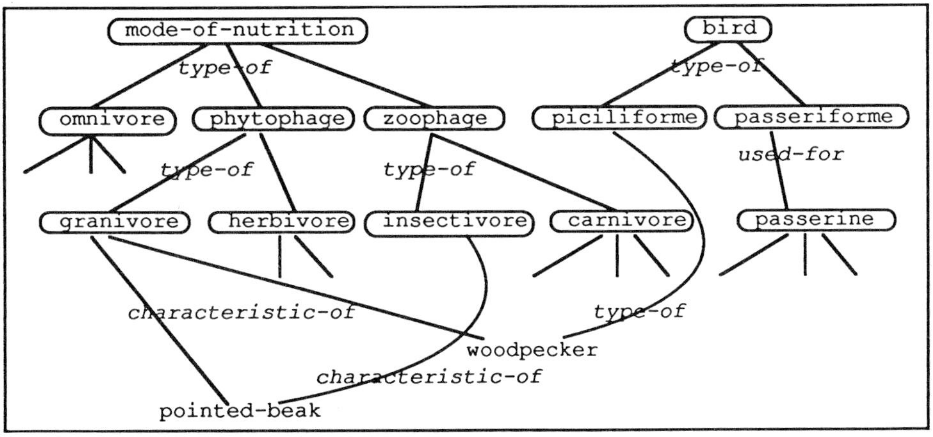


Fig. 2. Semantic network of the knowledge base.

not visible. For example, the term "phytophage" is a concept. However, there are objects that are considered concepts because of their use in a particular context. For example, beak, a visible object, can be considered as a concept if it is not followed by a qualifier (in the natural sciences).

In the network, circled nodes represent concepts or objects that we can consider as elementary knowledge. The arcs/lines represent the relationships between the elementary knowledge. For example, in the network:

— pointed-beak is at the same time a characteristic of *granivorous* and *insectivorous* birds,
— woodpecker is at the same time a type of *granivore* and *piciliforme*,
— "passeriforme" is used for "passerine".

We have chosen a semantic network representation because our principal interest is to know the relationships of the elementary knowledge. We are not preoccupied, for the time being, with other uses of the network. For instance, to obtain the fixed pedagogical objective, we leave out aspects such as property inheritance.

### 3.3. The Use of the Network and the Pedagogical Knowledge

The pedagogical strategy that we implement is the "discovery" type, where observation plays a central role. The chosen implementation method is based on progression within the system in four phases: observation, elementary abstraction, symbolization and reasoning, and creativity. Note that in the "discovery" type of strategy, it is the learner who directs the system. The system tries to understand the needs of the learner so as to guide him, particularly in the symbolization and reasoning phase. The learner gives his needs in the form of demands. For example, if he wants to see images which contain fish, and birds with long beaks, he will type "fish long-beak" as his demand. The system will then try to understand this demand. In order to realize this objective, we implement some heuristics that act on the demand and at the same time on the learner's behavior. We give below two heuristics that are implemented in the system:

*Heuristic 1*: If a term in the learner's demand is more general in sense than another one in the same demand, then remove the most general term, considering the term that is more specific as a more precise demand. For example, if the demand is *''granivore pointed-beak''*, the system will remove *''granivore''*, and consider *''pointed-beak''* as being more precise (cf. Fig. 2). This heuristic attempts to reduce the number of possible responses.

*Heuristic 2 (pedagogical)*: If a term is a concept, then establish a dialog with the learner so as to know the specific terms that allowed him to infer this concept. For example, if the demand is *''phytophage''*, either the learner really knows the significance of this term in the natural sciences, or he wants to have a better understanding of the term. In this case, there should be a dialog between the system and the learner.

We realize the importance of the need to develop an IICAE tool that is based on various pedagogical strategies. This is why we have developed some scenarios using different forms of learning (learning by ''memorization'', by ''instruction'', and by ''analogy''). These scenarios are implanted in the prototype BIRDS with the aim of helping the student to move from one stage to another during learning (cf. Sec. 2.3.).

## 4. THE ARCHITECTURE OF AN IICAE SYSTEM

Figure 3 shows the architecture that we defined for an IICAE system. It is composed of four modules.

— The *domain module* contains all knowledge related to the domain under study, such as the semantic network and the descriptive base (the description of the images used).

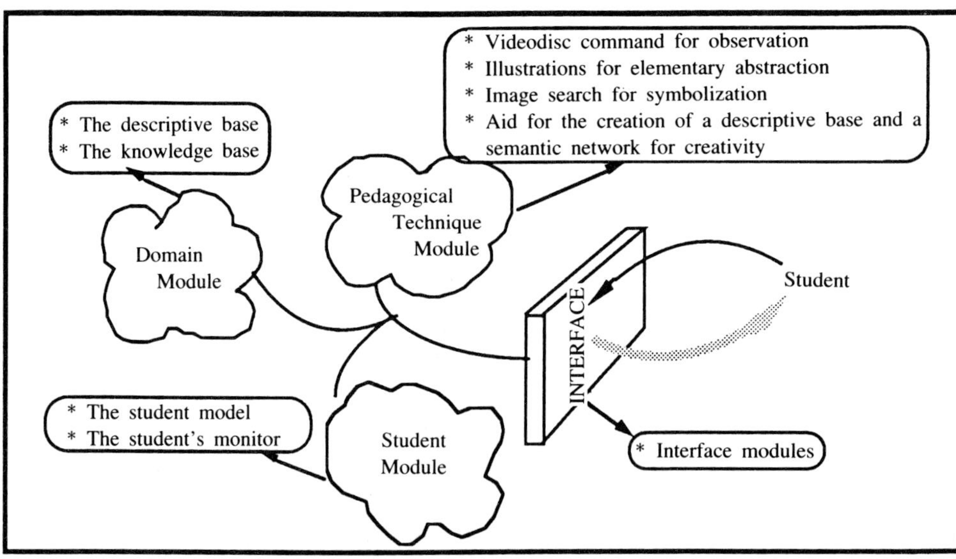


Fig. 3. The architecture of an IICAE.

— The *pedagogical technique module* defines the heuristics, the objective and the techniques of progression within the system.
— In order to individualize and be capable of evaluating the performance of the learner (student) as well as that of the system, the system should allow the creation of the *student module*. This module contains mainly the learner's model which is the representation or the profile of the learner. In traditional education, where the tutor has 20 to 30 students, individual attention has long been felt as an important means for achieving improved academic performance. Many studies have been devoted to the learner's model.[7,9–12] These concern what the module should be and for what it should be used. In our project, we want to use the student module mainly to meet the pedagogical need: to understand the student's need, to help change the pedagogical objective and to evaluate him and the system.
— The use of the system will be facilitated by the use of an *intelligent interface*.

## 5. THE STUDENT MODEL

Figure 4 shows two student models, proposed by de La Garanderie[7] and Self,[11] which served as the basis of our study. Our model integrates the aspects of cognitive science and that of pedagogy. The model that we propose is represented by the following components (or parameters):

$$(R, \quad A, \quad F, \quad C, \quad E, \quad N)\ .$$

These parameters allow us to effect some pedagogical functions and to follow the learner's cognitive evolution.

| **Model proposed by de La Garanderie** | **Model proposed by Self** |
|---|---|
| P1 : Observation | P : Procedural knowledge |
| P2 : Elementary abstraction | C : Conceptual knowledge |
| P3 : Symbolization and reasoning | T : Learner's particularities |
| P4 : Creativity | H : Historic |
| *(Cognitive science)* | *(Pedagogy)* |

**Our model**
R : Personal references
A : Activities/date of the session
F : Factual knowledge
C : Conceptual knowledge
E : The learner's types of error
N : The levels of evocative habits
*(Cognitive science + Pedagogy)*

Fig. 4. The student model and two other propositions.

### 5.1. What the Parameters Represent

R represents the learner's personal references. This parameter is formed initially by:
- the learner's name;
- the learner's age: this parameter can be significant during a long period of follow-up of the learner, by observing the evolution of his evocative habits in relation to his age.

A represents the learner's activities during all the sessions, and the date of the session. This parameter is indispensable for adapting the system to the learner's evocative habit. In fact, the evolution of the learner's evocative habit can only be measured over a long period; hence the need for the date of all the sessions.

F represents the learner's factual knowledge. By factual knowledge, we mean concrete or elementary knowledge or facts (as interpreted by the teacher) in the domain of study. For example, knowledge (such as objects) that is visible is considered as factual in the prototype.

C represents the learner's conceptual knowledge. By conceptual knowledge, we mean knowledge related to concepts. It is knowledge abstractions and is generally invisible.

E represents the learner's types of error. There are two types of error—lexical error and associative error. These two types of error occur in all domains. Lexical errors have the same form in all domains: omission, insertion, replacement of one or several characters. Associative errors do not have the same form in all domains. In certain domains, they occur by the use of a single term (for example, a term that has no meaning in the domain even though it is correctly written). In some other domains, they concern the application of bad rules in the resolution of problems (for example, in mathematics) or by wrong association of two terms using a semantic link (for example, to say that a hawk is a type of piscivore when it is a carnivore).

N represents the learner's evocative habit levels. In the prototype BIRDS the pedagogical module is constructed in such a way as to reflect each evocative habit. By this method, we can know the learner's evocative habit by observing his activities inside each module.

### 5.2. Implementation in the Prototype BIRDS

The learner's model has a very important role in the prototype. Its parameters allow us to determine the learner's evocative habit and therefore to propose some aids. For example, we use the information contained in the learner's model to gradually draw him into another cognitive phase (or another level of evocative habit), or to propose some scenario that allows him to correct his errors.

The prototype is developed on a PC/AT using C language and the inference engine OPS5+. We use the videodisc called *British Garden Birds*, edited by BBC London. The superimposing system that we have developed allows us to use a single screen (the television) on which images from the videodisc and graphics from the PC can be displayed.

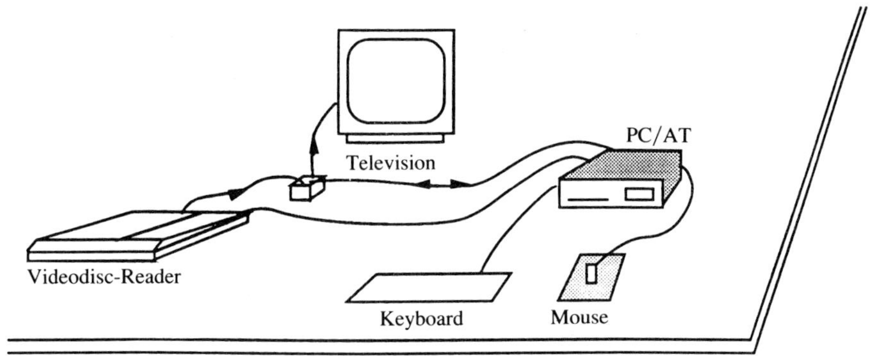


Fig. 5. The working environment.

## 6. CONCLUSION

We have tried by this work to marry cognitive science with computer science and pedagogical concepts. The pedagogical objective that we defined constitutes an objective in the secondary school. It is therefore a means for validating our learner's model. We are carrying out an experiment with the prototype in a school at Nancy in France, in collaboration with a teacher who has been our expert in the natural sciences since the beginning of the work. We believe that the model is applicable to any category of learner, from pre-school to university level, since the base of our concept is both pedagogical and cognitive.

## REFERENCES

1. V. J. Bassan, *Comment Intéresser l'enfant à l'école*, Presses Universitaires de France, Paris, 1976, pp. 17–75.
2. C. Hermant, *Enseigner apprendre avec l'ordinateur*, Paris, Cedic/Nathan, Paris, 1985, pp. 15–38.
3. M. Hennart, J. F. Berthon and M. Binse, *Ecrire des logiciels pédagogiques*, Cedic/Nathan, Paris, 1986, pp. 41–75.
4. M. Créhange *et al.*, "Semantics of user interface for image retrieval: Possibility theory and learning techniques applied on two prototypes", Congrès RIAO, Boston, Mar. 1988.
5. G. Halin, "Apprentissage pour la recherche interactive et progressive d'image: processus EXPRIM et prototype RIVAGE", Thèse de doctorat en Informatique, Centre de Recherche en Informatique de Nancy, Oct. 1989.
6. H. Bestougeff and J. P. Fargette, *Enseignement et ordinateur*, Cedic/Nathan, Paris, 1982, pp. 19–82.
7. A. De la Garanderie, *Les Profils Pédagogiques: Discerner les Aptitudes Scolaires*, Le Centurion Collection Paidoguides, Paris, 1988, pp. 70–157.
8. M. J. Coombs, *Developments in Expert Systems*, Academic Press, Glasgow, Scotland, 1983.
9. J. F. Nicaud and M. Vivet, "Les tuteurs intelligents: Realisations et tendances de recherche", TSI, Vol. 7, No. 1, Dunod/AFCET, Paris, 1988.

10. J. C. Durand and G. Moitrieux, *Lire Les Images*, CRDP Nancy, France, 1979.
11. J. Self, "Student models: What are they?", IFIP/TC3, FRASCATI, Eds. R. Lewis and P. Ecroli, North Holland, May 1987.
12. C. Dede, "A review and synthesis of recent research in intelligent computer-assisted instruction", *Int. J. Man-Machine Studies* **24** (1986) 329–353.

**Amos Abayomi David** obtained his B.Sc. in computer science from the University of Ibadan, Nigeria, in 1981, and his Ph.D. in computer science from the Institut National Polytechnique de Lorraine (INPL), Nancy, France, in 1990. He is now a research lecturer at the computer science laboratory centre, CRIN, Nancy, where he works on the application of artificial intelligence and images in computer-aided education. He is also a member of the research team EXPRIM (système EXPert pour la Recherche d'IMage: Expert system for image retrieval) at CRIN.

**Odile Thiery** obtained her Ph.D. degree in computer science in 1985, for work on the specification of information systems. She is the Director of Studies of IMAGe, Nancy. She has been working since 1985 on image-based computer-aided education, and is a member of EXPRIM.

**Marion Crehange** obtained her Ph.D. degree in computer science in 1975 for her work on data independence in databases. She is Director of the computer science department of IUT, Nancy. She is also Director of the research team EXPRIM. She works especially on interactivity in multimedia document retrieval.

# PLAYMAKER: A KNOWLEDGE-BASED APPROACH TO CHARACTERIZING HYDROCARBON PLAYS*

GAUTAM BISWAS, XUDONG YU
and WILLIAM HAGINS
*Department of Computer Science*
*Vanderbilt University, Nashville, TN 37235, USA*

JAMES BEZDEK
*Division of Computer Science*
*University of West Florida, Pensacola, FL 32514, USA*

JOHN STROBEL, CHRISTOPHER KENDALL
and ROBERT CANNON
*Department of Geology, Department of Computer Science*
*University of South Carolina, Columbia, SC 29208, USA*

Received 1 April 1990

This paper discusses the design and implementation of PLAYMAKER, a knowledge-based system for characterizing hydrocarbon plays. PLAYMAKER is a component of XX (eXpert eXplorer), a workstation-based tool that aids exploration geologists in a number of different tasks: sediment and carbonate simulation, play and field characterization, retrieval and storage of information in a geological database, comparison of the play or field under study with other fields in the database, and report generation. PLAYMAKER is implemented using MIDST (Mixed Inferencing Dempster-Shafer Tool), a rule-based expert system shell that incorporates mixed-initiative and inexact reasoning based on the Dempster-Shafer evidence combination scheme. This paper discusses the effectiveness of a two-level knowledge base structure adopted for the design and implementation of PLAYMAKER.

*Keywords:* Knowledge-based system; Multi-layer knowledge base; Mixed initiative reasoning; Dempster-Shafer belief functions; Hydrocarbon exploration.

## 1. INTRODUCTION

Oil exploration is a discipline where intuition and experience play a major role in decision making and analysis. A number of geological and exploration tasks can be appropriately handled by knowledge-based techniques. A significant proportion of geological information relevant to oil exploration is symbolic (e.g. lithologies, facies, and structure) rather than quantitative. Even for parameters that have quantitative definitions, such as age, porosity, and permeability, lack of precise information necessitates qualitative rather than quantitative analysis in decision making situations. Moreover, the lack of formal models, and the limitations of the ones that exist, result in exploration geologists developing and using heuristic procedures for problem solving and decision making.

* This research is supported by grants from Amoco, British Petroleum, Japan National Oil Corporation, Mobil, Texaco, and Union Oil.

Over the years a number of expert systems have been developed for use in the hydrocarbon industry. These include systems like PROSPECTOR, DIPMETER ADVISOR, SRPS, Gridding Advisor, EXPAL, muPETROL, and XEOD.[1] In general, however, this technology has not been considered a major success for problem solving applications. Several reasons may have contributed to this:

- A primary problem is the lack of standardized terminology, and the lack of agreement among explorationists in choosing common geological models to describe a phenomena.
- The geologist's expertise is often very regional in nature, and cannot be easily extrapolated to other geographic locations.
- Data used for exploration that comes from sources such as seismic lines, well logs, outcrops, field notes, and maps, is often incomplete, inconsistent, and non-uniform in both quantity and quality.
- The uncertainty that arises from the above characteristics is often ignored, thereby producing false estimates or unjustified confidence in the values of the estimates produced.

There is, however, one class of geological applications where knowledge-based techniques show great potential, viz. expert systems that operate as intelligent front-ends and knowledgeable catalogs to large database management systems. An example of the use of this approach is XEOD,[2] an expert system designed to assist in the identification and classification of microfossils. The eXpert eXplorer (XX) system plays a similar role in hydrocarbon exploration. The aim is to provide a knowledge-based system that facilitates data encapsulation, and which provides "navigational assistance" in acquiring salient data and information from a variety of sources. More specifically, two XX components, PLAYMAKER and CLUSPAK, are designed to play the role of an intelligent aide. They are linked to a catalog of derived data about plays, fields, and hydrocarbon prospects to perform the following tasks:

1. Help users organize available data in characterizing a play, field, or prospect in a standard form that takes into account the uncertainties associated with the source of the information.
2. Help users formulate queries to retrieve information about specific plays from the catalog.
3. Implement clustering schemes for comparing plays, fields, and prospects, which in turn provide the basis for identifying similar plays and fields.

This paper first presents an overview of the architecture of the XX system. The rest of the paper concentrates on PLAYMAKER: the component that aids in characterizing fields and plays. Section 2 reviews the geological model for characterizing fields and plays. Section 3 discusses the design and implementation of this model as a rule-based system. Limitations of the first version motivated the design of a second prototype which is discussed in Section 3.2. Section 4 contains a discussion and directions for future work.

### 1.1. XX: System Components

Figure 1 shows the architecture of the XX system. The major modules are the Graphics Interface, Database Manager, Field Database, PLAYMAKER, SEDPAK, CLUSPAK, and REPORT. SEDPAK is shown linked to the system with a dotted line because it runs as a stand-alone auxiliary to the XX system. Users interact with the system through the System Manager (not shown), which allows selection of various system functions by use of pop-up windows and a mouse. XX currently runs under Unix on engineering workstations, such as SUN 3 and SUN 4, DEC 3100, and APOLLO DN 3000. Graphics are built using the X Windows System,[3] and the code is primarily written in the C and Common LISP programming languages. The system is not a monolith. Rather, each of its components (System Manager, Database Manager, PLAYMAKER, CLUSPAK, SEDPAK, and REPORT) executes as a separate Unix process, thereby minimizing memory demands made by foreground processes.[4] Thus, the components of the system can be developed and tested autonomously, making system integration much more straightforward than if the system were developed as one large program.

The startup screen for the XX system utilizes pop-up menus. The user chooses to initiate a description of a new play, or to continue working on an existing play by selecting the appropriate function with a mouse. Each selection causes a new menu to pop up, and further selection from the subset of functions associated with each major function can be initiated. In this mode no keyboard activity is needed unless actual descriptive text is to be entered or a report is to be written. Processes for the secondary functions of the XX system will already be executing, e.g. the Database

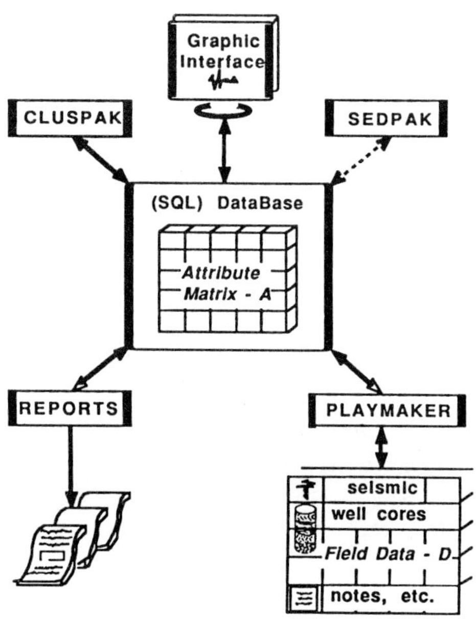


Fig. 1. XX system architecture.

Manager, or they may be forked,[4] e.g. CLUSPAK. The interface between processes is accomplished by sockets,[4] so that messages can pass between processes asynchronously. Host systems are designed for resident XX application and database files. The X Windows System (version 11.4) environment provides remote access to the host system from any location. Our goal has been to make the system as modular as possible, enabling further enhancements to one component with as few side effects as possible.

The rest of this section contains a brief overview of the components involved in play characterization and analogical analysis: the Attribute Matrix, the Database Manager, and CLUSPAK. A detailed description of PLAYMAKER is presented in Sec. 3. Other components of the XX system, e.g. SEDPAK, have been discussed in detail elsewhere.[5] A preliminary prototype of the Report Generator is discussed in Ref. 6.

### 1.1.1. Attribute Matrix (system kernel)

The primary repository of conceptual information is called the Attribute Matrix (matrix A, Fig. 1). Each column in A represents a previously explored oil field or a field that is currently being investigated. The rows of A are the attributes or exploration keys that are derived from structural and sedimentological exploration of a region, and relate to a field or prospect's reservoir, source, and seal. Figure 2 depicts the structure of a portion of the Attribute Matrix A.

The Attribute Matrix is effectively a relational database, and is linked to a rule-based system called PLAYMAKER that helps exploration geologists build each play column (hence the name). Associated with each geological attribute are a number of values that the attribute can assume. For example, the attribute *Depositional Setting*, can take on one of three values: *basin*, *slope*, and *shelf*. The attribute-value definitions can be hierarchical. Therefore, each of the above values can be specified in more detail, e.g. the basin can be further characterized in terms of the *distal*, *mid*, and *proximal* basins. The advantage of this is that depending on the data available, the system can then record information at various levels of detail. (For example, see the

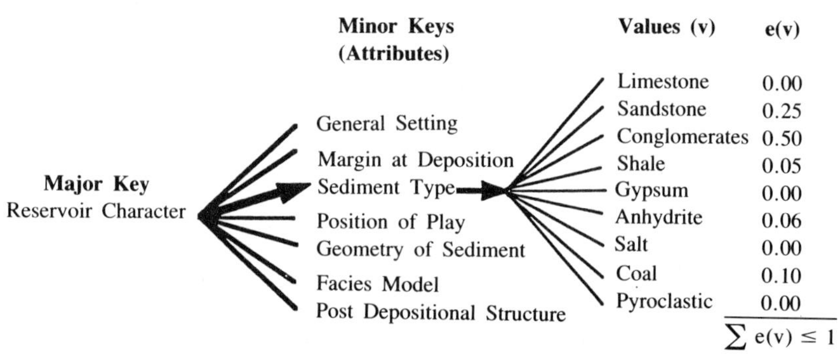


Fig. 2. Partial hierarchical structure of Attribute Matrix A.

*Clastic Facies* hierarchy shown in Fig. 5.) Each attribute value for a field has a numerical measure of belief or confidence in the value associated with it. This belief value is computed by PLAYMAKER, and will be discussed in greater detail later. Depending on the needs and desires of the user, the attribute matrix might contain all the plays in a geographic area, such as the North Slope of Alaska; or it might include all of the giant oil fields of the world.

### 1.1.2. Database Manager

The textual and numeric data in the attribute matrix are stored in a relational database. The Database Manager (DBM) performs insertions, deletions, and retrievals from the database using the SQL queries.[7] All database functions are centralized in this module of the system. We emphasize that although our system uses INGRES as the developmental DBM, the system can be interfaced with any relational database (e.g. ORACLE) that accepts SQL queries. Thus, the system is transportable to a wide variety of corporate database structures.

### 1.1.3. REPORT

REPORT enables the analyst to prepare a report describing characteristics of the target play and its analogs. The system examines the attributes of the target play, and based upon their values, it prepares a description of the play. Parts of the report are automatically generated by values associated with play attributes. The analyst may need to add to this report, so REPORT provides the standard editing functions of a word processor. Construction of a baseline report which will serve as a template for fields and plays in the attribute matrix is underway. Then, when the system is instructed to generate a report about a particular field or play, it will examine the attribute values for this field or play, and refill slots in the template as needed. REPORT is written as a stand alone LISP program, and will have a limited capability to learn how a particular company or user wants its exploration reports configured from examples. Each learning session will result in an updated report template which will then form the basic template for report generation for any field in the attribute matrix.

### 1.1.4. CLUSPAK

CLUSPAK is the module of XX that endows it with one of its major capabilities: assistance to the explorationist in reasoning by analogy. An important component in an exploration geologist's decision making about the potential of a prospect is a comparative process with past successes (and failures!). XX provides CLUSPAK as a tool for mimicking this facility. This package provides users with a means for exploring various clustering tendencies which may exist in (subsets of) columns of the attribute matrix. CLUSPAK combines conceptual and numerical clustering techniques to find known fields and plays in the resident database, that possess properties similar to the target play or prospect. Queries about analogs to target plays can be constrained in various ways, such as, but not limited to, analogs over: a single basin, a geographical region (e.g. the Gulf of Mexico), fields that possess similar properties over some subset of attributes, and so on.

## 2. THE GEOLOGICAL MODEL

Prospect analysis in the oil industry has evolved through time. In the earlier part of the century, wells were drilled wherever oil was found to seep out of the ground. Present day methods include structural analysis in the area of interest to identify traps, and facies analysis to locate subtle sedimentary variations related to sedimentary traps. Data for such analysis come from outcrops, well logs, and seismic lines. Given current technology and data collection resources available, a comprehensive method for prospect generation would be basin analysis. Using basin analysis the geologist tries to understand the geological history of the basin and determine where potential source rocks and traps could be located in the basin. On the basis of this more extensive geological understanding, drilling strategies can be recommended. The PLAYMAKER geological model follows this basin analysis scheme.

The geological model of PLAYMAKER aids exploration geologists in organizing information extracted from data sources, such as interpreted seismic cross sections, well logs, cores, and outcrops so that the characteristics essential to determining the hydrocarbon potential of a play or prospect can be determined. Some of these characteristics, such as the sediment type, geometry, and facies models, relate to most of the essential components of a hydrocarbon bearing prospect: the source rock, reservoir, and seal. Other characteristics, such as the tectonic setting, the structural style, and history of the basin in which the prospect or play is located, provide background information that helps in further understanding the play or prospect. Still others are specific to individual components, such as the qualitative parameters that allow geologists to predict reservoir porosity and permeability, the nature of the seal, and organic content of the source rock.

Relations between interpreted data sources and the required play characteristics are necessarily judgemental. They are developed into if-then rules with associated belief values to express the strength of the judgemental associations. Belief values are defined using the Dempster-Shafer framework,[8] and Dempster's combining formula is adopted to integrate the effects of individual pieces of observed evidence in determining the beliefs associated with overall play characteristics. The nature and reliability of the source which contributes the information (e.g. seismic lines usually provide very reliable information about subsurface features, but are poor indicators of vertical and lateral grain size variations) is also taken into account while designing rules. Another important feature incorporated into the model is heuristic schemes that provide the ability to deal with contradictory information.

## 3. DESIGN AND IMPLEMENTATION

PLAYMAKER assumes that the geologist interacting with the system has interpreted seismic, wells, and/or outcrop data available at the start of the consultation process. Following the geologic model, the system first attempts to characterize the basin in which the field or prospect is located by determining basin setting, history, and structural style of the trap. This general information forms the context for the comparison process which is used to retrieve analogs.[9] The second group of characteristics PLAYMAKER handles includes those for describing the source, seal, and the reservoir: sediment geometries, sediment lithologies, facies, and depositional setting. These features form the core for the comparison scheme. The third class of criteria PLAYMAKER infers deals with even more specific information—total organic content of the source rock, basin thermal history, reservoir size, porosity, and permeability, and seal impermeability. Whereas detailed information about these features could lead to quantitative estimates of oil reserves, in most situations the information available lends itself only to qualitative analysis and a rank ordering of the possible capacity of a new prospect with respect to already explored fields.

The PLAYMAKER system is implemented using MIDST,[10] a rule-based expert system shell for mixed-initiative reasoning. The first prototype of PLAYMAKER used the shell's facility to create partitioned rule bases so that the overall characterization problem could be broken down into component sub-problems. The idea was to improve overall inferencing efficiency by partitioning, however, once the prototype was complete a number of limitations were discovered. As a result, both the MIDST shell and PLAYMAKER have been redesigned into a more effective system. Section 3.1 discusses the design and implementation of Prototype 1 of PLAYMAKER, and Sec. 3.2 presents Prototype 2 of the system.

### 3.1. Prototype 1: Design and Implementation

Figure 3 illustrates the partitioning structure developed for Prototype 1 of PLAYMAKER. As discussed earlier, the initial partitions determine the quality of the *information sources: seismic*, *wells*, and *outcrops*, and the *general information* that pertains to the region in and around the prospect: *basin setting*, *basin history*, and *structure*. The rest of Fig. 3 illustrates the partitioning structure applicable to the *reservoir*; similar partitioning structures define information gathering for the *seal* and *source*. Note that the transfer of control between partitions implemented as simple rules allows branching into different partitions depending on the nature of information available and the conclusions drawn in previous partitions. A better picture of the overall effectiveness of this partitioning scheme is obtained from the case studies on actual field runs provided in Refs. 1 and 11.

The inferencing scheme uses a combination of forward and backward chaining to permit a mixed-initiative dialog. A belief function scheme based on Dempster-Shafer theory incorporates uncertainty arising from the reliability of the data sources and the judgemental nature of the expert-supplied rules. Rules in individual partitions are compiled into a network that facilitates efficient matching and retrieval both in the forward and backward chaining situations. This provides a network structure for propagating belief values from evidence to conclusions by means of an efficient computational algorithm. Details of the network structure are provided in Refs. 12 and 13. A set of graphics-based screens implemented in X Windows form the core for interactions with the user. Each screen is menu-based; it displays a query, possible responses to the query, and a set of icons that help explain query concepts. Users can

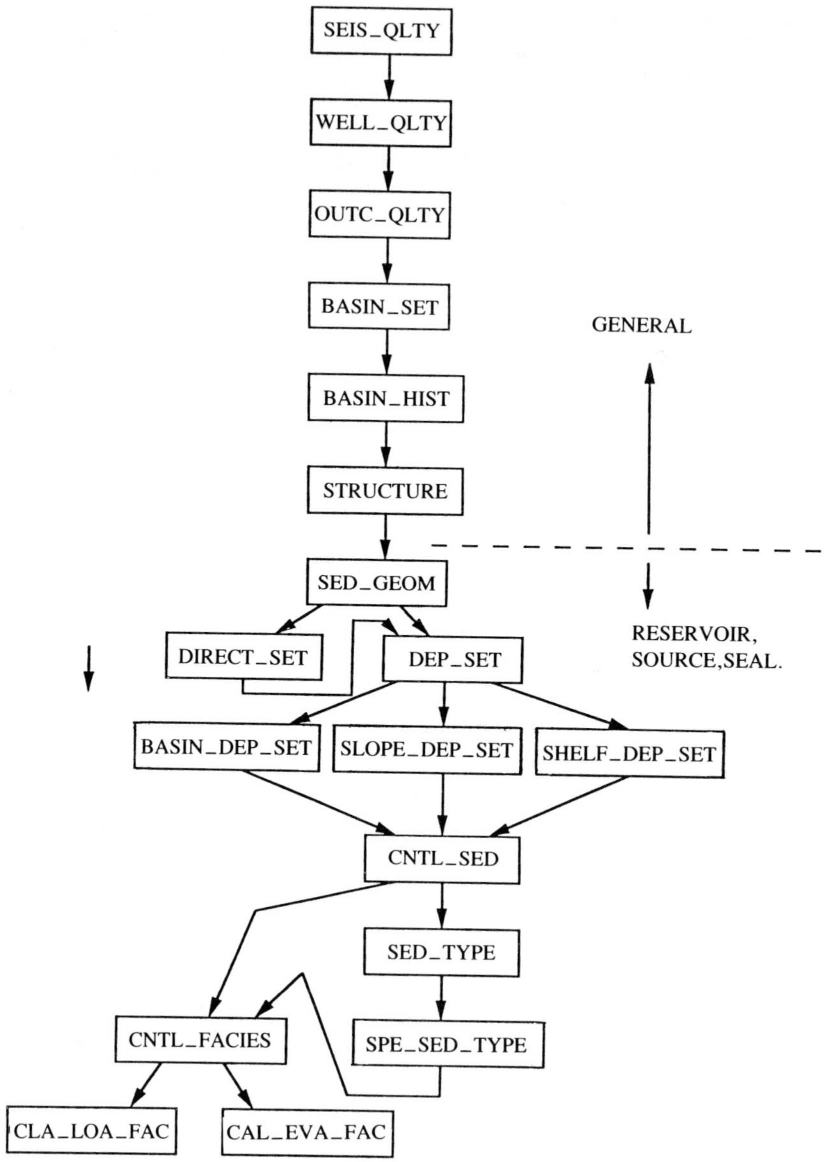


Fig. 3. Partitioning structure of PLAYMAKER (version 1).

pick responses from the menu of choices, and assign belief values to individual choices. An example of a menu-based query screen appears in Fig. 4.

In addition to an efficient implementation of the mixed-initiative reasoning scheme, MIDST also provides a sophisticated rule editor that allows domain experts to create, delete, and modify the partition structure, and also create, delete, and modify rules

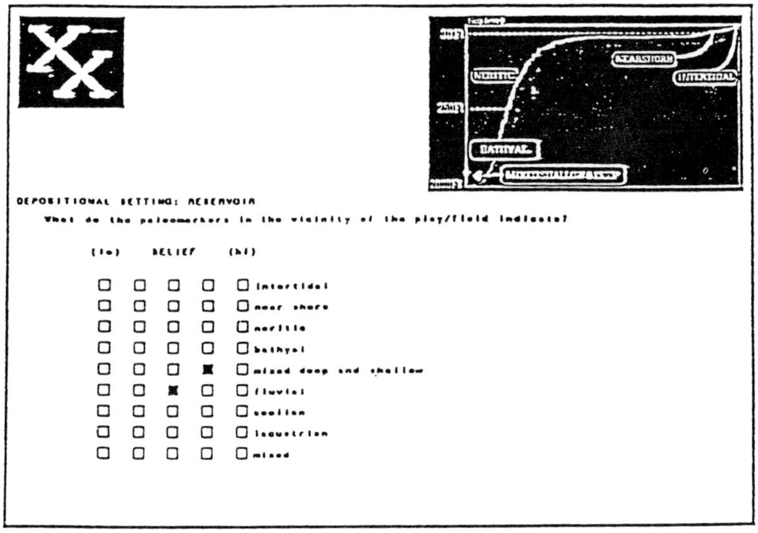

Fig. 4. Example of a menu-based query screen.

within partitions. An important feature of rule creation and modification is the use of a *ranking scheme* that facilitates the creation of belief functions.[14] The current prototype contains about 2,300 rules subdivided into the partitions (conceptual categories) illustrated in Fig. 3. Prototype 1 was tested on a number of known Gulf Coast fields.[11]

A number of important issues became apparent during the testing process. Some of these issues had to do with knowledge-based refinement because results produced by modifications: additions, deletions, and fine tuning of rule conditions, conclusions, and belief values. We are currently looking into techniques for simplifying and automating this process.

A second set of issues related more to knowledge base structures and knowledge organization. It was found that information acquisition from the user was quite repetitive and often a little disjointed. This was because different partitions (e.g. depositional setting, lithologies, and facies) sometimes required observed geological parameters in different forms, whereas all of these could in fact be inferred from a common primary data characteristic. Furthermore, inferences drawn in one partition, such as the lithology type and depositional setting, provided clues about relevant characteristics in other partitions, such as facies, and these relations were not fully exploited. As a result, the consultation process was often too long and appeared repetitive. In addition, because related data was not all acquired at the same time, the dialog appeared disjointed. This lack of focus annoyed and distracted geologists using the system.

### 3.2. Prototype 2: Design and Implementation

The second prototype overcomes some of the limitations attendant with the first prototype. The *sequential* partitioning scheme adopted in Prototype 1 has been replaced by a *hierarchical representational scheme* that defines a more complex multi-linked structure between various geological characteristics. This scheme allows for better representation of the relations among attributes, and for easier propagation of information (both user-supplied and that inferred by the system) among partitions to avoid repetitive querying. Among other benefits, it has resulted in a more efficient scheme for belief propagation and the development of techniques to verify the consistency of user-supplied information. In the following section, we first describe the framework for the knowledge base structure of the second prototype as a two level Markov network. This framework provides the basis for defining an efficient belief propagation scheme based on local computations.[15] The PLAYMAKER knowledge base is then developed in this framework, and examples are presented to demonstrate the effectiveness of the belief propagation scheme in deriving play characteristics. A short discussion of knowledge acquisition techniques based on this framework is also presented.

#### 3.2.1. The knowledge base structure

The knowledge base structure of Prototype 2 is based on the concept of a general Markov network as defined by Kong[16] and adapted by Shafer and Shenoy[15] for propagation and computation of belief functions. Following Shafer and Shenoy,[15] we define a set of variables $V = \{X_1, X_2, \ldots, X_n\}$ to form a belief function model, where the $X_i$, $1 \leq i \leq n$ are termed *individual variables* (i.e. attributes), each with a *frame of discernment* $\Theta(X_i)$. The geological attributes in our play characterization domain form the variables of the belief function model. Depositional setting (Dep_Set) is an example of a variable, and $\Theta$(Dep_Set) = {*basin*, *shelf*, *slope*}. Subsets of variables, e.g. $X = \{X_i, X_j, X_k\}$ are called *joint variables*, and their corresponding frame of discernment is defined as the Cartesian product, $\Theta(X) = \Theta(X_i) \times \Theta(X_j) \times \Theta(X_k)$.

In the PLAYMAKER domain, Primary_Bed_Shape [$\Theta$(Primary_Bed_Shape) = {Hor_Por, Hor_Cha, Dip_Par, Dip_Cha}], Area_Lithology [$\Theta$(Area_Lithology) = {homo, hetero}], and Dep_Set can together define a joint variable, $X$, with $\Theta(X_i \times X_j \times X_k)$ = {(Hor_Par, homo, basin), (Hor_Par, homo, shelf), . . . , (Dip_Par, hetero, Slope), . . .}.

Variables and joint variables can be interpreted as questions, e.g. "*What values of this variable are believed in and to what extent?*" and "*What conjunction of values of this variable are believed in and to what extent?*" In our application, the expert enters information about joint variables in rule form; for example,

If $(A, a)$ and $(B, b)$ and $(C, c)$ then $(Z, z)$

where $(A, a)$, $(B, b)$, $(C, c)$, and $(Z, z)$ represent attribute-value pairs. Note that $a$, $b$, $c$, and $z$ represent singletons or a subset of conclusions.

Belief functions are associated with individual rules. For example, the belief function associated with the rule shown above is associated with the frame $\Theta(A \times B \times C \times Z)$, and constructed as a function that maps from the set of all possible subsets of $\Theta(A \times B \times C \times D)$ to [0, 1]. The method for acquiring belief functions is similar to the method used for Prototype 1, i.e. the user enters rankings for individual conclusions. The MIDST system converts the expert-supplied rankings into appropriate belief functions.[14]

A second level hierarchical structure exists within nodes that define play characteristics. A variable usually takes on a number of possible values which can be represented as a classification hierarchy of the type discussed in Shenoy and Shafer.[17] (Actually Shenoy and Shafer term this hierarchy a diagnostic tree, but it can be applied to any classification scheme that can be represented as a tree structure). For example, Fig. 5 represents the classification structure for various Clastic Facies. The root node of the hierarchy represents the top of the classification structure, i.e. Clastic Facies (Clas_Fac). A first level of classification of this structure produces three kinds of facies: *marine*, *transitional*, and *non-marine*. Further subdivisions are shown in the figure. The leaf nodes, such as *basin*, *slope*, *delta*, *lacustrian*, and *alluvial fan*, represent the most detailed level at which information can be derived. The reason for using this kind of hierarchical structure is that different kinds of geological data (evidence) only provide a certain level of discernment among the different facies. For example, knowing whether the *fauna* is *marine* only helps distinguish *marine* from *non-marine* and *transitional* type of facies, whereas knowing *primary bed shape* (Horizontal_Chaotic), the type of *sediment* (sand or conglomerates), and *depositional setting* (basin) indicates a *fan* type of facies. The use of this hierarchical structure and the evidence combination scheme described in the next section provides an effective means for integrating evidence at different levels of detail, and deriving the most precise conclusion about an attribute value from within a node.

The top level network is shown in Fig. 6. The rounded nodes represent primary geological characteristics that are important for play characterization, and the boxed nodes represent joint variables. Unlike Prototype 1, where concepts were separated into disjoint partitions, this version retains the entire structure in a single partition to make the belief propagation process more efficient. After the primary geological characteristics are defined, the expert supplies relations among variables in the form of production rules with associated belief values. Examples of some rules appear in Fig. 7.

The attributes associated with individual rules define the joint variables of interest in our inferencing scheme. Unlike the Zarley approach,[18] where relations among joint values are expressed by enumerating truth tables of all possible attribute-value combinations, we found it more efficient to allow the expert to enter relations among variables as a set of rules with associated belief values.[18] Expert-supplied rules at each joint variable node define how belief values at one node will be propagated to neighboring nodes. Typically, propagation of belief values for this application occurs bottom up, from data characteristics to play characteristics. Further details of the propagation scheme are presented in the next section.

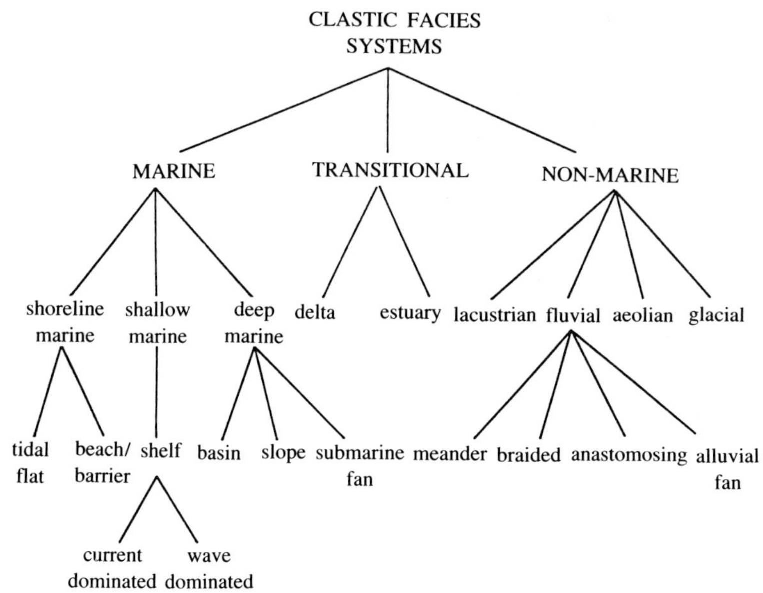


Fig. 5. Internal network for Clastic Facies.

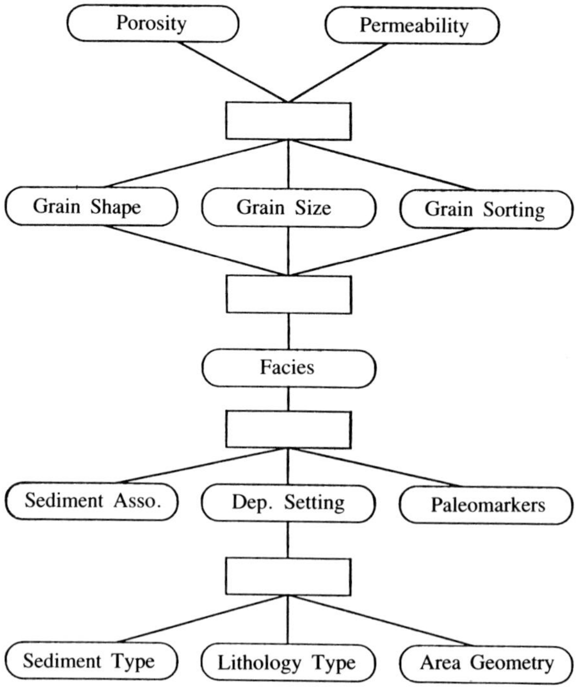


Fig. 6. The top-level network.

```
(|rule 100|
  ((((SED_TYPE) (SHALE))
    ((PRI_BED_TYPE) (HORIZ_PARA))
    ((LITHOLOGY_TYPE) (HOMOGENEOUS))
    ((BED_THICK) (THIN))
  BF)
  ((((DEP_SET) (BASIN))) 0.8)))

(|rule 103|
  ((((A_GEOMETRY) (CLINOFORM))
    ((BED_THICK) (THICK)
    ((A_LITHOLOGY) (HETEROGENEOUS))
    ((SED_TYPE) (CONGLOMERATE)))
  BF)
  (((((DEP_SET) (SLOPE))) 0.8)))

(|rule 104|
  ((((A_GEOMETRY) (CLINOFORM))
    ((BED_THICK) (MEDIUM)
    ((A_LITHOLOGY) (HETEROGENEOUS))
    ((SED_TYPE) (CONGLOMERATE)))
  BF)
  (((((DEP_SET) (SLOPE))) 0.6)))

(|rule 108|
  ((((PRI_BED_TYPE) (DIP_PARA))
    ((A_LITHOLOGY) (HETEROGENEOUS))
    ((SED_TYPE) (SAND)))
  BF)
  (((((DEP_SET) (SHELF))) (((DEP_SET) (SLOPE))) 0.5)))

(|rule 110|
  ((((A_GEOMETRY) (DISC_SHEET))
    ((SED_TYPE) (CARBONATE)))
  BF)

(|rule 114|
  ((((PALEOMARKER) (FRESH_WATER)))
  BF)
  (((((FACIES) (LACUSTRIAN))) 0.3)))

(|rule 115|
  ((((PALEOMARKER) (FRESH_WATER))
    ((PRI_BED_SHAPE) (FLAT_TOP_LENS)))
  BF)
  (((((FACIES) (FLUVIAL))) 0.6)))

(|rule 127|
  ((((DEP_SET) (SLOPE))
    ((PRI_BED_SHAPE) (CLINOFORM))
    ((PALEOMARKER) (MIXED_DEPTH_MARINE))
    ((SED_TYPE) (SHALE)))
  BF)
  (((((FACIES) (SLOPE))) 0.35) ((((FACIES) (DELTA))) 0.35)))
```

Fig. 7. Sample rules.

### 3.2.2. The propagation scheme

With the implementation of the new represented scheme, the belief calculation and propagation becomes much more efficient. Propagation of belief is carried out on both the top-level network and the internal network associated with each concept. A change in belief for a variable node is immediately propagated up and down in the internal network of that variable. Depending on the magnitudes of the belief values associated with nodes in the internal hierarchy of a concept node, a subset of node values is chosen. Corresponding values in the joint node are fired to propagate belief values in higher level nodes of the top network. This propagation process continues until sufficient evidence is accumulated to make definitive conclusions at the highest level nodes (*porosity* and *permeability*), or no further information is available for play characterization. Details of the overall inferencing scheme are presented in Refs. 10 and 14, and are not repeated here. This section concentrates on describing the propagation scheme that arises from the modified knowledge representation structures.

For propagating belief values, there are two possibilities: (i) to propagate belief values immediately after an update occurs in any part of the network, (ii) to concentrate on the local computation within a node and propagate beliefs values between top-level nodes only when attribute values within the node are established with a high level of confidence as determined by a prespecified threshold value. Within the lower layer (i.e. within each variable), a change in some belief value is propagated up and down the network immediately using the method outlined by Shenoy and Shafer.[17] After each up and down propagation in the internal node hierarchy, belief values at leaf nodes are checked to see if they have achieved certain set thresholds (see Ref. 14 for details). If the belief values at the left nodes exceed the threshold function, then belief values for all leaf nodes are propagated to the higher level. Otherwise, the inferencing mechanism continues to concentrate on the node by querying the user, until the left node belief value exceeds the threshold function or the user has no further relevant information to provide. At this point the system selects a group of nodes (based on a heuristic algorithm shown in Fig. 8), whose belief values are then propagated to higher level joint nodes, where belief values for other concepts are computed using rules of the type shown in Fig. 7. Note that the selection algorithm ensures that no duplicate information is passed from one node to another. Figure 9 is a snapshot of the belief value distribution for the variable node *Facies* at some point in the play characterization process.

Note that a number of leaf nodes have a zero belief value associated with them, but their parents which represent aggregates of values, have non-zero values. At this point, the next set of evidence supports the node *Tidal Flat* to an extent of 0.6. This information is immediately propagated up and down on the internal network; the new belief value distribution is shown in Fig. 10. As we can see from the two figures, the new evidence causes an increase in the belief value for the node *Tidal Flat* and its ancestors (*Shoreline Marine*, *Marine*). At the same time, belief value at the other nodes descrease proportionately. For the belief distribution of Fig. 10, the selection algorithm would choose the set {*Tidal Flat*, *Beach Barrier*, *Deep Marine*, *Aeolian*} to

```
Initialize a−lst to include all leaf nodes;
Repeat while a−lst is not empty
{  cur-node ← first in a−lst;
   f-node ⇐ father of cur-node;
   If f-node is marked 'NO or
     belief of cur-node > belief of f-node −0.15
   Then
   {  mark cur-node as 'YES;
      for all ancestor nodes a-node of cur-node
      (  mark a-node as 'NO;
         for all son s-node of a-node (except cur-node)
            if it is marked 'NO
            then mark s-node as 'NO;
      }
   }
   Else add f-node to a−lst;
   Delete cur-node from a−lst;
}
;
```

Note: a−lst contains all the nodes that are to be checked.

Fig. 8. The node selection algorithm.

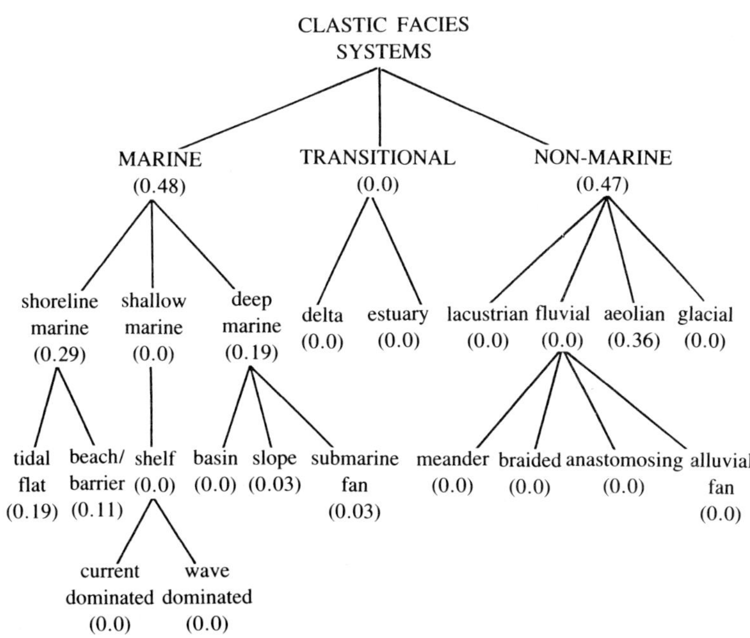


Fig. 9. Example of belief distribution I.

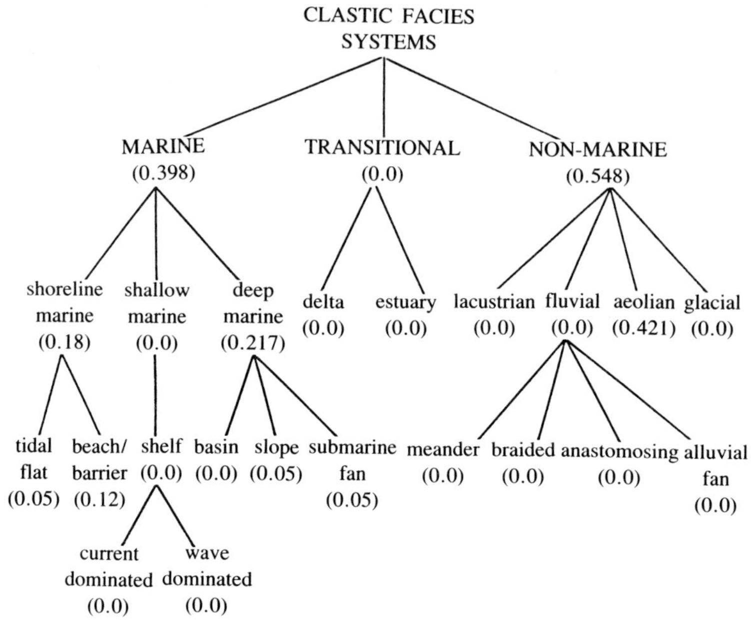


Fig. 10. Example of belief distribution II.

represent the variable, and propagate their belief values in the high-level network. The overall inferencing algorithm is summarized in Fig. 11. Note that from the user's point of view the interaction with the system follows a mixed-initiative format.

### 3.2.3. A comprehensive example

Partial transcripts of a case, run on the PLAYMAKER system, follow and illustrate the nature of the dialog between a user and the MIDST system, resulting in the determination of the porosity for a particular field. The actual system has a sophisticated user interface (see Fig. 4). This transcript just summarizes the key aspects of the interaction. The system queries and remarks appear in bold font. User responses are in medium font. Explanatory comments appear in italics. Additional output provided by the system is omitted for the sake of brevity and clarity.

**Welcome to the MIDST expert system developing environment.**
**End all responses with a bang.**
**Would you like to enter a new knowledge base?**

**Enter yes or no.**
no

**Enter a name for the knowledge base you would like to work with.**
yy4

```
Preliminary information collection

Forward-chain on information available

Repeat until problem solved

{  Pick top-ranked variable as the current hypothesis

   repeat until belief value at leaf node > threshold or
         no further relevant information available

   {  Query user;

      Fire rules, and update belief values;

      Propagate belief in the internal network;

   }

   Call Selection algorithm to select the set of attribute-value pairs for higher level propagation;

   Belief propagation on the top-level network;

   Update hypothesis rankings;

}
```

Fig. 11. The overall inferencing algorithm.

*As an expert system shell, MIDST can be applied to different knowledge base applications. YY4 is the knowledge base used to estimate the play characteristic for a particular field.*

**You have elected to work with the knowledge base "YY4"**
**Enter R to run a consultation**
**M to modify the knowledge base**
**E to end session with MIDST**
r

**Descending to level POROlevel7**

**Descending to level POROlevel4**

*Since the goal is to decide the porosity of the particular field, POROSITY is selected as the top ranked hypothesis variable. However, there are no queries directly associated with this variable, so the system descends to lower levels by backward chaining. The aim is to determine other characteristics from which POROSITY may be inferred.*

**WHAT IS THE FLUVIAL TYPE?**
**POSSIBLE RESPONSES —**
**0 – (FOR EXPLANATION)**
**1 – (BRAIDED)**
**2 – (MEANDERING)**
1,1.0

*For each query, MIDST provides a menu of possible responses, and some explanation, such as why the question is asked and how it will affect the reasoning process, etc. This question and the next two are used to collect some preliminary information so that the system can pick the appropriate variable node from among several candidate variable nodes.*

**Descending to level POROlevel2**

**WHAT IS THE LOCAL GEOMETRY?**
**POSSIBLE RESPONSES —**
**0 – (FOR EXPLANATION)**
**1 – (CON_SHEET)**
**2 – (CLINOFORM)**
**3 – (FLAT_TOP_LENS)**
**4 – (TOPO_FILL)**
3,1.0

**WHAT IS THE NATURE OF THE PALEOMARKERS?**
**POSSIBLE RESPONSES —**
**0 – (FOR EXPLANATION)**
**1 – (MIXED)**
**2 – (SHALLOW)**
**3 – (FLUVIAL)**
**4 – (LACUSTRIAN)**
**5 – (AEOLIAN)**
3,1.0

**rule 115 is being fired.**
**The new H_B is**
**(((FACIES) (FLUVIAL)) 0.6)**

*After preliminary information is acquired, the system established the FACIES node as the hypothesis on which to focus. Since the belief value for the leaf node FLUVIAL does not exceed the prespecified threshold, information acquisition is still concentrated on the variable FACIES.*

**WHAT IS THE SEDIMENT TYPE?**
**POSSIBLE RESPONSES —**
**0 – (FOR EXPLANATION)**
**1 – (SHALE)**
**2 – (SAND)**
**3 – (CONGLOMERATE)**
2,1.0

**Descending to level POROlevel1**

*At this point, there is no query directly related to FACIES so the system descends to a lower level and tries to establish DEP_SET, which, in turn, will help to establish FACIES.*

**WHAT IS THE LITHOLOGY OF THE AREA?**
**POSSIBLE RESPONSES —**
**0 – (FOR EXPLANATION)**
**1 – (HOMOGENEOUS)**
**2 – (HETEROGENEOUS)**
2,1.0

**WHAT IS THE BEDDING THICKNESS?**
**POSSIBLE RESPONSES —**
**0 – (FOR EXPLANATION)**
**1 – (THIN)**
**2 – (THICK)**
**3 – (MEDIUM)**
2,1.0

**WHAT IS THE GEOMETRY OF THE AREA?**
**POSSIBLE RESPONSES —**
**0 – (FOR EXPLANATION)**
**1 – (DISC_SHEET)**
**2 – (CONT_SHEET)**
**3 – (CLINOFORM)**
1,1.0

**WHAT IS THE PRIMARY BEDDING SHAPE?**
**POSSIBLE RESPONSES —**
**0 – (FOR EXPLANATION)**
**1 – (HORIZ_PARA)**
**2 – (HORIZ_CHAO)**
**3 – (DIP_PARA)**
2,1.0

**rule 109 is being fired.**
**The new H_B is**
**(((DEP_SET) (SHELF)) 0.7)**

**((DEP_SET) (SHELF)) cannot be sufficiently verified.**

**System Currently GUESSES**
**((DEP_SET) (SHELF)) 0.7**

*For the current variable DEP_SET, the system could establish no conclusion with belief value above 0.9. The top-ranked hypothesis SHELF, with belief value 0.7 is then regarded as the most probable conclusion. This information is then passed up to the higher level variable nodes.*

**rule 117 is being fired.**
**The new H_B is**
**(((FACIES) (FLUVIAL)) 0.768)**

*The establishment of DEP_SET as SHELF has increased the belief in the conclusion FLUVIAL FACIES.*

**WHAT IS THE SEDIMENT ASSOCIATION?**
**POSSIBLE RESPONSES —**
**0 – (FOR EXPLANATION)**
**1 – (DOWNDIP)**
**2 – (UPDIP)**
**3 – (INTERBEDDED)**
1,1.0

**rule 118 is being fired.**
**The new H_B is**
**(((FACIES) (FLUVIAL)) 0.91**

**System Currently DEDUCES**
**((FACIES) (FLUVIAL)) 0.91**

*With this additional information, the belief value for leaf node FLUVIAL exceeded the 0.9 threshold. This is established as the value for the variable FACIES, and the belief value is propagated to the upper level variable. The system has all the information it needs, and switches into the forward chaining mode.*

**rule 158 is being fired.**
**The new H_B is**
**(((G_SORTING) (GOOD)) 0.64)**

**rule 157 is being fired.**
**The new H_B is**
**(((G_SHAPE) (ROUNDED)) 0.64)**

**rule 156 is being fired.**
**The new H_B is**
**(((G_SIZE) (GRAVEL_COARSE)) 0.64)**

**((G_SIZE) (GRAVEL_COARSE)) cannot be sufficiently verified.**
**Look for some evidence.**
**System Currently GUESSES**
**((G_SIZE) (GRAVEL_COARSE)) 0.64**

*At this point PLAYMAKER found no additional evidence that could increase belief in GRAIN_SIZE. It makes a guess and moves on.*

**rule 162 is being fired.**
**The new H_B is**
**(((G_SIZE_QLT) (EXCELLENT)) 0.44)**

**((G_SIZE_QLT) (EXCELLENT)) cannot be sufficiently verified.**
**Look for more evidence.**
**System Currently GUESSES**
**((G_SIZE_QLT) (EXCELLENT)) 0.44**

**rule 170 is being fired.**
**The new H_B is**
**(((POROSITY) (GOOD)) 0.36)**

**System GUESSES**
**((POROSITY) (GOOD)) 0.37**

*After the forward chaining process, POROSITY-GOOD is established with a belief value 0.36. At this point, the system checks for other evidence that might help improve belief in the nature of porosity, but cannot find any. Note that the set of rules in the system are not quite complete. This results in a low belief in the final conclusion.*

The above example illustrates the nature of the interaction between PLAYMAKER and the user. The dialog process is streamlined because a number of relevant questions are asked together. In fact, using the X Window interface we plan to put up a number of related queries simultaneously in different windows on the screen. This will permit the user to provide more coherent and consistent responses, and will also result in less overhead in invoking and displaying the query-response screens. The system fires rules, establishes belief in variable values, and propagates them along the network. Based on the magnitudes of the belief values, the inferencing scheme then decides what further information may lead to more conclusive evidence in the hypotheses of interest. Further queries are displayed, and responses are collected. This process continues until definitive conclusions are reached (e.g. belief value $> 0.9$) or there is no further evidence to collect.

## 4. DISCUSSION

The single partition, multi-layer structure of Prototype 2 of PLAYMAKER has a number of advantages over Prototype 1. All geological parameters are represented in a uniform manner, and, when possible, inferred from a common primary data characteristic. The values inferred for a concept are transmitted immediately to connected nodes (i.e. other concepts) so that their belief values can be updated according to prespecified rules. In Prototype 1, information transferred from one partition to another only when the second partition was invoked. Transfer from one partition to another was sequential, with no backtracking. Often an inference drawn in one partition had to be transformed into another form to be useful in a different partition. Moreover, a lot of computational effort was expended in loading and saving individual partitions. In Prototype 2, computation time and effort is saved by eliminating sequential transfer and one-partition-at-a-time execution. Furthermore, the control mechanism has a more global picture of the impact of all evidence gathered on the overall set of play characteristics. As a result, the information acquisition process is more effectively focused.

Another aspect of Prototype 2 is that within a node concept, values are organized hierarchically by level of detail. Evidence bearing on different levels is accumulated and integrated using the up and down propagation scheme. The selection algorithm then picks the best set of nodes from which information is passed to neighboring nodes while ensuring that duplicate information is not transmitted. Depending on which node values are transmitted, a different subset of rules are selected from the joint variable node to update belief values of variables in adjoining nodes. Thus the upper layer network is really dynamic. Primary data does not have to be input repeatedly in different forms, and information acquisition from the user is not repetitive.

The new structure also provides a framework for developing a useful completeness and consistency checking mechanism.[19] Whereas the previous mechanism could only check for consistency within a partition, the current prototype uses a slightly extended algorithm which can be applied to the entire knowledge base.

The new structure is also better organized geologically, and provides better mechanisms for knowledge acquisition. This process can be user-driven, or system-driven. When the knowledge acquisition process is initiated by the user, usually a domain expert, it is the user who has control of the process. The expert studies the performance of the system on test cases, and when the system's results do not agree with the expert's belief, the system is asked for an explanation. An explanation can be in the form of a general description of why the system reached that particular conclusion, or it can be a very specific explanation of the function of certain rules and why certain rules fired and others did not. The expert may direct the system to add, delete, or change particular rules. When doing this, the existing network of each concept provides pointers to which concept values may be useful in formulating new rules.

In the case where the knowledge acquisition process is initiated by the system after a set of rules have been added, the system checks the consistency and completeness of the resulting knowledge base. If the system finds an inconsistency or incompleteness in the knowledge base, it will direct the domain expert to delete, or change specific rules. It may also suggest the addition of rules that match a specific functionality (i.e. lead to specific conclusions).

Currently, we are working toward extending and completing the knowledge base for play characterization. A sophisticated graphics-based rule editor has also been developed. A major effort is also underway to design and develop automated knowledge refinement and knowledge acquisition techniques.

## REFERENCES

1. J. S. Strobel, "The Simulation of the Sedimentary Fill of Basins and the Characterization of Hydrocarbon Plays by an Expert System", Ph.D. thesis, Dept. of Geology, Univ. of South Carolina, 1989.
2. A. W. Shultz, *et al.*, "XEOD: An expert system for determining clastic depositional environments", *Geobyte* **3** (1988) 22–32.
3. R. W. Scheifler and J. Gettys, "The X Windows System", *ACM Trans. Graphics* **5** (1986) 79–109.
4. M. J. Bach, *The Design of the Unix Operating System*, Prentice Hall, 1986.
5. J. S. Strobel, C. Kendall, G. Biswas, J. Bezdek and R. L. Cannon, "Interactive (SEDPAK) simulation of clastic and carbonate sediments in shelf to basin settings", *Quantitative Dynamic Stratigraphy*, Ed. T. A. Goss, Prentice Hall, 1989, pp. 433–444.
6. P. T. Reed, R. L. Cannon, G. Biswas, J. C. Bezdek and C. Kendall, "Syntactic learning by induction from examples and experiments", *Proc. Applications of AI VIII*, Orlando, FL, April 1990, pp. 645–653.
7. C. J. Date, *An Introduction to Database Systems*, 4th ed. Addison Wesley, 1986.
8. G. Shafer, *A Mathematical Theory of Evidence*, Princeton University Press, 1976.
9. M. Pai, G. Biswas, C. Kendall and J. Bezdek, "Towards the design of a system for hydrocarbon play analysis", *Methodologies for Intelligent Systems*, Eds. Z. W. Ras and M. Zemankova, Elsevier Science, 1987.
10. G. Biswas and T. S. Anand, "An expert system shell for mixed initiative reasoning", *J. Indian Institute of Science* **67** (1987) 465–490.
11. D. Cheong, C. Kendall and B. Bowen, "A Review of Gulf Coast Stratigraphy and Hydrocarbon Occurrence", Tech. Report, Dept. of Geology, Univ. of South Carolina, Columbia, SC, 1989.
12. G. Biswas and X. Yu, "A rule network for efficient implementation of a mixed-initiative reasoning scheme", *Proc. ACM Seventeenth Annual Computer Science Conference*, Louisville, KY, 1989, pp. 123–130.
13. W. Hagins and G. Biswas, "An improved rule network for mixed-initiative reasoning: updates", Tech. Report, Dept. of Computer Science, Vanderbilt University, Nashville, TN, 1989.

14. G. Biswas and T. S. Anand, "Using the Dempster-Shafer scheme in a mixed-initiative expert system shell", in *Uncertainty in Artificial Intelligence 3*, Eds. L. N. Kanal, T. s. Levitt and J. F. Lemmer, North-Holland, 1989, pp. 223–239.
15. G. Shafer and P. P. Shenoy, "Local Computations in Hypertrees", School of Business, Working Paper No. 201, The University of Kansas, Lawrence, KS, August 1988.
16. A. Kong, "Multivariate Belief Functions and Graphical Models", Ph.D. thesis, Dept. of Statistics, Harvard Univ., Cambridge, MA, 1986.
17. P. P. Shenoy and G. Shafer, "Propagating belief functions using local computations", *IEEE Expert* **1**, 3, (1986) pp. 43–52.
18. D. Zarley, Y. Hsia and G. Shafer, "Evidental reasoning using DELIEF", *Proc. Seventh AAAI (AAAI-88)*, St. Paul, MN, 1988, pp. 205–209.
19. X. Yu and G. Biswas, "CHECKER: An efficient algorithm for knowledge base verification", *Proc. Third Intl. Conf. on IEA/AIE*, Charleston, SC, July 1990, pp. 735–744.

---

**Gautam Biswas** is an Assistant Professor of Computer Science at Vanderbilt University, Nashville. He was previously on the computer science faculty at the University of South Carolina in Columbia. Dr. Biswas received a B.Tech. degree in electrical engineering from the Indian Institute of Technology, Bombay, in 1977, and M.S. and Ph.D. degrees in computer science from Michigan State University, East Lansing, in 1979 and 1982 respectively. His primary research interests are in artificial intelligence and knowledge-based systems, and more specifically in qualitative reasoning, model-based reasoning, and intelligent tutoring systems. He is currently applying qualitative modeling and multi-level reasoning techniques in designing knowledge-based systems for oil exploration and diagnosis of complex, electromechanical systems.

Dr. Biswas is an associate editor of the *International Journal of Approximate Reasoning*, and a member of the IEEE Computer Society, ACM, AAAI, and the Sigma Xi Research Society.

**Xudong Yu** received the M.S. degree in computer science from Vanderbilt University, in May 1989. He is currently working toward the Ph.D. degree in computer science at the same place. His current research interests are in model-based diagnosis, qualitative reasoning and knowledge-based systems.

**James Bezdek** received the B.S. from the University of Nevada, Reno, in 1969; and the Ph.D. from Cornell University in 1973. He has held academic positions at SUNY College/Oneonta, Marquette University, Utah State University and the University of South Carolina. At the latter, he was Chair of Computer Science. Dr. Bezdek was a visiting research scientist at Boeing Aerospace in 1982, and Director of the Information Processing Laboratory at the Boeing Electronics High Technology Center from 1987 to 1989. Currently, he occupies the Nystul Florida Eminent Scholar Chair in the Division of Computer Science at the University of West Florida. His research interests include pattern recognition algorithms, neural networks, image processing and machine vision, medical diagnosis, and expert systems. He is the founding editor of the *International Journal of Approximate Reasoning*, and an associate editor of the *IEEE Transactions on Systems, Man*

*and Cybernetics*, *International Journal of Man-Machine Studies*, *International Journal of Applied Intelligence*, *International Journal of General Systems*, and *International Journal of Fuzzy Sets and Systems*. He is a past president of IFSA (International Fuzzy Systems Association) and NAFIPS (North American Fuzzy Information Processing Society), and is an ACM lecturer for the 1990–91 academic year.

**John Strobel** studied geology and computer science at the University of Georgia, graduating in both fields in 1983. He studied geophysics at the University of North Carolina at Chapel Hill, and basin modeling and expert systems at the University of South Carolina, graduating in 1985 and 1989 respectively. Currently, he works with the CONOCO workstation group, designing and developing geologic software for the CONOCO basin modeling project. His current interests and research efforts are in basin modeling and palinspatic reconstruction.

**Christopher Kendall** graduated with a first class honors B.A. degree in geology in 1962, and an M.A. in 1965, from Trinity College, Dublin, and a Ph.D. in 1966 from Imperial College, London. From 1966–68 he was a Commonwealth Fund Harkness Fellow at the University of Texas; then in 1968–69 he was a Sydney University Post-Doctoral Fellow. He has been an Assistant Professor at the Department of Geology, Ohio State University, and a Research Associate Professor of the University of South Carolina. Dr Kendall also worked with Exxon Production Research and was a Research Associate and Director of Geological Research with Gulf Research, Pittsburgh. Presently, he is a Professor at the University of South Carolina in the Department of Geology and Marine Science. His main interests are sedimentology, particularly the carbonates, basin modeling, expert systems and hydrocarbon exploration.

**Robert Cannon** received the B.S. in mathematics from the University of North Carolina at Chapel Hill, the M.S. in mathematics from the University of Wisconsin at Madison, and the Ph.D. in computer science from the University of North Carolina at Chapel Hill. As a Woodrow Wilson Intern he taught mathematics at Philander Smith College and was also on the mathematics faculty at Wilmington College. Since 1973 he has taught computer science at the University of South Carolina, where he is now Chair of the department. He was Chair of the ACM Accreditation Committee for three years, and is Secretary of the Computer Science Accreditation Commission. His research interests include shared access to microcomputer text files for writing instruction, and expert systems and simulation for geological analysis.

# AN EXPERT SYSTEM FOR INTERPRETING MESOSCALE FEATURES IN OCEANOGRAPHIC SATELLITE IMAGES*

N. KRISHNAKUMAR and S. SITHARAMA IYENGAR
*Department of Computer Science*
*Louisiana State University*
*Baton Rouge, LA 70803, USA*

RON HOLYER and MATTHEW LYBANON
*Remote Sensing Branch*
*Naval Oceanographic and Atmospheric Research Laboratory*
*Stennis Space Center, MS 39529, USA*

Received 1 April 1990

Thermal infrared images of the ocean obtained from satellite sensors are widely used for the study of ocean dynamics. The derivation of mesoscale ocean information from satellite data depends to a large extent on the correct interpretation of infrared oceanographic images. The difficulty of the image analysis and understanding problem for oceanographic images is due in large part to the lack of precise mathematical descriptions of the ocean features, coupled with the time varying nature of these features and the complication that the view of the ocean surface is typically obscured by clouds, sometimes almost completely. Towards this objective, the present paper describes a hybrid technique that utilizes a nonlinear probabilistic relaxation method and an expert system for the oceanographic image interpretation problem. This paper highlights the advantages of using the contextual information in the feature labeling algorithm. The need for an expert system and its feedback in automatic interpretation of oceanic features is discussed. The paper presents some important results of the series of experiments conducted at the Remote Sensing Branch, of the Naval Oceanographic and Atmospheric Research Laboratory, on the National Oceanic and Atmospheric Administration Advanced Very High Resolution Radiometer (AVHRR) imagery data. The results clearly indicate the drastic improvement in labeling due to the oceanographic expert system.

*Keywords:* Expert system; Knowledge-based system; Feature labeling; Oceanic features; Relaxation; Infrared imagery.

## 1. INTRODUCTION

Satellite-borne sensors potentially offer many advantages for the study of oceanic processes. They provide global synoptic measurements of various oceanic surface properties, in contrast to the local measurements, possibly at a range of depths, provided by conventional oceanographic measurement techniques. Thermal infrared (IR) images of the ocean obtained from satellite sensors are widely used for the study of ocean dynamics. Figure 1 shows a sample infrared image of the Gulf Stream

* This project is funded by the Department of Navy under the contract number N00014-88-K-6002.

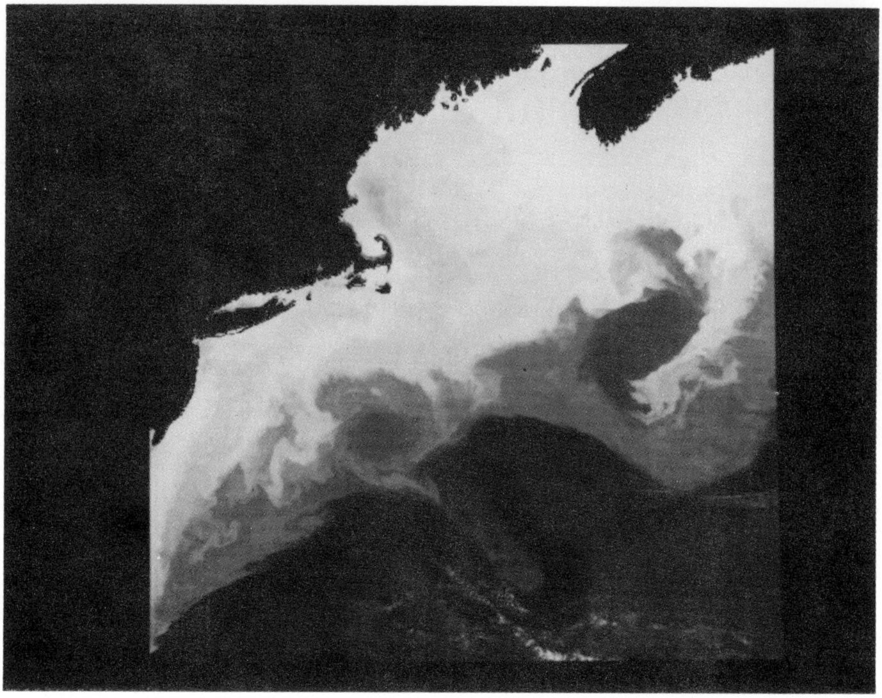

Fig. 1. Typical IR image.

obtained from the Advanced Very High Resolution Radiometer (AVHRR) aboard the NOAA-7 satellite. Brightness in this infrared image is inversely proportional to the ocean surface temperature (dark areas represent warmer temperatures and light areas represent colder temperatures). Vortices (areas of closed circulation) within this turbulent flow pattern are called *eddies*. The Gulf Stream and its associated eddies are examples of mesoscale features (''mesoscale'' is the name commonly applied to the features existing on spatial scales of the order of 50 to 300 km). Mesoscale features are important to the study of ocean dynamics, to fisheries and to many other diverse interests.

Current image analysis techniques rely on human interpretation of the satellite imagery. Human interpretation is obviously varied in its level of expertise and is highly labor-intensive. With the proliferation of high volume AVHRR image applications, it becomes highly desirable for certain applications to move from the labor-intensive manual interpretation of infrared imagery towards the capability for automated interpretation of these images. The complete automation of the oceanographic image interpretation function is probably not feasible, but one can begin to address certain subsets of the problem with the present-day image processing and artificial intelligence techniques. This was the motivation for the work reported by Lybanon *et al.*,[1] in the development of a prototype oceanographic expert system.

Several previous studies have addressed the automation of the analysis of infrared satellite imagery for mesoscale features. Gerson and Gaborski,[2] and Gerson *et al.*[3] investigated the detection of the Gulf Stream in infrared images from the Geostationary Operational Environmental Satellite (GOES). Gerson and Gaborski[2] used a hierarchical approach where 16 × 16 pixel (128 × 128 km) "frames" within the image were evaluated for the possibility of containing the Gulf Stream. Frames flagged as Gulf Stream possibilities were then further evaluated to determine the exact location of the Stream within the frame by looking at statistics based on 5 × 5 pixel "local neighborhoods". As an outgrowth of the work reported in Refs. 2 and 3, Coulter[4] performed automated feature extraction studies using the higher resolution Advanced Very High Resolution Radiometer data. Janowitz[5] studied the automatic detection of the Gulf Stream eddies using Advanced Very High Resolution Radiometer data. Nichol[6] used a region adjacency graph to define spatial relationships between elementary connected regions of constant gray level called atoms. Although satisfactory emulation of human extraction of eddy structure is claimed for this method, Nichol[6] did point out that not all enclosed uniform areas identified by the method will correspond to real ocean structure. Krishnakumar *et al.*[7] had earlier approached this problem and shown some preliminary results on the relaxation-based feature labeling scheme, the development of a prototype expert system and the interface between these two modules. Goodenough *et al.*[8] have developed an expert system for remote sensing applications. In Ref. 8 the knowledge is presented in the production rules and frame databases. The expert system given in Ref. 8 is used to study the spatial differences between maps and images.

## 2. MOTIVATION OF THE PRESENT WORK

Our primary objective is to build a powerful automatic image interpretation system for oceanographic satellite images. In order to make this difficult problem tractable, we divide the problem into two parts: *the feature labeling problem* and *the development of an expert system*. It is clear that the performance of the labeling algorithm depends heavily on the low level image processing algorithms. Particularly, the output of an edge detector algorithm plays a major role in the feature labeling process. In view of this, a new efficient edge detector algorithm proposed by Holyer and Peckinpaugh[9] is employed in our feature labeling technique. It is known that the conventional edge derivative operators are very sensitive to noise and are not suitable for analyzing oceanographic satellite images. The new edge detector algorithm proposed by Holyer and Peckinpaugh[9] is based on the gray level co-occurrence matrix, which is commonly used in image texture analysis. This algorithm[9] is found to exhibit the characteristics of fine structure rejection while retaining edge sharpness. In this paper we focus on the importance of an expert system in building an automatic oceanographic image interpretation system.

The objective of an oceanographic expert system is to correctly interpret the dynamics of the ocean process with minimal human interaction. Towards this objective, the development of a powerful oceanographic expert system is under way at the Remote Sensing Branch of the Naval Oceanographic and Atmospheric Research Laboratory (NOARL). However, we have already developed a prototype expert system for Gulf Stream regional dynamics.[1] One of the elements of an expert system is a database of knowledge about the subject matter, with the knowledge represented in a form suitable for manipulation by the "inference engine" of the expert system (i.e. the logical and heuristic procedures for solving problems in the problem domain). With the help of the knowledge gained from discussions at NOARL and from the literature in oceanography, a knowledge base about the nature of the mesoscale features (occurrence, mean lifetime, movement, etc.) was built.[1]

This paper describes a hybrid technique to label features in thermal infrared images obtained from satellites. The technique presented here exploits the advantages of using contextual information in the labeling algorithm. The remainder of the paper is organized as follows: Section 3 gives an overview of the architecture of the proposed image interpretation system. Section 4 introduces the probabilistic relaxation scheme and briefly discusses the application of this scheme to the oceanographic labeling problem. In Sec. 4.1 we develop a mathematical framework which is necessary for our labeling problem. Section 4.2 discusses the performance of our technique and describes the steps that are involved in implementing this technique. Section 5 describes the need for an oceanographic expert system and the implementation of the expert system. The improvement in feature labeling due to the feedback from the expert system is illustrated in Sec. 6 with the help of an example. Section 7 concludes with all the important features of this technique and proposes future extensions to the available scheme.

## 3. ARCHITECTURE OF THE INTERPRETER

In this section, we briefly describe the various components involved in the image iteratively updated using the nonlinear probabilistic relaxation scheme. Finally, the architecture of the proposed system. The IR image obtained from the satellite is the input to the feature labeling module. The feature labeling module consists of two submodules: one estimates the initial feature probabilities and the other implements the iterative updating scheme. The initial pixel probabilities are assigned with the help of the previous analysis and the ground truth data. These probability values are then iteratively updated using the nonlinear probabilistic relaxation scheme. Finally, the relevant features that are present in the image are labeled with the aid of a decision process.

The labeled features are then fed to the expert system module. This expert system is divided into two submodules. The first submodule consists of a knowledge base and an inference engine. The knowledge base has a thorough collection of facts and rules about the mesoscale features such as Gulf Stream, warm core rings, etc. Based on the positional information obtained from the feature labeling module and the knowledge base, the inference engine attempts to interpret the dynamics of these features. Basically the inference engine is a pattern matching module. The second submodule

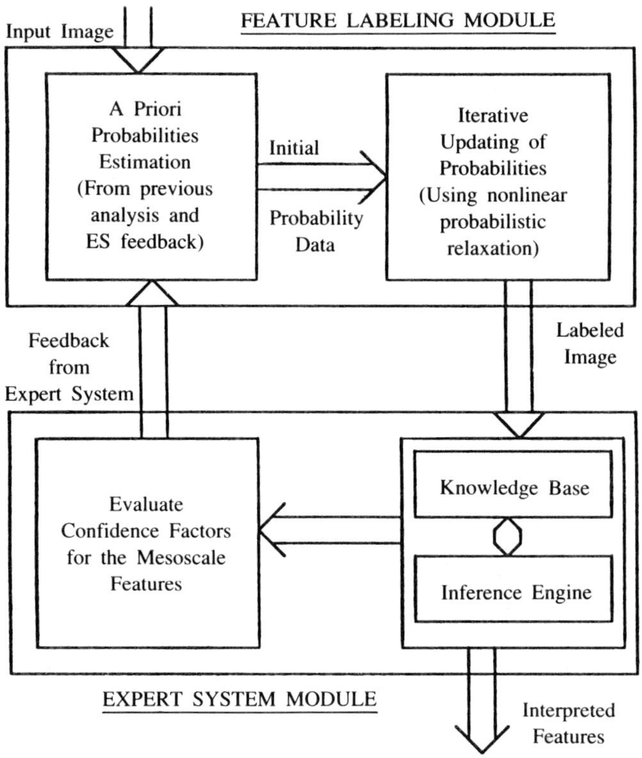


Fig. 2. Architecture of the hybrid system.

evaluates the consistency of the labeling process with the help of the knowledge base as well as from the input from the operator. This evaluation results in assigning a confidence factor to each of the features detected. This factor is them "fed back" to the feature labeling module, in addition to the previous data analysis, to improve the consistency of the labeling process in future.

A salient feature of this hybrid architecture is the feedback from the knowledge-based system to the labeling module. Due to atmospheric effects like cloud cover, the oceanic features may not be identified by the feature labeling module. Thus, the position of the Gulf Stream and eddies may not be determined correctly. In such cases, the expert system provides an approximate position of these features. This helps in interpreting the subsequent images. This is illustrated with the help of an example in Sec. 6. Another feature is the dynamic interpretation of the features. The hybrid architecture allows the expert system to learn from previous analysis. Also the modular approach allows the user to maintain the system and incorporate changes without much difficulty.

## 4. PROBABILISTIC RELAXATION LABELING

An important research area in image analysis and image interpretation technology is the development of methods that blend contextual information with conventional image processing algorithms. A literature survey clearly indicates that such a hybrid approach yields good results. Relaxation labeling is one such process. Relaxation labeling has been applied to a variety of image processing problems, e.g. linear feature enhancement,[10] edge enhancement,[11] image enhancement,[12] pixel classification.[13,14] A recent survey article by Kittler and Illingworth[15] on relaxation labeling highlights the importance of this area of research. The survey[15] also points out the advantages and possible applications of relaxation methods. More importantly, the relaxation labeling approach was elegantly described by Rosenfeld *et al.*[16] who investigated the problem of labeling the sides of a triangle and proposed a set of schemes to solve the problem. The paper[16] concluded with the result that the nonlinear probabilistic relaxation schemes yield better results than the others. The labeling algorithm presented in this paper is based on the nonlinear probabilistic relaxation technique.

The goal of the relaxation process is to reduce the uncertainty (and improve the consistency) in the assignment of one of the labels to each object in a set of related objects. In the oceanographic feature classification problem, the classes are the various oceanographic features, namely the north and south walls of the Gulf Stream, cold eddy, warm eddy, shelf front and coastal boundary. Refer to Fig. 3 to identify the positions of these oceanic features in a typical image. The objects are the individual pixels in a set of registered multi-temporal images. The uncertainty could be due to cloud cover or the overlap of features, features not belonging to one of the classes, noise in the image, or other factors. In this paper, we are attempting to label mesoscale features, but the ocean exhibits variability on all spatial scales. Thermal structure on scales smaller than mesoscale will interfere with the mesoscale feature labeling process. The underlying mathematical framework necessary for the relaxation labeling method is described in the next section.

### 4.1. Mathematical Framework For Relaxation Labeling

Let $\Lambda = \{\lambda_1, \lambda_2, \ldots, \lambda_m\}$ be the set of possible labels that may be assigned to each pixel $\mathbf{x}$ in the IR image. Also we let $p_\lambda^k(x)$ denote the probability that the pixel at $\mathbf{x}(\mathbf{i}, \mathbf{j})$ belongs to the object $\lambda$ after $k$ iterations of the relaxation algorithm. Note that the probabilities are functions of time unlike the conventional pixel relaxation labeling schemes where the probability is a function of position alone. This allows the relaxation labeling algorithm to utilize temporal continuity to reduce the ambiguity in labeling. The ambiguity may arise due to noise (cloud cover, for example).

There are two steps in executing the probabilistic relaxation algorithm. In the first step, *a priori* probabilities are evaluated with the help of ground truth data and/or a previous but recent mesoscale analysis. In the second step, these *a priori* probabilities are iteratively updated (relaxation) until a consistent labeling is reached. We now discuss these two steps in detail.

*Step 1. Estimating the a priori probabilities.*

Let $p_\lambda^0(x)$ denote the *a priori* value, that is, the probability that pixel **x(i, j)** belongs to the object $\lambda$ at the zeroth iteration. The Bayesian probability equation is used to evaluate this value. Equation (4.1.1) is used to calculate $p_\lambda^0(x)$.

$$p_\lambda^0(x) = \frac{p(x|\lambda)\ P(\lambda)}{\sum_\lambda p(x|\lambda)\ P(\lambda)} \tag{4.1.1}$$

where $p(x|\lambda)$ denotes the conditional density function and $P(\lambda)$ the probability of occurrence of the object $\lambda$.

To evaluate the conditional density function $p(x|\lambda)$, a set of parameters is measured at the pixel **x(i, j)**. Let $X$ denote the parameter vector. The following parameters are used to form the vector $X$:

(1) the vector from origin to pixel **x(i, j)** (both the magnitude and direction).
(2) gray scale intensity value at the pixel **x(i, j)**.
(3) the edge magnitude (Sec. 4.2 presents the chosen edge operator algorithm).

For each object, the mean vector $\mu_\lambda$ and the covariance matrix $\sum_\lambda$ are computed. Also it is assumed that the conditional density function follows a normal distribution. Hence the conditional density function $p(x|\lambda)$ is evaluated using Eq. (4.1.2).

$$p(x|\lambda) = (2\pi|\textstyle\sum_\lambda|)^{-1/2} \exp\left\{-\frac{1}{2}(X-\mu_\lambda)'\textstyle\sum_\lambda^{-1}(X-\mu_\lambda)\right\}. \tag{4.1.2}$$

To compute $P(\lambda)$, relative areas of the objects are considered. The number of pixels in the object $\lambda$ is $n_\lambda$. Then $P(\lambda)$ can be calculated using Eq. (4.1.3).

$$P(\lambda) = \frac{n_\lambda}{\sum_\lambda n_\lambda}. \tag{4.1.3}$$

*Step 2. Iterative updating algorithm.*

We now discuss the probability updating rule. The new estimate of the probability of $\lambda$ at **x(i, j)** is given by (4.1.4).

$$p_\lambda^{k+1}(x) = \frac{p_\lambda^k(x)\ (1 + q_\lambda^k(x))}{\sum_\lambda p_\lambda^k(x)\ (1 + q_\lambda^k(x))} \tag{4.1.4}$$

where $q_\lambda^k(x)$ is called the update factor.

The updating factor for the estimate $p_\lambda^k(x)$ at the $k$th iteration is given by Eq. (4.1.5).

$$q_\lambda^k(x) = \frac{1}{m}\sum_y \sum_{\lambda'} r_{\lambda\lambda'}(x, y) p_{\lambda'}^k(y) \tag{4.1.5}$$

where $m$ is the number of objects. In this equation, $r_{\lambda\lambda'}(x, y)$ denotes compatibility coefficients. These coefficients are computed as in Refs. 14 and 16. According to the relaxation scheme, $r_{\lambda\lambda'}(x, y)$ is a measure of the probabilistic compatibility between label $\lambda$ on point $x$ and label $\lambda'$ on point $y$, and has the following characteristics:

(1) If $\lambda$ on $x$ frequently co-occurs with $\lambda'$ on $y$, then $r_{\lambda\lambda'}(x, y) > 0$, and if they always co-occur, then $r_{\lambda\lambda'}(x, y) = 1$.
(2) If $\lambda$ on $x$ rarely co-occurs with $\lambda'$ on $y$, then $r_{\lambda\lambda'}(x, y) < 0$, and if they never co-occur, then $r_{\lambda\lambda'}(x, y) = -1$.
(3) If $\lambda$ on $x$ occurs independently of $\lambda'$ on $y$, then $r_{\lambda\lambda'}(x, y) = 0$.

### 4.2. Discussion of the Technique

The implementation of the above mentioned technique is carried out in two stages.

*Stage 1*

At the first stage, *a priori* probabilities are estimated using a manually prepared mesoscale analysis from a time period of two days prior to the test image. The objects present in the oceanographic IR image are identified with the help of previous analysis. A set of pixels on the north and south wall of the Gulf Stream are provided by the previous analysis. The center pixel and radii of the eddies are also given. From the parameter vector $X$ for a pixel $\mathbf{x}(\mathbf{i}, \mathbf{j})$, the mean vector $\mu_\lambda$ is calculated. Also for each object $\lambda$, the covariance matrix $\sum_\lambda$ is computed. Equation (4.1.2) is used to compute the conditional density function $p(x|\lambda)$. Finally the initial probability $p_\lambda^0(x)$ is computed using Eq. (4.1.1).

*Stage 2*

In the second stage, the iterative updating rule is implemented. The compatibility coefficients are calculated using the initial class probability values obtained in the first stage. These are fixed during the update process. As a concluding step in the second stage of the implementation, the iterative updating algorithm is implemented using Eq. (4.1.4). The iterative algorithm terminates when $(p_\lambda^{k+1}(x) - p_\lambda^k(x)) < \varepsilon$, where $\varepsilon$ is a very small quantity.

Now we discuss the features of the edge detection algorithm proposed by Holyer and Peckinpaugh.[9] The motivation behind the development of such a new edge detector algorithm is to aid the analysis of oceanographic satellite images. The popular derivative-based edge operators, viz. Sobel's operator, are shown to be too sensitive to edge fine-structure and to weak gradients to be useful in this application. The edge algorithm proposed by Holyer and Peckinpaugh[9] is based on the cluster shade texture measure, which is derived from the gray level co-occurrence (GLC) matrix. Holyer and Peckinpaugh[9] have suggested that the edge detection technique based on the GLC matrix can be effectively used in automated detection of mesoscale features. The $(i, j)$th element of the GLC matrix, $P(i, j|\Delta x, \Delta y)$, is the relative frequency with which two image elements, separated by distance $(\Delta x, \Delta y)$, occur in the image, one with intensity level $i$ and the other with intensity level $j$. The elements of the GLC matrix can be combined in many different ways to give a single numerical value that would be a measure of the edges present in the image. Holyer and Peckinpaugh[9] have used a cluster shade function which is found to be very effective in the edge detection process. The new edge algorithm computes the cluster shade function at each pixel. Then the edges are detected by finding the significant zero crossings in the cluster shade image. The advantages of this new edge algorithm over the conventional derivative-based techniques are discussed in Ref. 9. It is known that using large windows in derivative-based edge detector algorithms results in poor smoothing. This problem is circumvented in the new algorithm. Because edges are detected by finding zero crossings, precisely positioned lines result, even if the GLC matrix is calculated using a larger window. So, the desired edge detection characteristic of retaining sharp edges while eliminating edge detail is achieved with the help of the new algorithm. As an input to our feature labeling algorithm, we used the image output generated by cluster shade algorithm, with a window size of $16 \times 16$ pixels and zero crossing threshold of 50. The edge magnitudes obtained from this new edge detector algorithm are used as an input to the feature labeling algorithm. In particular the edge magnitudes are used to evaluate *a priori* probability values.

## 5. OCEANOGRAPHIC EXPERT SYSTEM

The Remote Sensing Branch of NOARL studies and develops methods to exploit satellite data to provide oceanographic information. The Navy needs to provide such information to the Fleet, so NOARL has an objective of transforming research techniques for the oceanographic interpretation of satellite data into operational procedures. From a large volume of satellite data, combined with non-satellite data, the shipboard user will be required to produce operationally useful tactical products. Dramatic improvement will be required in our ability to automate the image analysis process.

Interactive image processing is a powerful tool in the hands of an expert image interpreter. However, human interpretation is both varied in its level of expertise and is labor-intensive. Expert judgement is required for oceanographic image interpretation because there is little or no standardization in either image enhancement or interactive techniques. NOARL has conducted research in the use of concepts from the field of artificial intelligence to develop knowledge-based "expert systems" to automate some aspects of the oceanographic image interpretation task. That work is an attempt to remove human-labor-intensive and varying-skill-level elements from the interpretation of oceanographic image and other satellite data. Lybanon *et al.*[1] describe the motivation and some of the history of NOARL in this area.

The rule base of the expert system is derived from an unprecedented compilation of information, and the expert system's mode of operation is innovative. The rule base represents oceanographic knowledge about the evolution of mesoscale ocean features in the Gulf Stream region of the north Atlantic Ocean. The rules are applied in such a way that the expert system describes the kinematics of that evolution. The expert system is presently implemented in a combination of OPS83, C, and FORTRAN running on a VAX 8300. The expert system uses the rules about the features to evolve an initial "state" to a later time. The new, hypothesized state can then be used as a new initial condition and the process is repeated. This process can be usefully carried out for several steps. This mode of operation is different from expert systems which use a (sometimes lengthy) chain of reasoning to reach a single conclusion, such as a system for medical diagnosis.

The domain of the expert system is the Gulf Stream region of the north Atlantic Ocean. The expert system has different rules for ring and Gulf Stream behavior in each of nine geographical regions. Figure 3 shows the operating regions of the expert system. Aside from the lines that separate them, the regions are bounded only by land. A ring's behavior as hypothesized by the expert system depends upon which region its center is in at the beginning of a time step. Basically, the motion has a region-dependent velocity vector. However, a ring that is closer than a certain critical distance from the Gulf Stream undergoes a modification of the basic motion. The Gulf Stream interaction rules are also region-dependent. The details depend upon how close the ring is to the Gulf Stream; the Gulf Stream interaction may result in a deflection or a looping motion of the ring, with possible coalescence with the Stream in some cases. Ring sizes decrease with time. The rate of decrease depends on the region and on whether there is Gulf Stream interaction. A ring that shrinks below a certain size disappears. Gulf Stream motion is modeled as downstream propagation of meanders, with region-dependent phase velocities and amplitude factors. While this is only a first-order model, there is justification in the literature for this behavior. Refer to Ref. 1 for a complete description of the expert system.

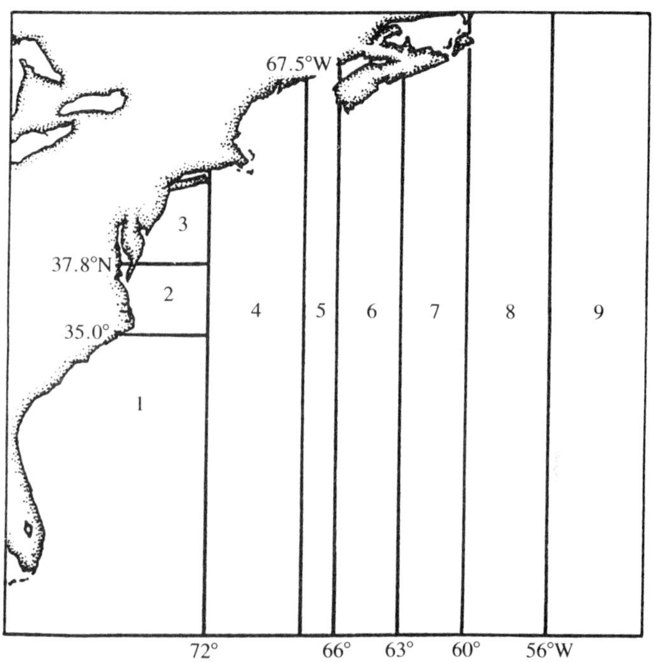


Fig. 3. Nine regions of expert system domain.

## 6. HYBRID FEATURE LABELING TECHNIQUE—AN EXAMPLE

In this section we present the results of our feature labeling technique. We show that the expert system greatly helps in labeling the features when the analysis of the previous sample image fails. This situation arises when the oceanic features are completely covered by cloud. In the following we describe the steps involved in the hybrid feature labeling technique.

The system starts up with the human interpretation of an image that is obtained two or three days before the current image. The initial probabilities are computed based on the analysis of the previous image. Nonlinear probabilistic relaxation technique is applied to label the features in the current image. Figure 1 shows the IR image with all the features. The output of the edge detector algorithm is given in Fig. 4. Figure 5 shows the IR image with all the edge features overlapped. The positional details of the features are then given to the expert system. Sometimes the IR image of the ocean may not be clear. That is, the features are covered by cloud. To analyze such an image, the feedback from the expert system is used. The position of the oceanic features is obtained by activating the inference engine of the expert system. This approach is different from the conventional one, in which the information is always provided by the low level module. The concept of getting feedback from a high level module (like an expert system) is totally new and justified in automatic image interpretation of oceanographic images. The output of the labeling algorithm is given in Fig. 6.

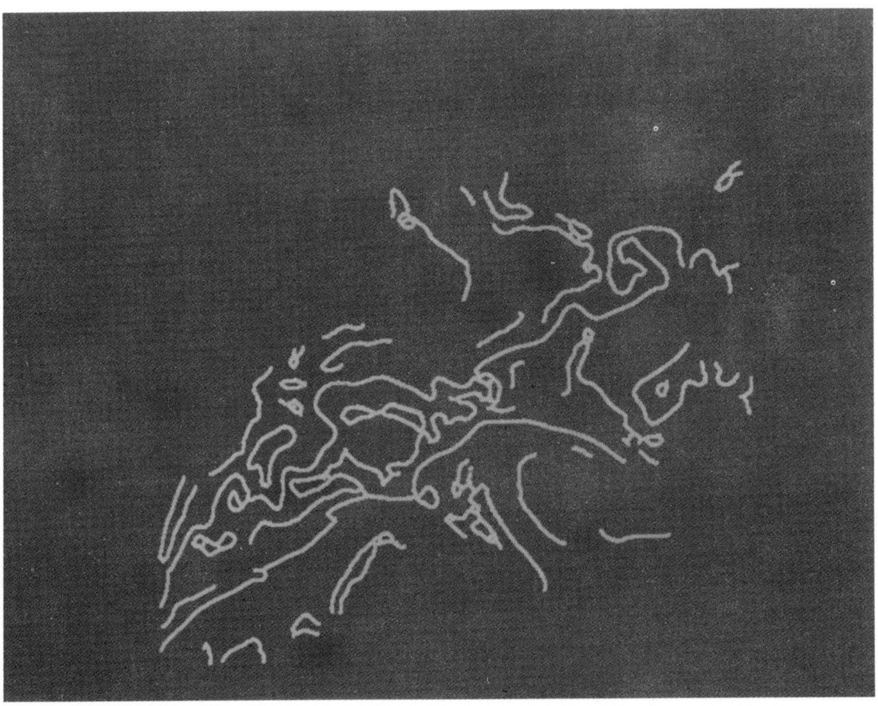

Fig. 4. Output of the edge detector.

Fig. 5. IR Image with edges overlapped.

Fig. 6. Output of the feature labeling algorithm.

## 7. SUMMARY AND RECOMMENDATIONS FOR FUTURE WORK

In this paper, the need for automatic interpretation of oceanographic images is emphasized. The advantage of exploiting the contextual information in feature labeling is highlighted. An efficient and simple technique for labeling of oceanic features is described. The underlying theoretical framework and the steps involved in estimating the probability functions are explained in detail. The overall architecture of the proposed image interpretation system is presented. The usefulness of an expert system in feature labeling is discussed. The concept of getting feedback from the expert system is a new approach and it is explained with the help of an example.

As a future extension to the present work we propose to:

(i) make the oceanographic expert system "learn" from its past experience in analyzing the satellite imagery data.

(ii) investigate the possibility of implementing a parallel relaxation labeling algorithm to speed up the labeling process.

## REFERENCES

1. M. Lybanon, J. D. McKendrick, R. E. Blake, J. R. B. Cockett and M. G. Thomason, "A prototype knowledge-based system to aid the oceanographic image analyst", *SPIE* **Vol. 635**–*Applications of Artificial Intelligence III* (1986) 203–206.
2. D. J. Gerson and P. Gaborski, "Pattern analysis for automatic location of oceanic fronts in digital satellite imagery", Naval Oceanographic Office, TN 3700-65-77, Oct. 1977.
3. D. J. Gerson, E. Khedouri and P. Gaborski, "Detecting the gulf stream from digital infrared data pattern recognition", *The Belle W. Baruch Library in Marine Science* **12** (1982) 19–39.
4. R. E. Coulter, "Application of the Bayes decision rule for automatic water mass classification from satellite infrared data", *Proc. 17th Int. Symposium on Remote Sensing of Environment*, Vol. II, 1983 pp. 589–597.
5. M. F. Janowitz, "Automatic detection of gulf stream rings", Technical report TR-J8501, Office of Naval Research, Contr N-00014-79-C-0629, June 1985.
6. D. G. Nichol, "Autonomous extraction of eddy-like structure from infrared images of the ocean", *IEEE Trans. Geoscience and Remote Sensing* **25** (1987) 28–34.
7. N. Krishnakumar, S. Sitharama Iyengar, R. Holyer and M. Lybanon, "A technique for feature labeling in infrared oceanographic images", *Fifth Int. Conf. on IIPS*, Jan. 1989, pp. 368–375.
8. D. G. Goodenough, M. Goldberg, G. Plunkett and J. Zelek, "An expert system for remote sensing", *IEEE Trans. Geoscience and Remote Sensing* **25** (1987) 349–356.
9. R. J. Holyer and S. H. Peckinpaugh, "Edge detection applied to satellite imagery of the oceans", *IEEE Trans. Geoscience and Remote Sensing* **27** (1989) 46–56.
10. S. W. Zucker, R. A. Hummel and A. Rosenfeld, "An application of relaxation labeling to line and curve enhancement", *IEEE Trans. Comput.* **26** (1977) 399–403.
11. B. J. Schachter, A. Lev, S. W. Zucker and A. Rosenfeld, "An application of relaxation methods to edge reinforcement", *IEEE Trans. Syst. Man. Cybern.* **7** (1977) 813–816.
12. L. S. Davis and A. Rosenfeld, "Noise cleaning by iterated local averaging", *IEEE Trans. Syst. Man. Cybern.* **8** (1978) 705–710.
13. J. O. Eklundh, H. Yamamoto and A. Rosenfeld, "A relaxation method in multispectral pixel classification", *IEEE Trans. Pattern Anal. Mach. Intell.* **2** (1980) 72–75.

14. L. S. Davis, C. Y. Wang and H. C. Xie, "An experiment in multispectral, multitemporal crop classification using relaxation techniques", *Comput. Vision, Graph. Image Process.* **23** (1983) 227–235.
15. J. Kittler and J. Illingworth, "Relaxation labeling algorithms—a review", *Image and Vision Comput.* **3**, 4 (1985) 206–216.
16. A. Rosenfeld, R. A. Hummel and S. W. Zucker, "Scene labeling by relaxation operations", *IEEE Trans. Syst. Man. Cybern.* **6** (1976) 420–434.

**Narayanan Krishnakumar** received the B.S. degree in applied sciences from Madurai University, India in 1981 and the B.S. degree in electrical and electronics engineering from the Indian Institute of Science, Bangalore, India in 1984. He is currently a Ph.D. candidate at Louisiana State University.

His primary research interests are in the areas of computer vision, digital image analysis, artificial intelligence, and parallel processing.

**S. Sitharama Iyengar** directs the Robotics Research Laboratory (RRL) at Louisiana State University. His area of research interest is in the design and analysis of algorithms for a wide variety of problems. Professor Iyengar's research at the RRL addresses problems that are fundamental to the implementation of autonomous intelligent machines. This research is comprehensive, covering most aspects of intelligent systems. For example, he has conducted important work on the problems of intelligent robot navigation, intelligent sensing, world-modeling using acoustic sensors, and real-time expert systems for the control of mobile robots, to name a few. Many of these projects have involved collaboration with NASA, Oak Ridge National Laboratory, Navy-NORDA, and JPL/Caltech.

Professor Iyengar has published over 100 papers in refereed journals and conference proceedings. He has served as a visiting research scientist at the Robotics and Artificial Intelligence Group, CESAR Division, Oak Ridge National Laboratory, as a member of the National Science Foundation select panel for reviewing research proposals on neural networks, as Guest Editor for a special issue on Autonomous Systems in *IEEE Transactions on Computers*, June 1989, and as Guest Editor for a special issue on Intelligent Image Databases in *IEEE Transactions on Software Engineering*, May 1988. He is presently a Guest Editor for a special issue on Distributed Sensor Networks in *IEEE Transactions on Systems, Man and Cybernetics*. He has won several research and teaching awards and is a senior IEEE member.

**Ronald J. Holyer** received the B.A. degree in physics and mathematics from Augustana College in 1964, the M.S. degree in physics from the South Dakota School of Mines and Technology in 1966, and the Ph.D degree in geology from the University of South Carolina in 1989.

He has conducted remote sensing and image processing research at Texas Instruments, Inc. and Lockheed Electronics Co., Inc. He is presently with the Naval Oceanographic and Atmospheric Research Laboratory at the Stennis Space Center, Mississippi, where he is a principal investigator in the field of automated image analysis and pattern recognition applied to remotely sensed oceanographic data.

**Matthew Lybanon** received the B.S. and M.S. degrees in physics from Georgia Institute of Technology, Atlanta, in 1960 and 1962 respectively. He has conducted research in remote sensing, image processing and pattern recognition while employed by the Computer Sciences Corporation at NASA's Marshall Space Flight Center and Stennis Space Center. A member of the Naval Oceanographic and Atmospheric Laboratory's Remote Sensing Branch, he is Principal Investigator for the GEOSAT Ocean Applications Program, for a project which is developing knowledge-based techniques for the automated interpretation of oceanographic satellite data, and for a project to provide analysis tools for Navy oceanographic centers. His current professional interests include artificial intelligence, neural networks, image processing, generalized nonlinear least squares methods, and applications of those topics to the extraction of information on ocean dynamics and sea ice from satellite observations.

Mr. Lybanon is a member of the American Physical Society and the American Geophysical Union. He is a reviewer for papers submitted to the American Journal of Physics. He was awarded a NASA commendation for image processing work to help assess the damage to Skylab's solar panel when they opened prematurely during launching.

# AN EXPERT SYSTEM FOR TUNING PARTICLE BEAM ACCELERATORS

DARREL L. LAGER, HAL R. BRAND
and WILLIAM J. MAURER

*Engineering Research Division, Electronics Engineering*
*Lawrence Livermore National Laboratory*
*University of California*
*Livermore, CA 94550, USA*

Received 1 April 1990

An expert system that acts as an intelligent assistant to operators tuning a particle beam accelerator was developed. The system incorporates three approaches to tuning: (1) Duplicating within a software program the reasoning and the procedures used by an operator to tune an accelerator. This approach has been used to steer particle beams through the transport section of Lawrence Livermore National Laboratory's Advanced Test Accelerator and through the injector section of the Experimental Test Accelerator. (2) Using a model to simulate the position of a beam in an accelerator. The simulation is based on data taken directly from the accelerator while it is running. This approach will ultimately be used by operators of the Experimental Test Accelerator to first compare actual and simulated beam performance in real time, then to determine which set of parameters is optimum in terms of centering the beam, and finally to feed those parameters to the accelerator. Operators can also use the model to determine if a component has failed. (3) Using a mouse to manually select and control the magnets that steer the beam. Operators on the Experimental Test Accelerator can also use the mouse to call up windows that display the horizontal and vertical positions of the beam as well as its current.

*Keywords:* Artificial intelligence; Expert systems; Accelerators; Tuning; Particle beams.

## 1. INTRODUCTION

Particle beam accelerators are members of a class of large, complex systems that must be operated by people rather than machines to be effectively controlled. When machines were used to control such systems in the past, they frequently failed, usually because the conventional approach of feedback control using a numerical model of the system failed. This failure occurs because the system is strongly nonlinear, continually changes due to component failures, involves physical phenomena for which satisfactory models have not been derived, or may be so complex that it is simply too expensive to derive the model.

Despite these problems, individual operators are able to run such complex systems effectively. The operators appear to have a set of small, rule-of-thumb (heuristic) models for the various components of the system and to know how to manipulate those components to achieve the desired control.

In an attempt to duplicate the expertise of operators of large accelerators, we have developed an expert system called MAESTRO (Model and Expert System Tuning

Resource for Operators) that models the procedures involved in tuning such accelerators and in fixing them when components fail (a frequent occurrence). MAESTRO is a software program that blends physics models of the system and operator heuristics. We chose the MAESTRO acronym to emphasize the metaphor of a conductor unifying and coordinating the activities of control, diagnostics, physics models, and post-run analysis—all activities that are critical to the success of physics experiments. Traditionally those activities would have been separated, and different people within different groups would have been responsible for them. However, one of the advantages of MAESTRO is that it imposes unity and consistency on the system while it also helps operators tune the system more efficiently. As an example of the latter, operators can make much more informed control decisions because they can observe the simulation while the machine is running. Also, physicists can quickly gain insight into a particular phenomenon and make appropriate changes to the model because discrepancies between the model and the machine are more readily apparent.

## 2. PARTICLE BEAM ACCELERATORS

A particle beam accelerator is a device that accelerates electrically charged atomic or subatomic particles, such as electrons, protons, or ions, to high energies. Laboratory researchers use accelerators to study high-energy physics problems that arise in the Weapons, Beam Research, and Magnetic Fusion Programs. We have focused our efforts on two accelerators, the Advanced Test Accelerator (ATA) located at Lawrence Livermore National Laboratory's Site 300, and the Experimental Test Accelerator (ETA) located at the Laboratory itself. The ATA is the more complex of the two and consists of an injector, an accelerator, a transport section, an emittance selector, a tuning dump, an achromatic jog (a-jog), and a wiggler. The injector produces a pulse of electrons and injects it into a beam pipe, an evacuated pipe a few inches in diameter running the length of the machine. (A beam pipe with its associated components is called a beam line.) The accelerator section increases the energy of the electrons in the beam pulse up to about 50 MeV. An alignment laser guides the beam through the accelerator section and delivers it to the transport section. The transport section steers and focuses the beam into the emittance selector which "strips off" the electrons with undesired energy. A bending magnet directs the beam either to the tuning dump which absorbs the energy in the beam while the operator is tuning, or to the a-jog which moves the beam onto the wiggler beam line. The wiggler couples energy from the electron beam to another laser beam, greatly increasing the energy in the laser beam. A typical experiment is to deliver an electron beam into the wiggler and investigate its characteristics for producing gain in the laser beam. The ETA is somewhat simpler than the ATA and consists of an injector, an accelerator, a transport section, and a wiggler. One of the differences between the two is that the ETA accelerator increases the energy of the electrons in the beam pulse to only about 6 MeV, without using laser guiding. Another difference is that the wiggler couples energy into a microwave beam, increasing the energy of the beam. In a typical experiment the ETA produces high-power microwaves that heat a magnetic fusion plasma. Both accelerators have a variety of diagnostic devices that determine the beam's position within the pipe and its energy distribution. Both systems also have ancillary components (vacuum pumps, safety systems, cooling systems, and pulsed power systems) in their beam lines, further increasing their complexity.

## 3. TUNING

The goal when tuning an accelerator is to produce a beam that has the desired temporal and spatial energy and charge distributions required for a given experiment. The optimum distribution or ''beam profile'' is depicted in Fig. 1, where the beam pulse traveling down the beam pipe is on center within a few millimeters. All the electrons in the pulse have uniform axial velocity and zero transverse velocity, and all are uniformly distributed within it. In reality the beam has non-uniform velocities and is subject to a variety of instabilities, causing it to disperse at the nose and tail. (A common instability is a corkscrew, named for the spiral shape assumed by the beam.) Serious instabilities cause the beam to break up or strike the wall of the beam pipe.

Figure 2 shows the devices used for tuning the beam line. The beam bugs shown at the left of the figure are diagnostic devices for determining the beam position and current profile. A beam bug produces three oscilloscope traces as the beam pulse passes through it, one for the current, one for the $x$ position, and one for the $y$ position. The operator determines if the beam has the desired axial charge distribution and total charge by observing the current waveform. The position waveforms give the beam position along the horizontal ($x$) and vertical ($y$) transverse axes of the pipe. Video cameras record the light emitted when the beam strikes foils inserted into the beamline. The resulting images give information on the transverse distribution of the beam pulse and are used to determine the beam focus.

Steering magnets change the direction of propagation of the beam. It requires a pair of steering magnets a distance apart to displace the axis of propagation without changing the direction. The first changes the angle of propagation and the second compensates for the angle introduced by the first. Quadrupole magnets focus the beam and have the usually undesirable side effect of steering the beam off-center when it enters. A general rule-of-thumb is to keep the beam on-center through the quadrupoles to suppress the unwanted steering.

### 3.1. Complications

The tuning task is complicated by things the operator can readily adapt to, but are difficult for computers to deal with. Since the machine is made up of a large number of components, and since many of them are highly stressed state-of-the-art designs operating at high voltage and high current, there are random failures in the hardware that occur each day. Common occurrences are power supplies failing and the alignment laser drifting out of position. Less often magnets will short- or open-circuit. The operator handles these by periodically observing the status of the machine. If he cannot correct the problem, he modifies his tuning strategies and attempts to tune anyway until the problem is fixed.

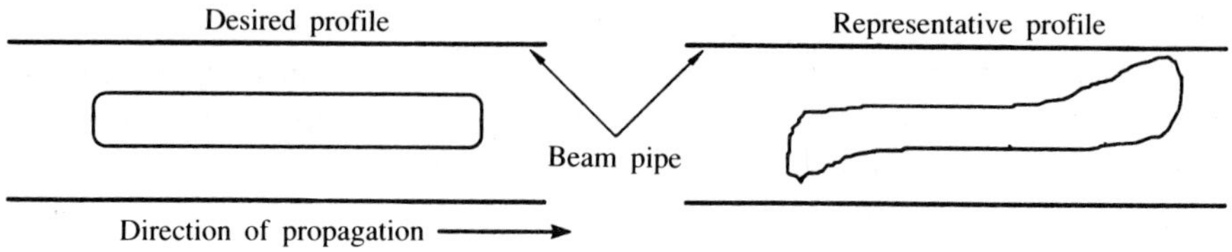


Fig. 1. Beam profile while tuning.

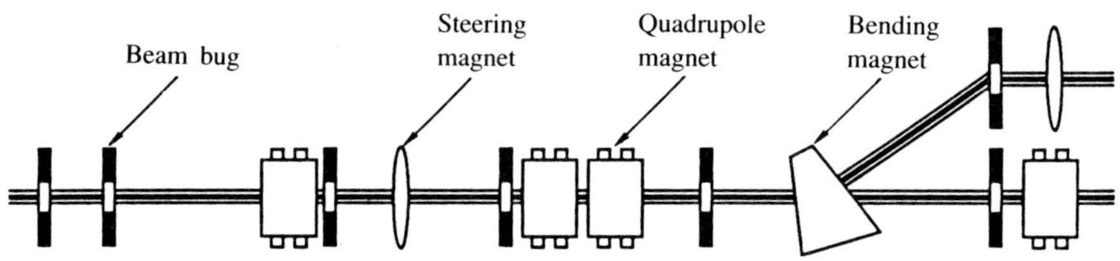


Fig. 2. Components affecting tuning.

The operator must also deal with unreliable diagnostics data. There is a high shot-to-shot variation in the characteristics of the trace data. There are also bad shots that must be ignored entirely when the machine misfires. As a result the operator observes several shots and determines an "average" of the beam characteristics. He will also devote one beam bug to watching the beginning of a section so he can determine if changes in the bug he is observing are caused by his tuning efforts or by changes in the beam characteristics at the input.

Since these accelerators are research tools the hardware is often reconfigured. Generally, the changes involve adding or deleting components, moving existing ones to different places or changing the relationships among them (e.g. connecting magnets to different power supplies). Another way the configuration can change is that during a run the beam may be directed down different beam pipes to do a desired experiment. The operator is usually told of the changes at the beginning of a shift and readily adapts to the differences. However, the expert system had to be designed with an interface that could tell it about the changes and could verify that the MAESTRO representation reflected the true machine.

Another complication the operator easily adapts to is that the machine is not built exactly as designed. Beam bugs may be installed with their measurement axes rotated away from being perfectly vertical or horizontal. The operator simply realizes this and instead of just using the $x$-axis knob to change beam position he will vary both $x$ and $y$ to do it. He will also move a knob and if the beam steers in the wrong direction, he will just move the knob the other way. The components are also imperfect so they all need calibration curves. The operator easily deals with these problems because much of the tuning is aimed at achieving a position equal to zero (on-center). However, a model needs more precise knowledge of the calibrations, positions, and orientations of the devices than an operator if it is to compute a desired change in one step (an operator can determine a change experimentally).

Finally, the machine does not measure the same way from one day to the next, even when all the hardware is unchanged. Various critical aspects of the machine are impossible to measure accurately enough. For example, the ion gauges that measure the vacuum profile along the beam path are not sufficiently accurate. As a result the benzene profile will not be the same as before and the propagation of the beam through the benzene is slightly different. The physics of transport of a beam through benzene are not well understood, so it is extremely difficult to compensate for the measurement system by modeling. The operator has evolved tuning strategies that are relatively insensitive to these phenomena.

### 3.2. Expert System Techniques

MAESTRO blends three distinct tuning approaches to achieve better performance than any one alone. A trade-off among these approaches can be made as the machine is modified or grows more complex, as the operators learn more of its idiosyncrasies, or as more is understood about its physics. In the first approach, called "cloning the operator," the procedures and reasoning followed by the operator are encoded as faithfully as possible. This was the approach taken for tuning the ATA because it was not possible within the alloted time to develop an accurate model for the beamline. A disadvantage of only using this approach is that operators may not be able to develop successful procedures for the far more complex machines being designed, such as the Superconducting Supercollider. A second approach, model-based tuning, simulates the beam propagating through the sections of the machine. The notable aspect of this approach is that the model is hooked into the actual system and is running at the same time the machine is running, so the simulation is based on measurements that are being made by the machine at the moment the machine is making them. This approach allows the operator to compare the simulation with the actual beam position, to choose an optimum set of parameters for centering the beam, and to download those parameters onto the real machine at a substantial savings in time. The disadvantage is that it may not be economically feasible to develop a sufficiently accurate simulator, either because the machine may be too complex or because it changes too often due to component failure. The third approach is to tune the system manually, but provide the operator with more powerful tools for tuning the machine. For example, this might take the form of displays derived from the raw data or different interfaces that make it easier to control the machine. The goal is to achieve a blend of these approaches that minimizes the time required to tune and maximizes the time available for performing physics experiments. Each of these approaches is discussed below.

Actually, no matter which approach we stress, we will always need the manual approach because operators will almost always have more knowledge of the machine than is economically feasible to encode into a computer program. Moreover, they can take into account information that may not be readily accessible to the computer, such as the "sound" the machine makes when it is not running quite right. They may also be able to instantly diagnose a failure because they remember what happened when that same situation arose on a machine they were tuning 20 years ago.

## 4. CLONING THE OPERATOR

The operators of the Lab's accelerators go through a set of procedures when their machines are first powered up. The procedures reflect two different kinds of reasoning by the operator. In the first instance, the operator is concerned with the overall tuning of the machine ("global strategy"). Global strategy is made up of many lower-level "local strategies" that are each concerned with the tuning of a small section of the machine.

When operators are performing a local strategy, they reason about components upstream (opposite the direction of propagation) and downstream from a chosen diagnostics device. For example, as shown in Fig. 3, when steering through the transport section, the operator observes the trace data and determines there is a position error at a bug. He reasons about the devices downstream and decides whether it is desirable to correct the error at this bug or to ignore it and examine the next bug. He reasons about devices upstream to decide which can be used to correct the error. He usually chooses a steering magnet and changes its field strength until the position error is zero.

In pseudo-English form this strategy can be described as:

Walk the bugs of the transport section moving downstream from the one nearest the injector—

if the position error at a bug is too large and the error cannot be ignored then reduce the error to zero by tweaking the steering magnets upstream;
if there are none, align the laser;
if there are two with no quadrupole between them, use them as a pair;
if the first upstream steerer is too close, use the second one upstream;
otherwise use the first upstream steering magnet.

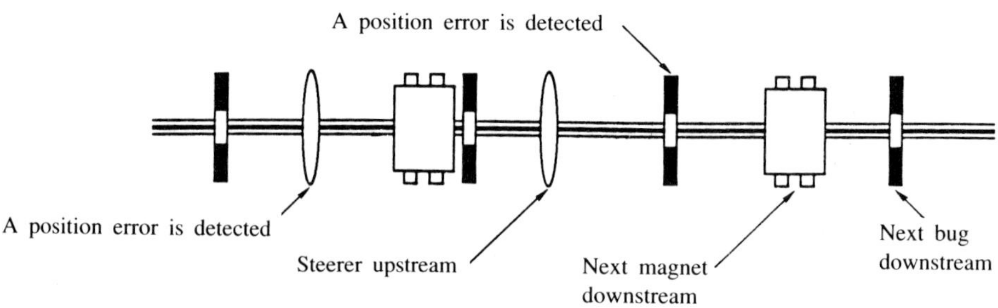


Fig. 3. The operator reasoning about devices upstream and downstream from a bug.

Note that this strategy is relatively unaffected by component failures, since a failed component is simply deleted from the beamline and is no longer considered as an upstream or downstream component.

The global strategy is concerned with properly applying local strategies, based on the present state of tune of the machine. The guiding philosophy is ''focus and steer the beam but don't put the beam into the wall.'' Given that philosophy, the operators first check each major section of the accelerator to see if the beam has arrived from the previous section. If it has not, the operators go back to the previous section and use a coarse steering technique to get the beam through the section. Once the beam has made it all the way to the tuning dump (that portion at the end of the accelerator that can absorb the full energy of the beam without disrupting the system or damaging components), the operator goes back to the beginning of the transport section and meticulously centers the beam while monitoring the beam current at the tuning dump. We have encoded the local strategies followed by the operator in a representation we call a Monitored Decision Script (MDS). An MDS is an extension of the notion of scripts introduced by Schank.[1] Scripts are used to represent step-by-step procedural knowledge. The canonical example is the script for eating at a restaurant—first you are seated, then you order, then you eat, then you pay, and then you leave. These things have to be performed in order, but exactly what is done at each step is decided when you visit a particular restaurant. We use the Script part of an MDS to represent the procedures involved in performing the local strategies. The Decision part of the MDS name comes from the decisions that must be made when errors are detected (say when a magnet does not respond to a request to change its field because the supply connected to it has failed). The Monitor portion of the name comes from monitors that are periodically examined to check the health of the system. This emulates the behavior of the operator, for example, when he periodically checks to see if the laser alignment has drifted off position.

To implement the global strategy, we have written a number of separate MDSs that are grouped according to what state the accelerator is in; that is, whether the accelerator is in the start-up, coarse, or fine-tuning states. One of these states is listed in a so-called pre-condition field of each MDS. Each MDS also contains a post-condition field, within which is listed the result of successfully executing the MDS. For example, if a particular MDS has a pre-condition field that lists initial start-up, then the post-condition field would state that the beam has reached the tuning dump. We have also developed an AI program called an inference engine to manipulate the MDSs and perform the global strategy. The engine first checks to see which state the accelerator is in; next, it matches that state with one of the MDSs that lists the state in its pre-condition field; next, it selects one of these MDSs and executes it. Executing the MDS puts the machine in a new state (not necessarily the one listed in the post-condition), then the cycle of match, select, and execute is repeated until the accelerator is tuned.

The MDS and inference engine programs were applied to the problem of centering the beam in the transport section of the ATA accelerator. Our initial approach was to decompose the steering problem into two simpler, decoupled problems; namely, centering the beam in $x$, then $y$. We thought this was possible because our system had "knowledge" of the beam bug rotation angles and other information that would enable decoupling of the $x$ and $y$ steering. Unfortunately this approach was unsuccessful because there was coupling between the vertical and horizontal steerers that we were unable to represent given our time constraints. Instead we modified our approach to more faithfully incorporate the strategy used by the operator. This was performed in two phases. In the first phase we diagnosed a pair of steerers and determined which more strongly influenced the $x$ position and which the $y$. In the second phase we centered the beam using the steerers by repeatedly halving the error in $x$, then $y$, using an optimization algorithm.[2] This approach successfully automated the centering of the beam.

### 4.1. Model-Based Tuning

For the ATA discussed above, we chose to clone the operator as the best way to automate the system, given the complexity of the accelerator and the limited amount of machine time available to us. For the ETA we chose to model the system because the ETA is less complex than the ATA and there has been more of an opportunity to get onto the system and model the various components. Consequently, this fiscal year we are much closer to a tuning model of an accelerator.

Making use of such a model involves two distinct phases. The first is the "commissioning" phase[3] during which the simulator is matched with the real accelerator by measuring what effect each component has on the beam. This phase forces proper bookkeeping because the effect of each component on the beam trajectory must be calculated accurately for the model to work. Any rotations, tilts, offsets, and miscalibrations must be eliminated or incorporated into the model during this phase so the simulator and real machine produce the same beam trajectory. As part of the commissioning phase we have developed procedures to measure various beam parameters. For example, we measure the effects that steering magnets have on beam position by sweeping horizontal and vertical steering magnets through a range of values, producing the cross-shaped pattern in Fig. 4. Similarly, we measure the effects that solenoid magnets have on focus by sweeping through a range of settings, producing the spiral-shaped pattern shown in Fig. 5. We have started the commissioning phase on the injector section of the ETA accelerator and have chosen the smallest subset possible: one magnet followed immediately by a beam bug. Once the effects of these components have been measured, we will commission the remaining injector magnets and then proceed down the accelerator beginning with the first ten-cell set. Once we are finished with the accelerator, we will tackle the remaining beamlines.

As discussed above, during the commissioning phase, we bring the simulation model and the accelerator into relative agreement. In the second operational phase we can actually begin to tune the accelerator and diagnose failure. To tune the accelerator, the first step is to turn the system on and measure the actual beam position in the accelerator. Given these measurements, the initial beam energy, and the commissioned

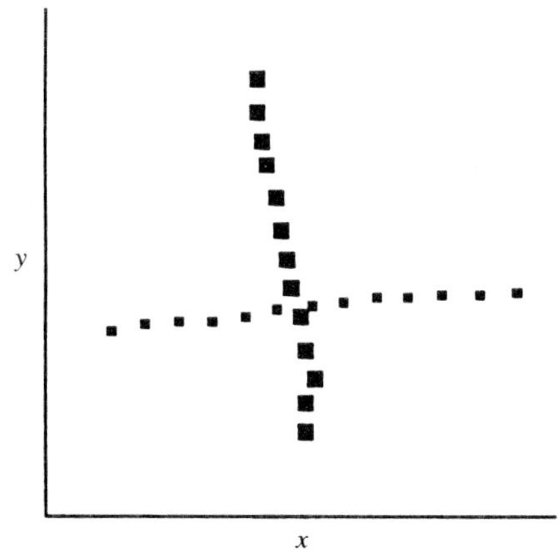


Fig. 4. Variation of $x$ and $y$ beam positions as the vertical and horizontal steering magnets are swept through a range of values.

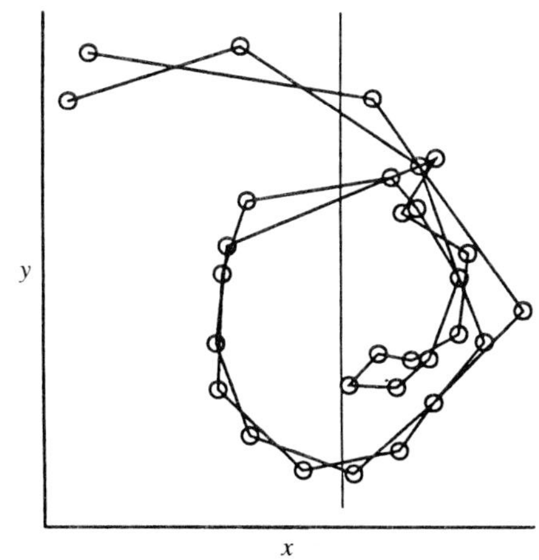


Fig. 5. Variation of $x$ and $y$ beam positions as the solenoidal field is varied through a range of values. The solenoidal field causes the beam to spiral as it passes through the magnet. As a result, varying the field causes the locus of points representing the beam position to assume a spiral shape. The spiral becomes tighter as the field increases.

model, we can estimate the launch conditions of the beam—its initial position and transverse velocities (denoted as $x$, $x'$, $y$, $y'$). These conditions are estimated by fitting the measured data to simulated data and then varying the launch conditions to get the best fit. Finally, we can use a nonlinear parameter estimator (part of the simulation model) to select tuning parameters that will center the beam. Obviously, a very large number of tuning parameters are available. Initially, an experienced operator will select a subset of these for tuning, and iterate the process with different subsets. Eventually, the operator's knowledge and experience will be encoded into an expert system that will select the subset of tuning parameters and will decide how much iteration is necessary.

When the simulation model and the accelerator go out of relative agreement (due to component failure), the model can be used to find those regions within the accelerator where there is still agreement. For a single component failure, there will be two regions of agreement roughly surrounding the failed component. From this information, a list of suspect components can be compiled. With the aid of an expert operator (or eventually, an expert system), a number of possible failures can be proposed. The nonlinear parameter estimator is then used to estimate both the magnitude of the proposed error and the improvement in the model's predictive ability, given the proposed error and the data currently available from the accelerator sensors. With this information, many proposed errors can be rejected because either the magnitude of the error is beyond reasonable limits, or the improvement in the model by the addition of the error is too small. In the ideal case, one is left with only one reasonable error. In the other cases, one is normally left with only a few possibilities. Beam redirection experiments can then be performed to further isolate the accelerator-model discrepancy. Selection of these experiments will initially be done by experienced operators, but will eventually be included within the expert system's capabilities. When the problem is finally found, then the accelerator can be fixed and/or the model can be updated with the (fit) error information, and tuning can proceed as before.

In conclusion, model-based tuning promises to put more science into the art of tuning, and leads to a more rigorous understanding of the machines. The model enables operators to "see" the effects of their tuning in the regions between (not covered by) sensors. Given sufficiently accurate models it should be possible to determine a set of parameters that will change the present state of the machine to a desired (tuned) state in a single step. Experiments can be performed off-line using the model to determine, for example, the effects of adding new components to the beamline at far less expense than would be the case if the real machine were used.

### 4.2. Manual Interface

The manual interface for MAESTRO is shown in the screen dump in Fig. 6. The interface consists of several windows that become visible on the screen as necessary. The Machine Interrogation and Control (MICI) window is the main one for interacting with the system. It consists of two panes, one above the other. The top pane displays the output from the simulator, showing the horizontal beam position as a thick line and the vertical position as a thin line. The lower pane shows a set of icons depicting the components in the beamline. The locations of the icons and their shape are derived from the information describing the beamline in the MAESTRO knowledge base. Components added to the beamline are automatically included in the MICI display once the information has been added to the knowledge base.

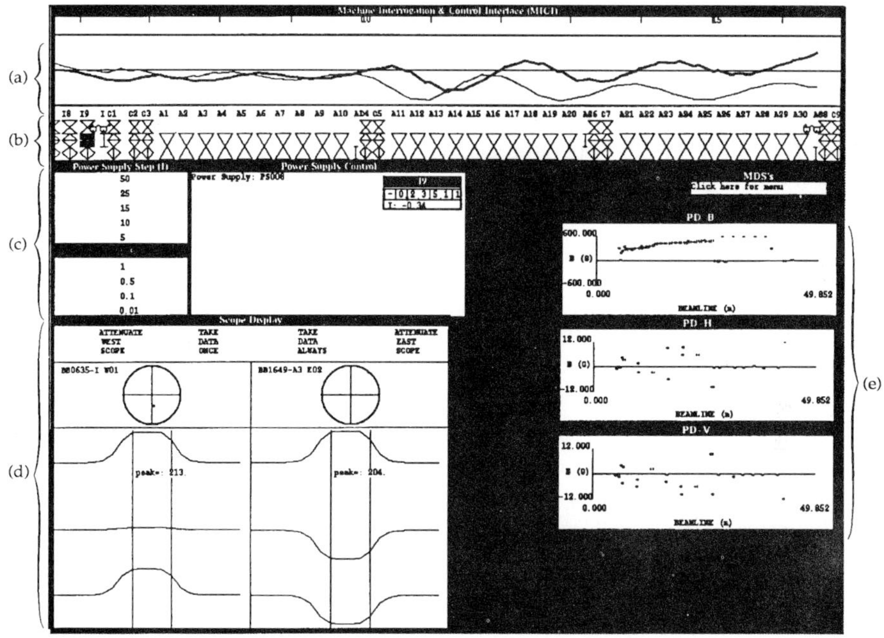


Fig. 6. Screen dump of the windows associated with the manual interface to MAESTRO. The windows are: (a) simulated beam position vs. distance down beamline. The $x$ position is the thin line and the $y$ position is the thick line; (b) icons depicting the components according to their positions in the beamline; (c) power supply control window; (d) scope display showing the $I$, $x$, and $y$ waveforms from the selected beam bugs; (e) field strength vs. distance down the beamline for the solenoids, horizontal steerers, and vertical steerers.

The operator controls the magnetic fields by positioning a cursor over an icon with a mouse. Clicking over a vertical steering magnet icon, for example, causes power supply control windows to become visible below the MICI window (Fig. 6). By clicking the mouse as the cursor is positioned in the windows we can increase or decrease the current in the appropriate power supply by a given increment.

The Scope Display window is used to control and display data acquisition. Clicking the mouse over the appropriate label in the window causes data to be acquired and displayed as a set of three traces in the window: the time history of the beam current, $x$ position, and $y$ position. The actual location of the beam within the pipe is derived from the trace data after accounting for sensor misalignment and is displayed in the circular "bull's-eye" displays in the upper part of the window.

There are other windows that display additional derived data. A "position display" window shows a value vs. position down the beamline. A "bug-walk," for example, makes position displays that show peak current, $x$ position, and $y$ position at the locations of the beam bug position monitors along the beamline. Similarly a "magnet-walk" shows the fields at the centers of the magnets vs. their location in the beamline. Three magnet-walks appear in Fig. 6 showing the solenoidal fields (labeled

PD-B), the horizontal steering fields (labeled PD-H), and the vertical steering fields (labeled PD-V) vs. distance down the beamline.

There are also windows for displaying historical data. Clicking the mouse over a beam bug icon causes a ''shot history'' window to appear. By clicking the mouse over buttons on the window the operator can view all the oscilloscope traces acquired for that bug for that day's run.

## 5. FUTURE

We are planning to improve the shot history mechanism so that it can not only manipulate past shot data but also past machine configuration data. For example, we want to have the ability to re-do the signal processing with different control parameters. We also want to be able to ask such questions as, ''During the last three months what was the highest current magnitude measured when the machine had the long collimator installed?'' Our approach is to develop an unstructured database based on the artificial intelligence representation scheme known as a semantic network.

We are also developing the ability to acquire image data from cameras observing the beam striking foils inserted into the beamline. We will apply image understanding techniques (the ability of an AI program to interpret or judge a visual image) to determine the position and focus of the beam.

## 6. SUMMARY

The MAESTRO software environment was developed to function as an intelligent assistant to an operator tuning complex systems such as particle-beam accelerators. It incorporates three approaches to tuning. The ''cloning the operator'' approach uses an inference engine and the MDS representation to encode the strategies and reasoning followed by the operator. The model-based approach makes use of a beamline simulator and a nonlinear least squares parameter estimator to first ''commission'' the model and then determine optimum tuning parameters. The third approach lets the operator perform tuning manually and provides him with displays that easily let him determine the machine status. Finally, a history mechanism lets the operator view past data to compare the present tune with ones previously obtained.

## ACKNOWLEDGEMENTS

The authors gratefully wish to acknowledge the contributions of Doyle Rogers and John Clark, the tuning experts. Their ability to make order out of chaos is truly amazing.

The work was performed jointly under the auspices of the U.S. Department of Energy by Lawrence Livermore National Laboratory under contract W-7405-ENG-48, for the Strategic Defense Initiative Organization and the U. S. Army Strategic Defense Command in support of SDIO/SDC MIPR No. W43-GBL-0-5007.

REFERENCES

1. R. C. Schank and R. P. Abelson, *Scripts, Plans, Goals, and Understanding*, Lawrence Erlbaum, 1977.
2. P. G. King and S. N. Demming, ''UNIPLEX: Single factor optimization of response in the presence of error'', *Analytical Chemistry* **46**, 11 (1974) 1476–1481.
3. M. Lee and S. Clearwater, ''GOLD: Integration of model-based control systems with artificial intelligence and workstations'', Workshop on Model-Based Accelerator Controls, Brookhaven National Laboratory, Upton, New York, Aug. 1987.

**Darrel L. Lager** received the B.S.E.E. from the California Polytechnic State University at San Luis Obispo in 1968. Since that time he has been at Lawrence Livermore National Laboratory, and is now the Project Engineer for Expert Control Systems. His professional interests revolve around the design and implementation of expert systems with major control and signal processing components.

**Hal R. Brand** obtained the B.S. in chemistry at San Jose State University in 1974, and the M.S. in engineering – applied science at the University of California at Davis, in 1976. He has been an employee at Lawrence Livermore National Laboratory since 1974, working in real-time data acquisition and display, real-time instrument control, and the application of knowledge-based systems to instrument control problems.

**William J. Maurer** received the B.S. in computer science from San Diego State University, 1984, and the M.S. in computer science from the University of California at Davis, 1988. He has been at Lawrence Livermore National Laboratory since 1984. His main interests are AI applications in engineering, decision support systems, and image understanding.

# EXPERT SYSTEM APPROACH TO ASSESSMENTS OF BLEEDING PREDISPOSITIONS IN TONSILLECTOMY/ADENOIDECTOMY PATIENTS

NICOLINO J. PIZZI
*National Research Council of Canada, IME,*
*Robotics and Automation Section*
*435 Ellice Avenue, Winnipeg,*
*Manitoba, R3B 1Y6, Canada*

JON M. GERRARD
*Department of Pediatrics, Health Sciences Centre*
*University of Manitoba*
*100 Olivia Street, Winnipeg,*
*Manitoba, R3E 0V9, Canada*

Received 1 April 1990

The purpose of this expert system is to assess a predisposition to bleeding in a patient undergoing a tonsillectomy and/or adenoidectomy, as may occur with patients who have certain blood conditions such as hemophilia, von Willebrand's disease, and platelet function defects. This objective is achieved by establishing a correlation between the patients' responses to a medical questionnaire and the relative quantities of blood lost during their operations.

Three major modules constitute the system: the automated questionnaire to be completed by the patient, the expert system proper, and the patient database. The questionnaire is divided into fourteen sections on topics such as the occurrence of bruises and positive familial history. The expert system takes the responses to the questionnaire and determines risk categories for patients undergoing the operations. The patient database contains the patients' questionnaire responses, personal data and the risk assessments generated by the expert system.

Subsequent to the development of the expert system prototype, inductive learning techniques were examined to automatically classify patients as either normal or abnormal. Specifically, Quinlan's ID3 induction algorithm was used whereby a training set of patient data generates a classification tree whose leaf nodes correspond to the classification outcomes.

This paper presents the architecture of the hematology expert system, identifies some problems encountered during the knowledge engineering process and presents some statistical data pertaining to the accuracy of its risk assessments. It also offers a comparative review of the expert system and inductive learning methodologies.

*Keywords:* Expert systems; Machine learning; Hematology; Induction; Medical artificial intelligence.

## 1. INTRODUCTION

The development of the Hematology Expert System for Tonsillectomy/ Adenoidectomy Patients[1] (HES) is a project being undertaken by the Robotics and Automation Section of the National Research Council of Canada, and the Pediatrics and Child Health Department of the Health Sciences Centre (Winnipeg, Canada). HES determines any propensities that a patient may have towards suffering greater than normal blood losses during a tonsillectomy and/or adenoidectomy (T/A) as well as any predispositions towards certain blood abnormalities such as: hemophilia, a hereditary hemorrhagic diathesis due to deficiency of the coagulation factor VIII; von Willebrand's disease, a diathesis associated with deficiencies in the von Willebrand factor protein antigen (vWAg) or in the activity measured as the restocetin cofactor (vWRCo); and thrombopathy (a platelet function defect measured as the occurrence of at least two abnormal platelet aggregation measurements). The intention is to use this system as a preoperative filter to recognize these high risk patients so that they may have subsequent coagulation tests performed. As a research instrument, HES is being used as a key component of a longer-term investigation into the advantages and limitations of an interactive questionnaire approach for the detection of bleeding problems in patients.

Parallel investigations were also conducted concerning the effectiveness of machine learning strategies. Preliminary experimentation led to the selection of Quinlan's ID3 algorithm[2] for the comparative portion of this study because of the performance and reliability of the specific implementation of the algorithm that was available.

## 2. HISTORY

The complexity of many modern surgical procedures, although beneficial to most patients, can be associated with severe complications in those patients with certain types of hemostatic defects. When these defects are suspected by specialists, they have a sizeable assortment of accurate but costly coagulation tests which may be performed at their discretion. For instance, assaying techniques, such as microtitration, provide rapid and accurate means of determining von Willebrand's disease.[3] Such tests are invaluable in determining whether or not a patient will bleed excessively during an operation. If a predisposition to excessive bleeding is suspected, preoperative coagulative agents may be administered. Nevertheless, considering the expense of these tests it would be expedient if a filter, such as HES, could be created to preoperatively classify patients as normal, abnormal, or ambiguous, thereby reducing the frequency of tests being administered to patients who are, in fact, hematologically normal. The initial HES prototype which automated this process was developed on a Symbolics 3650 workstation using Common Lisp. The prototype was subsequently ported, with some revisions and user interface enhancements, to a 286-based personal computer using Pascal.

The subject population of HES is T/A patients, primarily because the tonsils and adenoids are extremely vascular regions and patients with even mild hemostatic defects are at significant risk of excessive bleeding during their operation.[4] The original method (prior to the development of HES) made use of a written questionnaire which was administered to these patients whose responses were reviewed by a clinical specialist, and an assessment was made with regard to the patients' predispositions to excessive bleeding. The risk assessments were then compared against the estimated blood loss during the patient's T/A and, if applicable, against the known hemostatic condition of the patient as established by data gathered at the coagulation laboratory. An improved version of this questionnaire which removed certain existing anomalies was incorporated into HES. An expert system design approach was selected as the

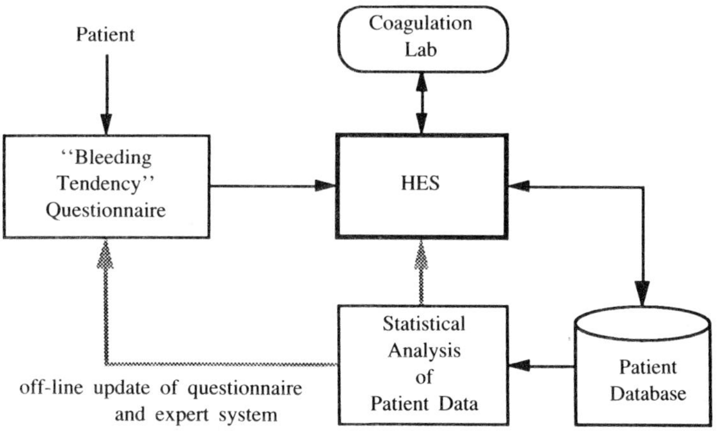


Fig. 1. Functional outline of HES.

development methodology for several reasons: a number of initial knowledge acquisition sessions with the principal hematologist indicated a particularly knowledge-intensive domain; an analysis of the methodology which he employed in the assessment of patient predisposition to excessive bleeding followed a rule-based paradigm; and a review of some of the relevant literature indicated some success with conceptually similar problems.[5–7]

## 3. FUNCTIONAL DESCRIPTION OF HES

Three major modules constitute the Hematology Expert System (Fig. 1): a self-administered "Bleeding Tendency" (BT) questionnaire; the expert system proper which analyzes the responses from the questionnaire and, if available, data from the coagulation laboratory; and the patient database. A sub-component of HES is a set of statistical utilities including frequency distribution analysis and a HES to SAS (Statistical Analysis System) translator which converts the patient database into a large data file which can subsequently be analyzed with SAS. The typical methodology employed in HES for patient data collection is as follows: A patient sits at a console and enters responses to the BT questionnaire (since the majority of patients are between the ages of two and sixteen years, it is often the patient's guardian who is requested to provide this information). He/She is then assigned a group number which indicates HES's assessment of the patient's predisposition to excessive bleeding during a T/A operation. Any time after the operation has been performed, any available medical data may be entered into HES by a clinical specialist who may subsequently analyze the information in the patient database using either HES or SAS.

### 3.1. "Bleeding Tendency" Questionnaire

The accurate diagnosis of patients with bleeding disorders can best be made in the context of the knowledge of bruising and bleeding symptomatology in patients without bleeding disorders. The BT questionnaire, based upon the original ''Bleeding Tendency'' questionnaire developed at the Department of Pediatrics and Child Health, is the front-end interface between the patient and the expert system portion of HES which provides this symptomatology context. Apart from some incidental enhancements to, and the removal of some anomalies from the original questionnaire, the most significant difference between the two is that patients usually have the option of indicating they are unsure of the appropriate response for a specific question. The inability of the original manual system to allow for uncertain responses made it difficult to delineate between responses which were negative and those which were intended to be equivocal. The HES questionnaire is intended to be self-administered but for the sake of the study and an analysis of the system as a whole, it is currently being administered by a clinical supervisor.

The BT questionnaire (Fig. 2) comprises fourteen principal sections totalling approximately eighty questions in all. The ''Personal'' section queries the patient for his/her age, blood type, sex, MHSC number (Manitoba Health Services Commission medical number), and so on. Two sections contain questions concerning the nature, severity, and occurrence of bruises and nosebleeds respectively. Two other sections pertain to unusual incidents of bleeding involving the teeth and gums and bleeding into the joints. The ''Operations'' section queries the patient about bleeding histories of any previous major operation (one requiring a general anaesthetic) or minor operation (such as a liver biopsy or suturing a laceration under a local anesthetic). A section incorporates questions about bleeding and bruising after any serious accident or trauma while another concerns bleeding from the bowel and urinary tract. The ''Family History'' section allows the patient to enter information regarding the bleeding histories of close relatives who have bleeding conditions such as bruising, excessive bleeding during tooth extractions or operations, hemophilia, or platelet function disorders. The ''Personal History'' and ''Other Medical Problems'' sections include

**Bruises Section**

Do noticeable bruises occur on AVERAGE:

1. At least every other week.
2. At least every other month.
3. At least once a year.
4. Less than once a year.
5. I do not know.

. . .

**Operations Section**

If the patient ever had an appendectomy:

1. Did he/she need a blood transfusion?
2. Did he/she have lots of bleeding?
3. Did he/she have little or no bleeding?
4. I am not sure.
5. The patient never had this operation.

Fig. 2. Excerpts from the ''Bleeding Tendency'' questionnaire.

questions on disorders such as kidney disease, high blood pressure, and anemia. Two sections query the patient about his/her diet and drug intake in the recent past. Finally, a section is included for females concerning bleeding patterns during menstruation (if applicable) and bleeding histories of any childbirths (if applicable).

Any time during the completion of the questionnaire, the patient is offered the option of backtracking to previous questions to review or modify his/her responses. The responses to the questionnaire are constantly monitored and validated against previous responses to ensure that neither inappropriate queries are made (for instance, detailed questions about the nature, severity, and occurrences of nosebleeds are not made of a patient who does not typically suffer from nosebleeds) nor incongruous responses solicited (prepubertal females are not asked questions concerning childbirths). The patient typically responds only to a small subset of these questions. However, personal and historical factors such as age and sex, the occurrence and nature of bruises and nosebleeds, and the number of positive responses (with respect to bleeding predisposition), may force the patient to answer a larger subset of questions.

### 3.2. Coagulation Laboratory Data

The coagulation laboratory of the Health Sciences Centre performs many tests on patients referred to the institution due to suspected bleeding abnormalities. These tests include the patient's bleeding time, aggregation counts of blood components such as collagen, epinephrine (a hormonal vasopressor), ADP (adenosine diphosphate), and arachidonic acid, as well as blood cofactors (components with which others must unite in order to function) such as vWRCo, vWAg, and FVIIIC. If these data are available for a particular patient they are entered into the HES database for future analysis. Occasionally, not all of the prescribed hematological tests are performed on these patients (for example, the amount of blood drawn is sometimes insufficient to perform all of the tests). Consequently, HES was made capable of handling missing coagulation data and determines the patient's condition as accurately as possible given the data at hand. Furthermore, since the data from the coagulation laboratory are usually not available for analysis at the time the questionnaire responses are recorded, the system can modify its patient assessments whenever new information becomes available.

HES classifies patients with coagulation laboratory data into one of thirty different hemostatic conditions including: von Willebrand's disease; platelet function defect; von Willebrand's disease or platelet function defect with normal bleeding times; mild, moderate, and severe forms of hemophilia; possible combinations of the above hematological conditions; isolated prolonged bleeding time; normality (with respect to the above); and, finally, an undetermined abnormal condition classification. The undetermined abnormal condition indicates that, although the patient did not have normal test results, he/she could not be classified into any of the other abnormal groups. For this study, the portion of the subject population which was selected as having "definite" hematological disorders was selected from those patients who had coagulation tests performed and did not have a normal classification as indicated in the results discussed below. It is important to note that although HES has the facility to classify patients into one of these thirty hemostatic conditions if the data are available, these generated results are in no way used in determining the patient's predisposition to risk, otherwise, it would violate the intent of HES as a preoperative filter (the data are stored solely as a matter of convenience for use by the clinical investigators).

### 3.3. Statistical Routines

HES provides frequency distribution analysis of responses stored in the patient database as compared against a specified diagnostic group. The investigator may select up to nineteen questions from the BT questionnaire (for instance, questions on the nature and severity of nosebleeds and bruises, the occurrence of dental or joint bleeding, family history, menstruation, and bleeding from the bowel and urinary tract) as well as a diagnostic group (for example, subjects with a specific hemostatic condition, subjects with any known hematological defects, subjects with an indeterminate bleeding disorder, normal subjects, or the entire subject population). The output includes the total number of patients in the database, the number of patients in the selected diagnostic group and a listing for each question from the user-selected subset. Each listing contains the diagnostic groups' responses to the selected questions and the absolute and relative totals of those responses. The investigator may require that complex statistical analysis be performed on the patient data—an analysis which usually exceeds the present capabilities of HES. Consequently, HES provides a translation utility which converts the records in the patient database into a text file which can be ported to SAS for subsequent off-line analysis.

### 3.4. Expert System

The expert system module takes a patient's responses from the BT questionnaire as well as any available coagulation laboratory data and yields three parameter values for the patient. First, the patient is designated by one of seven possible group assignment values: an integer value ranging from one, which indicates a very low hematological risk, up to six, which corresponds to a very high risk; or "?", which indicates that there was insufficient data or inconclusive evidence to derive an unequivocal group assignment value. If the patient's group assignment is equivocal then a clinical specialist may require that additional medical tests be conducted to determine the true physiological condition of the subject with respect to his/her hemostatic mechanisms. The hematologist selected group assignment values five and six to indicate a possible predisposition to excessive bleeding during a patient's T/A operation. The second parameter the expert system may generate is a non-physiological warning condition. If the patient has consumed certain types of drugs (for example, those of an anti-coagulative nature) or has ingested certain types of food, then the system flags the patient with a drug/diet alert. This alert status is used simply to indicate that the patient should not be immediately operated upon because of an increased risk of excessive bleeding during the operation due to the nature of the chemical substances present within the drugs and/or food the patient had recently consumed. In this case, the surgery would be rescheduled for a later date to ensure that the anti-coagulative effects of such substances had worn off. The final parameter value is a unique code number to identify the patient for future reference.

The expert system's explanation facility operates in two modes. The first mode generates a comprehensive description of the responses to the BT questionnaire and a listing of the final risk, intermediate risks (see the following section), point score, and group assignment, as well an any drug and/or diet alerts which were present when the patient filled out the questionnaire. The second mode is useful to surgeons who are interested only in positive indicators, if any, of the patient's predisposition to excessive bleeding as well as any drug and/or diet alerts.

### 3.5. Risk Assessments, Point Scores, and Rule Sets

Patient group assignments are based upon their risk assessments (Fig. 3) and point scores (Fig. 4). The risk assessment values are derived from an inverted decision tree where the top nodes are the patient's responses to essential questions from the BT questionnaire interface (Fig. 5). Even though only these essential query responses are used to determine risk assessment values, all query responses are recorded in the patient database in the event that they may be of interest in future extensions to HES. The Results section below discusses the incorporation of data from ten questions which, while originally considered non-essential, nevertheless proved to be of significant value in better discriminating between normal and abnormal subjects. Each intermediate level of the tree corresponds to intermediate risk assessments. For example, the responses to six questions from the bruising section (ease, frequency, and

**Nosebleed Risk Table**
IF the patient required hospitalization for a nosebleed
& the patient has nosebleeds monthly
& the patient is uncertain about the duration of an average nosebleed
→ assign the patient a bruise risk of "VERY HIGH". . . .

**Sex Risk Table** (Menstruating)
IF the patient is a menstruating female
& the patient's bruise risk assessment is "HIGH"
& the patient's menses risk is "HIGH"
→ assign the patient a sex risk of "HIGH". . . .

Fig. 3. Risk assessment decision tables.

**Point Scores**
IF there was no sign of bleeding during a previous operation
→ the patient scores $^{-}3$ points. . . .

IF the patient's hair color is blonde
→ the patient scores 3 points. . . .

Fig. 4. Point scoring subsystem rules.

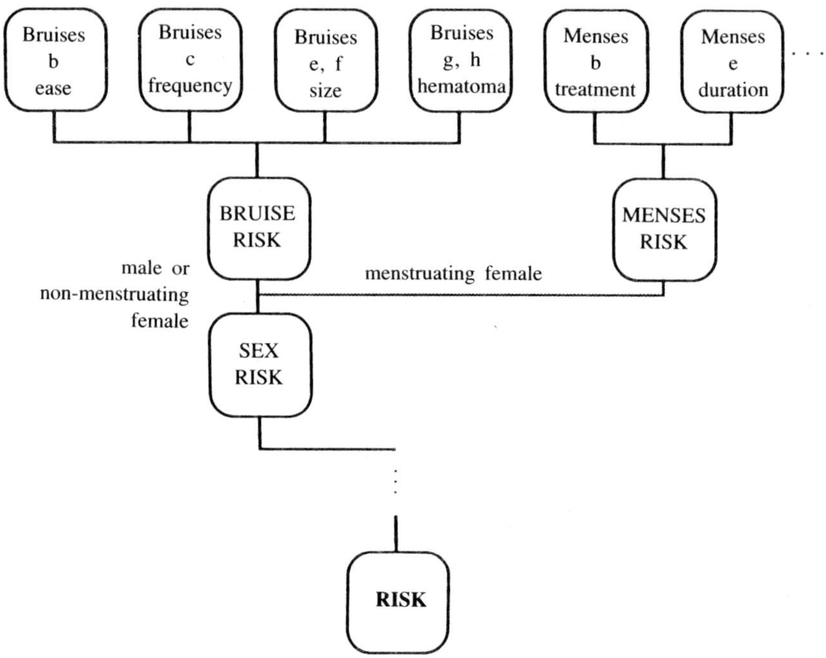


Fig. 5. Risk assessments' decision tree.

size of bruises, and the presence of hematomas under the bruise) of the BT questionnaire are used to determine the patient's bruise risk, which in turn is used singly or, if female, in conjunction with the menses risk to determine the patient's sex risk—another intermediate risk assessment value. The root node is a composite of the final risk assessment (a compendium of all the intermediate risks) and the non-physiological drug and/or diet alerts (if any). The final composite risk assessment may be one of seven values: very high, high, high medium, low medium, low, very low, or uncertain.

Each node of the risk assessment tree is a value which was returned from a corresponding risk assessment decision table. The 22 decision tables contain an average of 114 rows ranging from 2 entries to 240. Ten decision tables are directly associated with the patient's query responses, eleven correspond to the intermediate risks (for instance, age risk, sex risk, modifier risk, and rare event bleeding risk), and the final table is the composite risk assessment (and any non-physiological indicators). Decision tables were selected as the representational scheme because: they may be processed efficiently and, if required, updated easily; they are a convenient map from the pre-HES methodology created by the hematologist, which was already in place to determine patient risk assessment values; and equivalent rule classes may be easily derived (the tables represent a total of 1,251 rules).

The point score (or tally) is the other constituent which figures in the final group assignment of a patient. The tally is dependent upon the patient's responses to a small core of questions and was included in the expert system because, if the group assignment relied solely upon the patient's risk assessment, it was found that even a few positive responses to some of the queries would cause a disproportionate increase in the patient's final composite risk assessment value. The tally score was an effective method to smooth the group assignment distribution curve. This subsystem is based on eleven questions: highly positive responses increase the point tally, and strong negative indicators decrease it. Regardless of the effectiveness of the point score component, it is possible for a patient's final point tally to be invalid if more than four of the eleven queries were answered indecisively. In this event, the group assignment is based solely upon the risk assessment criterion. A set of thirteen group assignment rules (Fig. 6) amalgamates the criteria of risk assessments and point scores. If the first dozen rules are not triggered then the last (default) rule generates a group assignment value of "?".

Coagulation laboratory data are sometimes obtained for a patient because: they were previously compiled due to problems associated with a past operation; the patient was referred to the hospital with the suspicion of having a hemostatic defect; or the patient was flagged by HES as a high risk candidate and, as a result, blood tests were recommended. As previously discussed, several blood components are measured and the results may be stored in the HES database any time after the BT questionnaire is completed and a patient code number is generated. HES incorporates a bleeding disorder rule set of twenty rules (Fig. 7) to subsequently classify the patient with respect to one of the thirty hematological classifications. This rule set is capable of dealing with scenarios in which not all of the laboratory data are available.

## 4. INDUCTIVE LEARNING APPROACH

Inductive learning involves the automated formulation of generalizations based on a training set of specific events in a given domain. Quinlan's ID3 algorithm (Iterative

**Assignment Rules**

IF the point score is between $^{-}3$ and 0 {inclusive}
& the risk assessment is "VERY LOW"
OR the risk assessment is "LOW"
→ the patient's group assignment is 1. . . .

IF the point score is between 15 and 20 {inclusive}
& the risk assessment is "VERY HIGH"
OR the risk assessment is "HIGH"
→ the patient's group assignment is 5. . . .

IF the point score is not valid
& the risk assessment is "VERY HIGH"
→ the patient's group assignment is 6. . . .

Fig. 6. Group assignment rules.

**Blood Disorders**

IF FVIIIC $\leq$ 49.9%
& FVIIIC $>$ 14.9%
$\rightarrow$ the patient definitely has Mild Hemophilia. . . .

IF the Bleeding Time $>$ 9 minutes
& the Collagen Aggregation $<$ 60%
& the Arachidonic Acid Aggregation $<$ 60%
$\rightarrow$ the patient definitely has a Platelet Function Defect. . . .

IF the Bleeding Time $\leq$ 9 minutes
& Epinephrine Aggregation $<$ 60%
& ADP Aggregation $<$ 15%
$\rightarrow$ the patient definitely has a Platelet Function Defect with Normal Bleeding Time. . . .

Fig. 7. Bleeding disorder rules.

Dichotomiser 3), an implementation of which was used for this study, generates a classification tree whose leaves are the specific classification outcomes. All other nodes correspond to decisions which led to those outcomes. Consequently, a depth-first traversal of the tree produces a set of classification "rules" (Fig. 8). The algorithm has the following major steps: select the "best" attribute on which to split (at a decision point) so as to create a new sub-tree; divide the training events by the selected attribute's values into sets; for each newly created set recursively iterate to form a new sub-tree; continue until all of the events in the set have been properly classified.[8] The order of attribute splitting is based on the information gains achieved by the potential splits. In other words, the "best" attribute on which to split is the one which yields subsets that have minimum entropy. The training set of events may be represented as a number of $k + 1$ vectors. The first $k$ columns of this "matrix" represent the attributes in the training set and the $(k + 1)$th column of the matrix denotes the respective classifications. Each cell in the matrix represents the corresponding event's value for the corresponding attribute (or its classification if the cell is in the $(k + 1)$th column). That is, $v_{ij}$ is the value of attribute $j$ for event $i$ for $j \leq k$, or $v_{ij}$ is the event's classification for $j = k + 1$. For a training set that has $m$ classes, and $k$ attributes, the algorithm, at each decision point, splits on the attribute $A_k$, which yields the minimum entropy. The specific formula is:

$$E(A_k) = \sum_{j=1}^{\alpha} p(a_{kj}) \left[ -\sum_{i=1}^{m} p(c_i \mid a_{kj}) \log_2 p(c_i \mid a_{kj}) \right] \tag{1}$$

where $\alpha$ is the number of distinct values of attribute $A_k$, $E(A_k)$ is the entropy caused by splitting on $A_k$ at the current decision point, $p(a_{kj})$ is the probability that an event has the value $a_{kj}$ for attribute $A_k$ at the current decision point, and $p(c_i \mid a_{kj})$ is the probability that class $c_i$ obtains if attribute $A_k$ has value $a_{kj}$. The calculation for the minimum $E$ (entropy) is:

```
All Attributes and All Abnormals
... If Nosebleed-d is 3 then
        Classification is 1 : 5 events
If Trauma-a is 3 then
    Classification is 1 : 40 events
If Trauma-a is 1 then
    If Bruise-d is 3 then
        Classification is 0 : 15 events
    If Bruise-d is 2 then
        If Trauma-d is 3 then
            Classification is 1 : 1 events
        If Trauma-d is 2 then
            Classification is 0 : 5 events
    If Bruise-d is 6 then
        Classification is 0 : 2 events
    If Bruise-d is 5 then
        Classification is 0 : 1 events
    If Bruise-d is 4 then
        Classification is 1 : 9 events      ...
```

Fig. 8. Classification rules generated by ID3.

$$\min(E(A_1), E(A_2), \ldots, E(A_k)) \ . \tag{2}$$

For the subject population used in this study, an event was a specific patient's responses from the BT questionnaire and his/her diagnostic classification—the classification outcomes were normal or abnormal. Attributes were the questions and an attribute's values were the specific responses to the corresponding query. Four different subject populations were submitted to the ID3 implementation for classification. The first training set included samples from all normal and abnormal subjects. The second set did not include any patients who had an undetermined abnormal condition. These two sets contained twenty-two attributes and the classification outcome. The remaining two sets were the same as those above except that ten additional attributes were included in these sets that were not used by HES in the original determination of excessive bleeding risk. These attributes included additional questions on bruising and nosebleeds as well as queries on bleeding and bruising caused by traumas and/or accidents, and frequency of drug intake. Two-thirds of the subject population were used as the training set to generate the classification trees and the remaining one-third was used to measure the generated trees' respective sensitivities and specificities.[9]

## 5. RESULTS

The subject population comprised 595 patients who completed the BT questionnaire between July 1987 and July 1989. Normality was characterized by those patients who had an estimated total blood loss of less than 10% during their T/A operation, did not require a subsequent return to the operating theatre, and had neither significant bleeding nor a transfusion during any previous operation. The abnormal group was composed of patients who were diagnosed with a definite hemostatic defect. Only children between the ages of 2 and 16 were selected for either classification. Using these criteria, 236 patients were identified as normal ("non-bleeders") and 114 patients were classified as abnormal ("bleeders"). Sensitivity and specificity were measured for both risk assessment and group assignment values. Sensitivity is a measure of the system's ability to identify subjects who were known to have a hematological disorder *vis-à-vis* an assignment of an abnormal group/risk value. On the other hand, specificity is a measure of the system's ability to identify subjects who did not have any hematological condition *vis-à-vis* an assignment of a normal group/risk value. Abnormal group assignment values were either 5 or 6 whereas abnormal risk assessment values were considered to be "very high" or "high". The specificity of HES was 71% and 82% for risk assessments and group assignments respectively (Fig. 9), while the sensitivity was 77% and 61% for risk assessments and group assignments respectively. For the sake of comparison against the inductive learning approach, sensitivity was also measured for another group of abnormal subjects. All patients who were classified as having an undetermined abnormal condition were removed from the abnormal group—these patients could not be medically diagnosed to have any specific hemostatic defect but were definitely not normal. Sensitivity for this group was 78% and 65% for risk assessments and group assignments respectively (Fig. 10).

For each iteration of the ID3 algorithm the following data were collected: the system's sensitivity, the system's specificity, the total number of leaf nodes (classification outcomes) generated, the number of leaf nodes which had mixed (equivocal) classification outcomes, and the total number of attributes that were actually used to produce the classification tree (see Table 1).

## 6. DISCUSSION

Sensitivity and specificity measurements indicate that HES is generating statistically significant results; however, some deficiencies are also evident. The risk assessments demonstrate a tendency to capture more abnormal patients but at the expense of some "non-bleeders" being identified as abnormal (sensitivity is gained at the expense of specificity). The introduction of the point scoring system is an attempt to improve the specificity but it skews the results too far in the other direction. Nevertheless, these results are promising in that: they correspond to initial observations and predictions; and it appears that the deficiencies can be rectified with some "fine-tuning" of the point scoring system and the risk assessment decision tables. For example, HES's sensitivity and specificity can, of course, be improved by making some adjustments to its knowledge base. Table 2 presents some results concerning some initial attempts to fine-tune the system by modifying the decision tables and the point scoring and group assignment rules. Specifically, modifications were made to some of the risk assess-

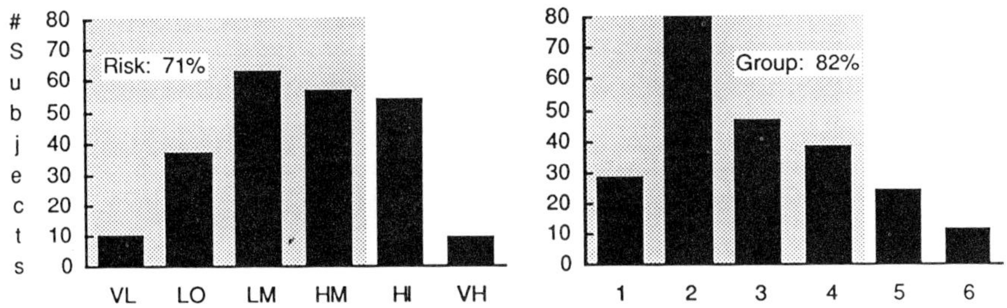


Fig. 9. Risk assessment and group assignment specificities.

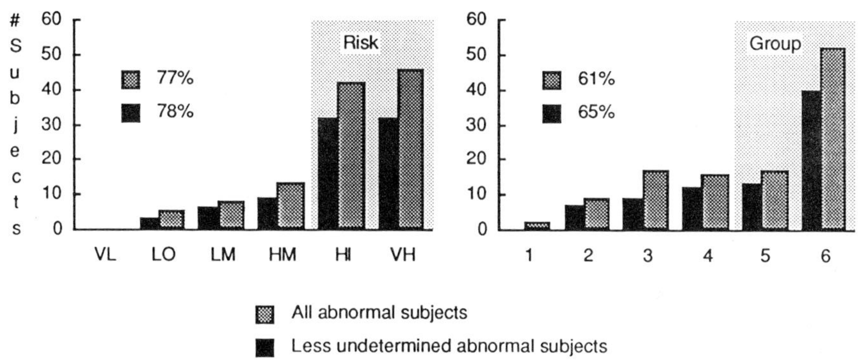


Fig. 10. Risk assessment and group assignment sensitivities.

Table 1. Results from ID3 runs.

| | No. of Leaves | Mixed Classes | Specificity (%) | Sensitivity (%) | Attributes Used (%) |
|---|---|---|---|---|---|
| All attributes<br>All abnormals | 49 | 0 | 85 | 92 | 44 |
| All attributes<br>No undetermined abnormals | 41 | 0 | 90 | 78 | 34 |
| Original attributes<br>All abnormals | 80 | 1 | 80 | 50 | 82 |
| Original attributes<br>No undetermined abnormals | 55 | 1 | 80 | 37 | 59 |

ment decision tables, point scoring rules, group assignment rules (some tables and rules were modified more than once), and finally two combinations of changes. Moreover, by adjusting some of the upper and lower bounds of conditions pertaining to the selection of abnormal subjects, the sensitivity can be increased to 65%. The specificity can also be increased to 83% by simply changing a rule in the point

Table 2. Results from knowledge base modifications.

| Modifications | Risk Sensitivity (%) | Group Sensitivity (%) | Risk Specificity (%) | Group Specificity (%) |
|---|---|---|---|---|
| Unchanged | 77 | 61 | 72 | 83 |
| Bruise Risk Assessment (1) | 78 | 62 | 63 | 81 |
| Bruise Risk Assessment (2) | n/c* | 62 | 74 | 82 |
| Bruise Risk Assessment (3) | 79 | 62 | 67 | 82 |
| Nosebleed Risk Assessment (1) | 76 | 62 | n/c | n/c |
| Nosebleed Risk Assessment (2) | 76 | 62 | n/c | n/c |
| Dental Bleeding Risk Assessment | n/c | 63 | 75 | n/c |
| Family History Risk Assessment (1) | n/c | 63 | n/c | n/c |
| Family History Risk Assessment (2) | 79 | 63 | 69 | 82 |
| Menses Risk Assessment (1) | 76 | 62 | n/c | n/c |
| Menses Risk Assessment (2) | 76 | 62 | n/c | n/c |
| Modifier Assessment | 76 | 62 | n/c | n/c |
| Points – Nosebleed Rule (1) | n/c | n/c | n/c | 82 |
| Points – Nosebleed Rule (2) | n/c | 62 | n/c | n/c |
| Points – Family History Rule (1) | n/c | n/c | n/c | 84 |
| Points – Family History Rule (2) | n/c | 62 | n/c | n/c |
| Points – Hair Rule | n/c | 62 | n/c | 85 |
| Group Rule Set (1) | n/c | 65 | n/c | 82 |
| Group Rule Set (2) | n/c | 67 | n/c | 89 |
| Group Rule Set (3) | n/c | 72 | n/c | 74 |
| Group Rule Set (4) | n/c | 74 | n/c | 73 |
| Group Rule Set (5) | n/c | 77 | n/c | 71 |
| Point Score and Group Rules | n/c | 65 | n/c | 84 |
| Point Score, Group and Risk Sets | n/c | 67 | n/c | 85 |

* n/c = no change

scoring subsystem pertaining to the patient's hair color. Furthermore, if the T/A surgeon variable is controlled, specificity can be increased to a minimum of 85%.

As indicated in Table 1, the sensitivity and specificity measurements for ID3 classifications were not as high as the unmodified results from HES (80% versus 82% for specificity and 50% versus 61% for sensitivity, respectively). The sensitivity measurement was even worse (37%) when patients with an undetermined abnormal condition were excluded from the training set. However, when the additional ten attributes were introduced the outcome was reversed. The classification trees of ID3 produced sensitivity and specificity measurements of 92% and 85% respectively when all the abnormals were used, and 78% and 90% when the undetermined abnormals were excluded. It should also be noted that the sensitivity measurement degrades significantly from the training set with all abnormal subjects to the set with the more restrictive abnormal classification. This may be explained by the fact that although the number of normal subjects in both training sets did not change, fewer abnormal subjects were used in the more restrictive training set. Therefore, the normal events tended to play a more significant role during the creation of the classification tree than the abnormal events and hence the subsequent improvement in specificity and degradation in sensitivity. To remedy this situation, a training set should contain the same (or similar) number of events for each classification. Fewer leaf nodes were generated for the classifications which used the ten additional attributes and yet less than one-half of the total number of attributes were used in constructing the tree (for example, 14 of the total 32 attributes were used for the former set versus 18 of 22 for the latter).

It appears that ID3 is able to produce smaller trees if given a larger number of potentially significant attributes on which to split. Moreover, some of the additional attributes were subsequently found to have greater domain-specific import than some of the original attributes used exclusively by HES. In fact, post-analysis of the first HES prototype showed that some of the original attributes were not clinically significant in the determination of patient risk to excessive bleeding during a T/A operation. The menstrual bleeding and childbirth section did not provide significant results because the vast majority of the females in the patient population were of a pre-menstrual age and thus never answered any questions from this section. The section on bowel and urinary tract bleeding was not statistically significant because the event rates for the occurrence of these types of bleeding problems were too low and/or other causes of such bleeding may have obscured these bleeding defects as causes proper. Another point of contention is that the techniques used for estimating blood loss—which is our delineator for normal patients—are themselves prone to error due to evaporation, loss of blood in the site where the surgeons dispose of gauze and loss of blood in surgical gloves and coats.[10] Inherent error is also present in the determination of a patient's total blood volume which was calculated using the constant, 70 cc/kg of body weight, which, in fact, is a constant only for a specified age range.[11] Finally, a parallel study[12] has indicated that one of the additional attributes concerning the location of bruises is a significantly more useful discriminator than the original queries above (only 5% of "non-bleeders" indicated that they usually bruise on more than one part of the body as opposed to 36% of "bleeders"). The parallel investigation has also concluded that if specific combinations of old and new queries are examined and the definition of abnormality is slightly altered, sensitivity and specificity measurements of 68% ad 87% may be achieved.

## 7. CONCLUSION

The Hematology Expert System for Tonsillectomy/Adenoidectomy Patients has been shown to generate statistically significant results with respect to both sensitivity and specificity. Nevertheless, a number of improvements should be incorporated into the system. The selection of essential questions needs to be modified—certain questions that were initially believed to be useful discriminators, such as those concerning bleeding from the bowel and urinary tract, now seem to require modification, while others are more significant than initially suspected. Therefore, the risk assessment decision tables need to be altered to indicate the changed import of those questions and the point scoring sub-system needs to be "fine-tuned" in order to more accurately correlate group assignments with hemostatic defects. Finally, while still maintaining

Table 3. HES versus ID3.

| | Sensitivity (%) | Specificity (%) |
|---|---|---|
| HES | 61 | 82 |
| HES (best modified) | 77 | 89 |
| ID3 (best results) | 92 | 90 |

the HES to SAS conversion utilities, the next version of HES itself should include greater statistical capabilities than are currently available.

The comparative review of the original HES/knowledge engineering approach and the ID3/inductive learning methodology has also produced some interesting conclusions. (Table 3 encapsulates the key sensitivity/specificity measurements.) First, the ID3 classification approach, and the inductive learning methodology in general, is considerably effective. Many knowledge-based or expert system projects in which domain events must be properly classified (those which serve a diagnostic function, for instance) can probably successfully utilize an inductive learning tool such as ID3—perhaps through the incorporation of the algorithm as a module within the system. Furthermore, development time was significantly reduced when the inductive learning approach was used, as compared against the traditional expert system development cycle. Since many clinical studies involve the discrimination of a subject population between normal and abnormal diagnostic groups, an automated discrimination analysis system would serve to speed this process of medical classification. With respect to the original HES prototype, and the preliminary results from the ID3 implementation, it is now necessary to study how the classification trees generated by the ID3 implementation can be appropriately added to the original HES environment. The initial results presented in this paper are encouraging. Moreover, once the above tentative changes have been thoroughly examined and tested, their possible incorporation should yield a clinical instrument with even greater accuracy.

## ACKNOWLEDGEMENTS

We would like to thank Barbara Nosek-Cenkowska, with the Department of Pediatrics, University of Manitoba, who assisted in the analysis of the patient database results. Our gratitude is also extended to Sandhya Kapoor and Lori Klassen for their assistance in gathering the data for the questionnaire. We would also like to acknowledge Dick Jackson's contribution of his implementation of the ID3 algorithm and Gord Sawatzky and Moe Barakat's constructive reviews of the final draft of this paper.

## REFERENCES

1. N. J. Pizzi, S. Kapoor, and J. M. Gerrard, "Hematology expert system (HES) for tonsillectomy/adenoidectomy patients", *Proc. Seventh Annual Conf. Applications of Artificial Intelligence*, SPIE, Orlando, 1989, pp. 884–893.
2. J. R. Quinlan, "Induction of decision trees", *Machine Learning* **1** (1986) 81–106.

3. R. Ramsey and B. L. Evatt, "Rapid assay for von Willebrand factor activity using formalin-fixed platelets and microtitration technique", *American J. Clinical Pathology* **72** (1979) 996–999.
4. G. Livingstone and F. C. Johnstone, "Tonsillectomy in patients with coagulation defects", *The Lancet* **2** (1963) 378–379.
5. J. M. Long *et al.*, "An example of expert systems applied to clinical trials: Analysis of serial graded exercise ECG test data", *Controlled Clinical Trials* **8**, 2 (1987) 136–145.
6. E. W. Salzman, "Measurement of platelet adhesiveness", *J. Laboratory and Clinical Medicine* **62**, 5 (1963) 724–735.
7. A. S. Elstein, J. Dod and G. B. Holzman, "Estrogen replacement decisions of third-year residents: Clinical intuition and decision analysis", in *Cognitive Science in Medicine: Biomedical Modeling*, eds. D. A. Evans and V. L. Patel, MIT Press, Cambridge, Massachusetts, 1989, pp. 21–49.
8. J. R. Quinlan, P. J. Compton, K. A. Horn and L. Lazarus, "Inductive knowledge acquisition: A case study", in *Proc. Second Australian Conf. Applications of Expert Systems*, Sydney, 1986.
9. N. J. Pizzi and D. Jackson, "Comparative review of knowledge engineering and inductive learning using data in a medical domain", *Proc. Eighth Annual Conf. Applications of Artificial Intelligence*, SPIE, Orlando, 1990, pp. 671–679.
10. E. Cáceres and G. Whittembury, "Evaluation of blood losses during surgical operations", *Surgery* **45** (1959) 681–687.
11. D. G. Nathan and F. A. Oski, *Hematology of Infancy and Childhood: Volume 1*, W. B. Saunders Company, Toronto, 1981.
12. B. Nosek-Cenkowska, M. S. Cheang, N. J. Pizzi, E. D. Israels and J. M. Gerrard, "Bleeding/bruising symptomatology in Children", unpublished.

---

**Nicolino J. Pizzi** is a research officer with the Robotics and Automation Section of the National Research Council of Canada where he leads the Cognitive Systems Group. He is currently involved in the design and development of an expert system that will assist oncologists in preparing comprehensive chemotherapy treatment plans, and an automated diagnostic system for the detection of deep vein thrombosis. Mr. Pizzi's current interests lie in connectionist architectures and the incorporation of inductive learning techniques within knowledge-based systems. He received the M.Sc. and M.A. in computer science and philosophy, respectively, at the University of Manitoba. He is a member of AAAI and SPIE.

**Jon M. Gerrard** is Professor and Head of the Section of Blood Diseases in Children in the Department of Paediatrics at the University of Manitoba. He graduated with an M.D. from McGill University in 1971. This was followed by an internship, residency, and a Ph.D. in paediatrics and pharmacology at the University of Minnesota, awarded to him in 1978. Dr. Gerrard is currently involved in research on children with bleeding disorders.

# EXPERT SYSTEM APPROACH USING GRAPH REPRESENTATION AND ANALYSIS FOR VARIABLE-STROKE INTERNAL-COMBUSTION ENGINE DESIGN

STEWART N. T. SHEN
*Center for Artificial Intelligence*
*Old Dominion University, Hampton Blvd.*
*Norfolk, VA 23529-0162, USA*

MENG-SANG CHEW
*Mechanical Engineering and Mechanics Department*
*Old Dominion University, Hampton Blvd.*
*Norfolk, VA 23529-0162, USA*

GHASSAN F. ISSA
*Computer Science Department*
*Old Dominion University, Hampton Blvd.*
*Norfolk, VA 23529-0162, USA*

Received 1 April 1990

Even though AI technology is a relatively new discipline, many of its concepts have already found practical applications. Expert systems, in particular, have made significant contributions to technologies in such fields as business, medicine, engineering design, chemistry, and particle physics.

This paper describes an expert system developed to aid mechanical engineering designers in the preliminary design of *variable-stroke internal-combustion engines*. Variable-stroke engines are more economical in fuel consumption but their design is particularly difficult to accomplish. With the traditional design approach, synthesizing the mechanisms for the design is rather difficult and evaluating the mechanisms is an even more cumbersome and time-consuming effort. Our expert system assists the designer by generating and evaluating a large number of design alternatives represented in the form of graphs. Through the application of structural and design rules obtained from design experts to the graphs, good quality preliminary design configurations of the engines are promptly deduced. This approach can also be used in designing other types of mechanisms.

*Keywords*: Expert system; Design; Graph representation; Engine.

## 1. INTRODUCTION

The popularity of expert system technology is continuously growing among researchers as well as practitioners of different fields. Such efforts often require close interdisciplinary collaboration. Research in and applications of expert systems in engineering design are particularly interesting for their novelty and potential value. There have been numerous research projects in meeting the challenges in dealing with many aspects of the engineering design problem.[1–6] However, in spite of such efforts, expert systems for engineering design in general are still at an early stage in terms of practicality. This fact is mostly due to the complexity and creativity required of engineering design. Engineering design generally involves diverse problem solving techniques and a significant amount of expert domain knowledge.[7] It also needs the aid of heuristics, planning, and experience. Much of these ingredients can be captured by expert systems, though significant difficulties often arise. Thus research in this area is particularly challenging and can be very rewarding.

Facing the problem of national dependence on imported oil, the country has found conserving oil to be an urgent task for consumers as well as engineers who design the engines for automobiles, these engines being one of the major culprits of the problem. Variable-stroke internal-combustion engines provide one alternative for reducing this problem. These engines can adjust piston strokes in relation to the power requirement without throttling. As a result, the loss of energy due to throttling, the method with which conventional fixed-stroke internal-combustion engines use to provide different amounts of power, is generally eliminated.

However, the variable-stroke internal-combustion engine design problem is a rather abstract and difficult one. Fortunately, Freudenstein and Maki cleverly represented the problem with graphs and formulated kinematic structural specifications and engine design rules over the graphs.[8] With such an approach, the design problem becomes much more concrete and manageable though still laborious and somewhat error-prone. Our expert system automates this approach by generating alternatives according to the set of kinematic structural specifications, and then selecting an appropriate preliminary design configuration according to the set of engine design rules. The system is implemented with the expert system shell EXSYS[9] and several external programs in Pascal. The *main external program* provides graphic user-interface to support the graphic representations of engines and to perform certain required calculations. The inference system is a rule-based system with a knowledge base consisting of the engine design rules. Some of the rules are attached to external programs which are executed upon the firing of the rules. These *rules external programs* provide some graphical representations and perform additional complex calculations.

Exploring the advantages of using graphs for design representation and analysis in expert system implementation and the potential benefits of variable-stroke engines were the main motivations for this research effort.

## 2. ENGINE DESIGN PROBLEM

We shall first briefly introduce the properties of variable-stroke internal-combustion engines and then describe the basic methodology for the engine design process using the expert system approach.

### 2.1. Fixed-Stroke vs. Variable-Stroke Internal-Combustion Engines

Load control in a conventional fixed-stroke internal-combustion engine is achieved by throttling (choking) the inlet to reduce the amount of oxygen flow for burning. Throttling consumes a significant amount of energy. By simply eliminating inlet throttling, one can avoid the energy loss due to this effort, thus improving engine efficiency. But by simply doing so one cannot allow the engine's output to change according to the load,[8] while in all the operational environments, an automobile engine has to operate under varying loads.

A better approach for load control would be to avoid throttling by varying the piston strokes depending on the changing loads. With short-stroke operation, only sufficient fuel-air mixture is inducted to satisfy light-load operations; whereas, with high-load conditions, long strokes are used to provide for more incoming charge into the cylinder. By doing so throttling loss is practically eliminated and fuel efficiency is greatly improved. This type of engine is called a variable-stroke engine and is more complex than fixed-stroke ones. Improvement in the fuel economy of a variable-stroke engine over a comparable fixed-stroke engine has been estimated to approach twenty percent.[8] Thus variable-stroke engines are definitely one alternative into which engine designers should look in order to design more efficient engines.

### 2.2. Engine Design Methodology Using Graphs

The basis of the design methodology using graphs is that kinematic structures can be defined precisely with the aid of graphical structures, which are analyzed in a relatively systematic manner for designing the mechanisms. In other words, the structural aspects of an engine design can be directly represented by a distinct graph which contains sufficient information for evaluating its feasibility. This means that we can focus our evaluation and study the simplified graphical representation of mechanisms instead of the actual designs, which would be much more complicated. Thus, the basic idea underlying the creation of mechanisms in this methodology is in separating the structural aspects from the functional aspects of a given design. The kinematic structure of a mechanism describes the connection schemes of a design such as which *link* connects to which other link and by what type of *joint*. Figure 1 shows a drawing of a slide-crank mechanism and its associated graph of the kinematic structure.

In Fig. 1, the graph has vertices (corners) that correspond to the links of the mechanism and edges (lines) that correspond to the joints. Note the correspondence between the labeling of the mechanism with that of the graph. A joint is a mechanical device which connects a number of links together, while a link is the part of a mechanism which is connected to another part by joints. A link could be a piston, a crank, or just a connection mechanism. Joints and links are the two basic components of a kinematic structure. This convention (graph vertices ⇔ links, and graph edges ⇔ joints) is widely accepted in the mechanisms field. Figure 1 illustrates that the essential knowledge of the structure of a mechanism can be represented compactly by a graph.

Joints are usually classified according to their degrees of freedom ($f_i$). The degree of freedom of a joint is the type of motion permitted by that joint. It is equal to the number of allowable free movements of that joint. Joints are also classified according to the type of contact and closure. This classification determines the type of a joint as being any one of the following: sliding pair (P), turning pair (R), ball joint (E), and so on. Links are classified by their number of connections; a singular link is connected to only one other link; a binary link is connected to two other links; and so on.

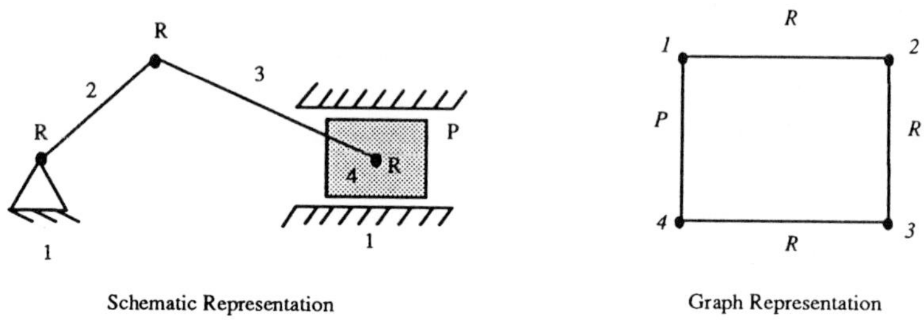


Fig. 1. Slider–crank mechanism and graph of kinematic structure.

A very important property of a mechanism is its overall degree of freedom ($F$). This degree of freedom imposes a constraint on the type of allowable structure of a mechanism. For instance, according to the specifications of our project, we are only interested in plane mechanisms with a single degree of freedom. This property can be calculated using the following equation[8]:

$$F = \lambda(l - j - 1) + \sum_{i=1}^{j} f_i$$

where:

$F$: degree of freedom of mechanism.

$l$: number of links in mechanism.

$j$: number of joints in mechanism.

$f_i$: degree of freedom (relative motion) permitted by the $i$th joint.

$\lambda$: mobility factor which is equal to 3 for plane and 6 for spatial mechanisms

Figure 2 illustrates the graphic representations of two different variable-stroke engine designs. Each of the mechanisms shown has one degree of freedom. To understand how we arrived at such a conclusion, we need to first understand the representation scheme.

Examining the scheme of the mechanism in Fig. 2(a), we see that it consists of links (each of which is given a distinct number) connected together by joints. There are several types of links shown in the graph. For example, $link_6$ represents a piston,

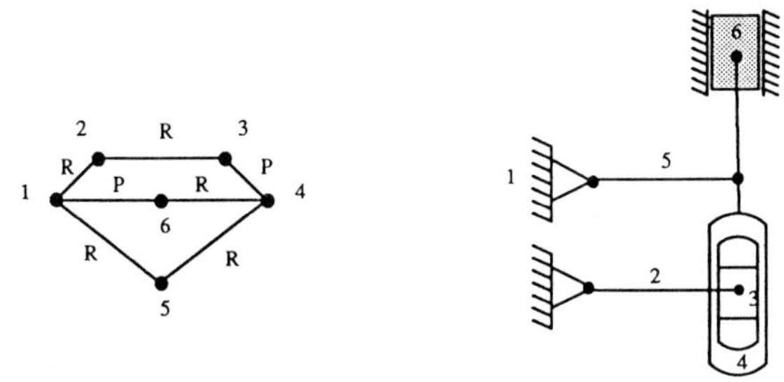


(a)

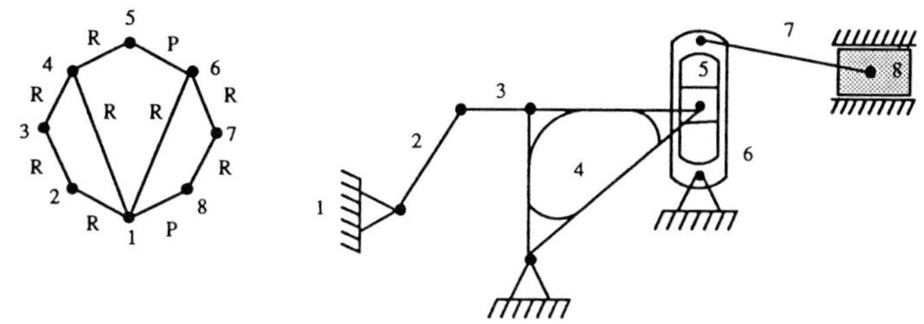


(b)

Fig. 2. Graphical representation of variable-stroke engines. (a) Six-link mechanism. (b) Eight-link mechanism.

the slashes represent one common ground which is denoted by $link_1$, $link_4$ is just a connecting link, and other links may be either cranks or just simple connecting links. There are two types of joints in the graph: turning pair joints (R) represented by circles, and sliding pair joints (P) represented by the connections between $link_1$ and $link_6$ and between $link_3$ and $link_4$. Every joint has a single degree of freedom ($f_i = 1$). The mechanism contains six links and seven joints. Now if we apply the formula to calculate the overall degree of freedom for the mechanism, we get:

$$F = \lambda(l - j - 1) + \sum_{i=1}^{j} f_i$$

$$F = 3(6 - 7 - 1) + 7$$

$$F = 1 \ .$$

It is important to note that generating graphs by connecting a number of nodes in different ways could lead to a large number of different configurations. But if the number of alternatives is too large, this could lead to the well-known problem of combinatorial explosion. To avoid this problem, a set of *kinematic structural specifications* is used to limit the number of possible graphs and to prune out unwanted alternatives before actually involving the expert system with testing design rules. Using the set of constraints and specifications, the search space is reduced to what are called graph chains. A graph chain is the set of all feasible graphs, with respect to the specifications, having the same connection schemes but differing in the way the edges are labeled. Looking back at Fig. 2(a), one sees that each edge within the graph is labeled with either an "R" or a "P". An edge labeled with an "R" is called a turning pair joint. An edge labeled with a "P" is called a sliding pair joint. The labeling is explained in detail in later sections.

Our expert system will then generate different graph chains according to the user request, and perform an evaluation process on the graphs belonging to that chain.

### 2.3. Kinematic Structural Specifications

The system makes use of a set of specifications given by engine design domain experts in generating the kinematic structural representations of engine configurations using graphs. These specifications allow the system to eliminate large numbers of inappropriate graphs and prevent the expert system from having to generate graphs blindly, which may lead to the problem of *combinatorial explosion*, causing a hang-up in the design process.

The following is a list of some of the specifications used, shown as illustrations:

1. The search is limited to plane, single degree of freedom mechanisms (i.e. $F = 1$ and $\lambda = 3$).
2. Joints are limited to those with surface contact—turning pair (R) and sliding pair (P). This limitation is due to their high load-carrying capability.
3. The search is limited to six-link with seven joints and eight-link with ten joints mechanisms. This limitation is to avoid increased mass and hence large inertia forces.
4. The maximum number of sliding pairs cannot exceed two. This is to limit the amount of sliding in the mechanism.
5. The ground link ($link_1$) of all six-link structures should be ternary (connects three joints). This is to avoid control via a floating-link connection.
6. All eight-link structures which do not have at least one link with four joints are excluded. This limits the number of floating links to three as desirable for dynamics and balance.

### 2.4. Engine Design Rules

The system also uses a number of *engine design rules* given by engine design domain experts to evaluate and determine the component types of engine configurations. These rules are closely related to the specifications described in the previous section. In a way, the rules are what constitute the main knowledge base of the expert system. They are used to evaluate structures resulting from applying the specifications and the user input data. Since the power of an expert system relies on the knowledge presented in its rules, the rules should be complete and clear. Each rule should be followed by a clear explanation so that when the final decision is made by the expert system, the user can obtain a good understanding of the reasoning process. According to these rules, a given preliminary design alternative will be classified as accepted or rejected.

Some of the fundamental engine design rules used by the system are listed below as illustrations:

1. Any link connected to the ground ($link_1$) by a turning pair (R) is considered a crank.
2. The crank must be binary (two-jointed). This limitation is to avoid complicated cranks and high piston side-thrust.
3. The crank cannot be directly connected to a sliding pair. This is to avoid the resulting high piston thrust, and the difficulty in varying the engine stroke.
4. Any link connected to the ground by a sliding pair (P) is considered a piston.
5. The piston must be binary (two-jointed—the sliding and the wrist-pin joints). This restriction is to avoid excessive side-thrust and high piston friction.
6. The piston cannot be directly connected to the crank. This results in high piston side-thrust, and difficulty in varying the piston stroke.
7. Multiple cranks result in multiple drive loops. This situation is not permitted, since one of the loops must be the control loop.

## 3. EXPERT SYSTEM IMPLEMENTATION

The primary objective of this project is to explore the feasibility of applying expert systems to assist in high level engineering design problems. We focus our attention on selecting a problem with practical value. Using graphical representation of variable-stroke engines is a relatively new idea to mechanical engineering and we try to promote such a novel approach through the automation of the preliminary design process. The approach is to automate such a process using an expert system, and then compare the results with existing results generated by human experts. The end product would be an expert system capable of generating results consistent with or better than those generated by experts. In the tedious process of generating and evaluating the various kinematic structures of variable-stroke engines, it is quite easy for experts to overlook some of the design rules. It is also possible for the expert to develop a bias towards a certain design configuration, resulting in its improper acceptance or rejection. In addition, the time and effort needed to evaluate the hundreds of design alternatives to produce a few feasible designs may be physically and mentally too demanding, should that be possible in the first place.

For the reasons given above, we therefore use the specifications and design rules proposed in the paper by Freudenstein and Maki[8] and described in previous sections, as the basis for constructing our expert system. With these rules our system operates at least as efficiently as an expert. The system tests all preliminary design alternatives, produces a comprehensive analysis of each configuration, states whether that configuration is accepted or rejected, and finally, shows all the steps and rules that contributed to its decision.

In the implementation of this expert system we decided not to start completely from scratch, but rather to take advantage of an existing expert system shell. An expert system shell is a program which provides many facilities for building expert systems and allows the knowledge engineer to devote most of his efforts to the knowledge base proper. The knowledge engineer selects the search strategy, the probability system, plus a few other features, and may include specialized external programs or procedures. He then enters the rules and modifies them as needed.

The expert system described in this paper is implemented using the EXSYS expert system shell to work with the knowledge base, and Turbo-Pascal external programs for user interface and for complex calculations.

### 3.1. EXSYS Expert System Shell

Some important features of EXSYS relevant to our project are described here. The reader is recommended to refer to the EXSYS user manual[9] or any other expert system shell manual to get a better understanding of how such packages work.

EXSYS is an expert system development package which can be used on any IBM PC-compatible or on VAX/VMS computers. EXSYS requires a minimum of 320K bytes of RAM with an additional 64K for every 700 rules. An expert system with up to 5,000 rules can be developed to run on a PC. Expert systems can be developed with EXSYS for problems that involve a selection from among a definable group of choices where the decision is based on logical rules. The rules can involve relative probabilities in one of three different ways. Expert systems by EXSYS deal with knowledge rather than data. This knowledge, as mentioned before, consists of IF-THEN-ELSE rules and is stored in the knowledge base. A rule in EXSYS is made up of a list of IF conditions containing English sentences or algebraic expressions and a list of THEN and ELSE consequences which may contain more statements, the probability of a particular choice, or maybe a request to run an external program to perform tasks such as calculation, reading or updating data files, and displaying graphics. If EXSYS determines that all the IF conditions in a rule are true it adds the rule's THEN consequences to what it knows to be true. If any of the IF conditions are false, the ELSE consequences are then added to what is known. A rule can have up to 128 conditions in its IF part.

At present, the expert system described in this paper contains only 53 rules. More rules will be added in the future upon our gaining more knowledge about the design process. These rules, described in Sec. 2.4, are the criteria under which a design configuration is recognized and is either accepted or rejected, followed by a probability factor. EXSYS provides three probability systems. We have chosen to use the $0-10$ system which uses a denominator of 10. In this system, a probability of 0/10 means absolutely NO, a probability of 10/10 means absolutely YES, and probabilities between 1 and 9 denote a confidence factor. Probabilities with confidence factors $(1-9)$ are averaged to produce the final result. The following example illustrates how this probability system works.

Suppose we have the following three rules:

1. IF $condition_1$ THEN $choice_1$ with probability of 4/10.
2. IF $condition_2$ THEN $choice_1$ with probability of 6/10.
3. IF $condition_3$ THEN $choice_1$ with probability of 8/10.

Assuming that all the three conditions are true, the final result would be $choice_1$ with a probability factor averaged to 6/10. If any one of the above rules has a probability factor of 0/10, the final result would not be averaged and would be equal to 0/10. Similarly, if any rule has a value of 10/10, the final result would not be averaged and would have a probability of 10/10.

Rules are used in several ways by EXSYS. In a **Forward Chaining** mode, each rule in the knowledge base is examined in the order of its occurrence. However, if there is information missing from the IF condition part of a rule, then backward chaining is used to derive that information.

In a **Backward Chaining** mode, EXSYS searches all rules for desired goals in the THEN or ELSE parts. When such a rule is located, the conditions in the corresponding IF part are evaluated and a conclusion may result.

Other available modes in EXSYS are the **FinalPass** mode which is just a normal backward chaining with an additional final forward pass through the rules, and the **Nobackward** mode which is similar to forward chaining except that no backward chaining is used to derive information.

EXSYS can receive data from monitoring equipment, databases, spread sheets, and dedicated external programs. Dedicated programs could be written in different languages (Pascal, Fortran, Basic) but have to be in their object code to be used with EXSYS. In our expert system, we use a main external program written in Pascal (described in more detail in the next sub-section) for initial user interface by displaying graphics, menus, and some help capabilities. In addition, this external program also provides for mathematical calculations and complicated analysis on arrays, matrices, and other data structures. Several other external programs and procedures are called by some rules in the knowledge base. The results generated by the external program are passed back to EXSYS for testing and evaluation.

### 3.2. Main External Program for Working with Graphics

The main external program is implemented using Turbo-Pascal to provide the facilities for manipulating graphics, carrying out lengthy mathematical calculations, and performing data structure analyses which cannot be done by EXSYS directly. Thus, the external program stands between the user and EXSYS. Its job is to get the input data, manipulate it, and then present some information from the resulting data to EXSYS. The external program uses a set of specifications (see Sec. 2.3) to create graph templates ready for use. According to these specifications, only six-link and eight-link structures are thought to be appropriate for study. For six-link structures, two possible templates are produced, and for the eight-link structure, six possible templates are generated. Labeling a template in all the feasible ways produces a chain of distinct graphs, each of which has a different characteristic equation. As mentioned before, a chain is a set of graphs having the same structural configurations but differing in the way the edges are labeled with Rs and Ps. The importance of using a set of specifications or constraints is to produce a small number of templates and thus eliminate hundreds of meaningless configurations which would otherwise dramatically slow down the performance of the design process.

Upon generating the graphical templates, the user can choose to work on either six-link or eight-link structures. According to his selection, a menu is displayed containing the available templates (unlabeled structure) from which a desired template is selected for labeling and producing a chain of different graphs (refer to Fig. 3). The user is allowed to label each arc in the graph with either an "R" (turning pair) or a "P" (sliding pair). The number of allowable Ps is set by the specifications and must not exceed two. The graph will not be tested by the expert system until it satisfies this constraint and all other specifications.

The graph shown in Fig. 4 is an example of using the labeling process described above. At this point, this graph actually represents a variable-stroke engine configuration. The duty of the external program is to perform an initial analysis to understand this graph and extract the information regarding the kinematic structure. Appropriate information is then transferred to EXSYS to determine the feasibility of such a preliminary design configuration.

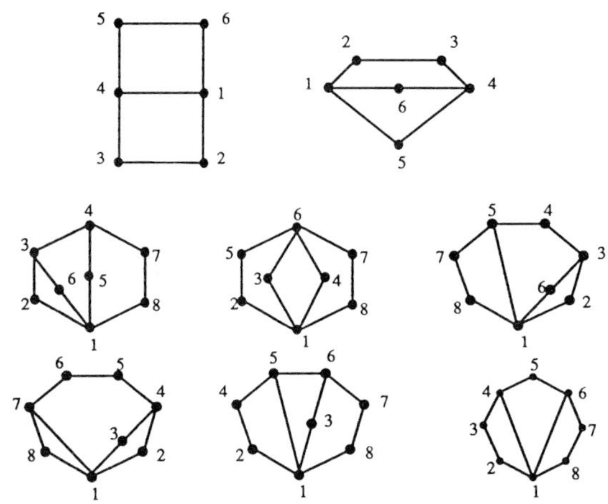

Fig. 3. Menus containing possible graph templates.

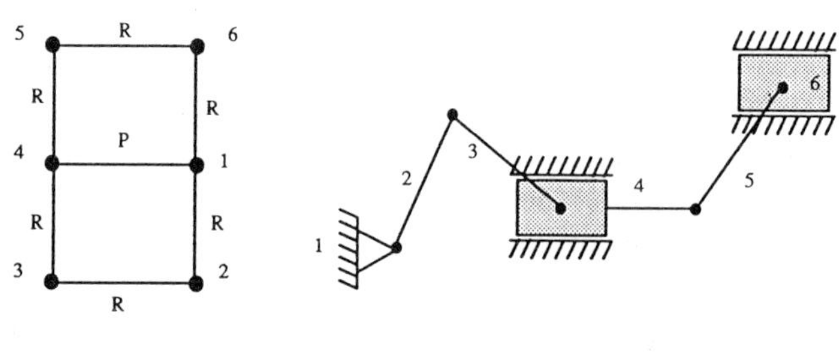


Fig. 4. A labeled graph and its corresponding engine schematic representation.

| | 1 | 2 | 3 | 4 | 5 | 6 |
|---|---|---|---|---|---|---|
| 1 | | R | | P | | P |
| 2 | R | | R | | | |
| 3 | | R | | R | | |
| 4 | P | | R | | R | |
| 5 | | | | R | | R |
| 6 | P | | | | R | |

Fig. 5. Matrix representation of the structural diagram in Fig. 4.

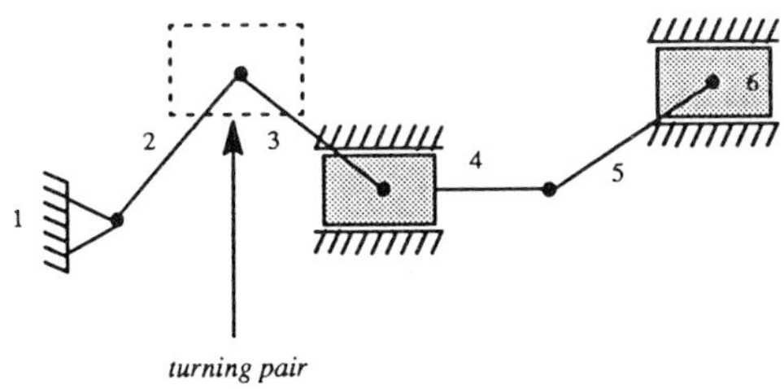


Fig. 6. Correspondence between location (2, 3) of Fig. 5 and schematic representation of the mechanism.

## 3.3. Representation and Analysis of the Structural Graphs

In Fig. 4, the graph contains six links represented by dots, and seven joints labeled with Rs and Ps. To represent such a graph in the computer, we use a 6 × 6 matrix as shown in Fig. 5. In general, a structural graph with $n$ links is represented by an $n \times n$ matrix. The rows and columns in the matrix correspond to the links in the structural graph. The non-empty entries in the matrix correspond to connecting joints and are assigned values of Rs and Ps. Therefore, a link represented by a row number is connected to another represented by a column number by a connecting joint which is located at the intersection of that row and column. For example, $row_1$ represents $link_1$ which is set by the specifications to denote the ground. To examine the characteristics of the ground link ($row_1$) in this case, we examine each entry within that row. The number of entries in a row denotes the number of joints connected by that link. Thus in this example, $row_1$ contains three entries, which means that the ground link connects three joints of the types denoted by the entries (R for a turning pair and P for a sliding pair). For example, the "R" at location (1, 2) denotes that $link_1$ is connected to $link_2$ via a turning pair. Similarly the "P" in location (1, 4) denotes that $link_1$ is connected to $link_4$ by a sliding pair. Note that the matrix below is symmetric. If $link_1$

is connected with $link_2$ by a turning pair (location (1, 2) = R), then $link_2$ is connected with $link_1$ also by a turning pair (location (2, 1) = R). These observations are important to establish the types of these links.

To show how this connection scheme relates to the original design (schematic representation of mechanism), we take, for example, location (2, 3) in the matrix which denotes that $link_2$ is connected to $link_3$ by a turning pair, and vice versa, by symmetry. This connection represents the part of Fig. 6 enclosed in the dashed box.

Table 1 presents a complete summary of the analysis performed on the structural graph of Fig. 4 and its matrix representation in Fig. 5 discussed above.

The example described above deals with one of the six-link structures. To gain further understanding of the analysis process we present a second example that deals with an eight-link structure. The analysis is similar to that of the previous example, except that some rules which are applicable to the eight-link structures may not apply directly to the six-link structures and vice versa. The structural graph and its matrix representation are shown in Figs. 7 and 8 respectively. A summary of the matrix analysis is presented in Table 2. Information such as that presented by the tables is stored in a file for later access by the knowledge base. Most of the rules in the knowledge base contain variables that have to be instantiated with values stored in the file.

Table 1. Summary of matrix analysis.

| Row # (Link #) | Analysis |
|---|---|
| 1 | — Ground.<br>— Contains one R joint and two P joints.<br>— Total number of joints is three.<br>— Connected to $link_2$ by an R, $link_4$ by a P, and $link_6$ by a P. |
| 2 | — Contains two R joints.<br>— Connected to ground by an R and to $link_3$ by an R.<br>(This link could be considered as a crank by the expert system according to the rules.) |
| 3 | — Contains two R joints.<br>— Connected to $link_2$ by an R and to $link_4$ by an R. |
| 4 | — Contains one P and two Rs.<br>— Total number of joints is three.<br>— Connected to ground and $links_{2,5}$ by Rs.<br>(This link could be considered as a piston by the expert system.) |
| 5 | — Contains two Rs.<br>— Connected to $links_{4,6}$ by Rs. |
| 6 | — Contains one P and one R.<br>— Total number of joints is two (binary).<br>— Connected to ground by a P and to $link_5$ by an R.<br>(This link could be considered as a second piston by the expert system.) |

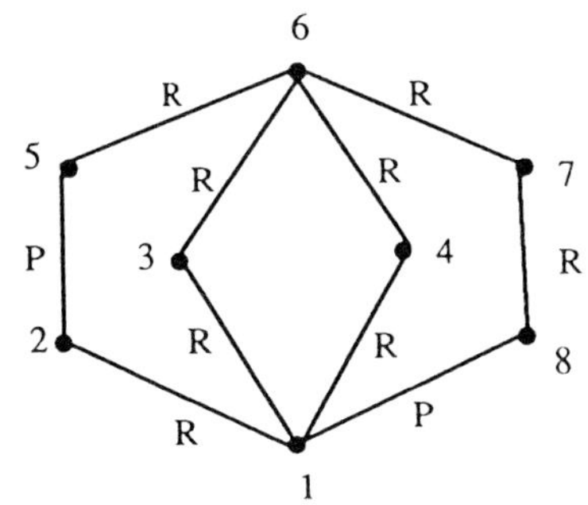


Fig. 7. Eight-link structural diagram.

| | 1 | 2 | 3 | 4 | 5 | 6 | 7 | 8 |
|---|---|---|---|---|---|---|---|---|
| 1 | | R | R | R | | | | P |
| 2 | R | | | | R | | | |
| 3 | R | | | | | P | | |
| 4 | R | | | | | R | | |
| 5 | | R | | | | R | | |
| 6 | | | P | R | R | | R | |
| 7 | | | | | | R | | R |
| 8 | P | | | | | | R | |

Fig. 8. Matrix representation of Fig. 7.

to the six-link structures and vice versa. The structural graph and its matrix representation are shown in Figs. 7 and 8 respectively. The summary of matrix analysis is presented in Table 2. Information such as those presented by the tables are stored in a file for later access by the knowledge base. Most of the rules in the knowledge base contain variables that have to be instantiated with values stored in the file.

Table 2. Summary of matrix analysis of Fig. 7.

| Row # (Link #) | Analysis |
|---|---|
| 1 | — Ground.<br>— Contains three R joints and one P joint.<br>— Total number of joints is four.<br>— Connected to $links_{2,3,4}$ by R joints and to $link_8$ by a P. |
| 2 | — Contains two R joints.<br>— Connected to ground by an R and to $link_5$.<br>(This link could be considered as a crank by the expert system according to the rules.) |
| 3 | — Contains one R and one P.<br>— Connected to ground by an R and to $link_6$ by a P.<br>(It could also be considered as a crank.) |
| 4 | — Contains two Rs<br>— Connected to ground and to $link_6$ by Rs.<br>(This link could also be considered as a crank.) |
| 5 | — Contains two Rs.<br>— Connected to $links_{2,6}$ by Rs. |
| 6 | — Contains one P and three Rs.<br>— Total number of joints is four.<br>— Connected to $link_3$ by a P and to $links_{4,5,7}$ by Rs. |
| 7 | — Contains two Rs.<br>— Connected to $links_{6,8}$ by Rs. |
| 8 | — Contains one P and one R.<br>— Total number of links is two.<br>— Connected to ground by a P and to $link_7$ by an R<br>(This link could be considered as a piston). |

## 4. ARCHITECTURE AND OPERATION OF THE EXPERT SYSTEM

In the last two sections, we described the main external program and EXSYS as two separate entities, and the few relationships from one to the other. In this section we expand on the interactions between the external programs and EXSYS. These interactions constitute the complete expert system. We will use the two examples described in Sec. 3 to illustrate how the expert system would treat the facts concerning a given design configuration, and how it would arrive at a conclusion to accept or reject that design. We will also show some of the rules used in the evaluation process. Figure 9 shows a layout of the main components of this expert system.

Upon running the expert system package, the user is asked to choose between six-link and eight-link chains. According to the user's choice, a menu containing the

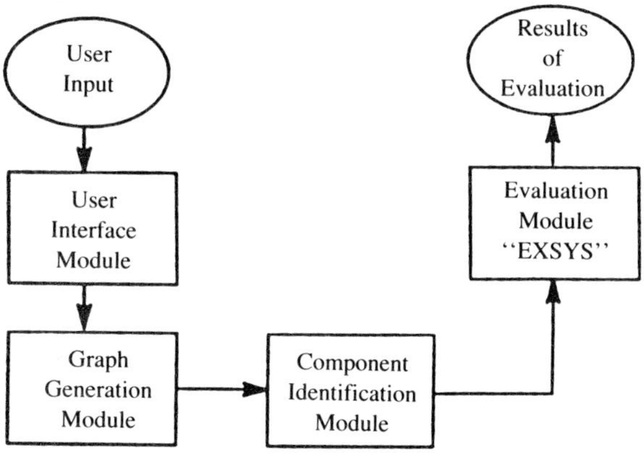


Fig. 9. System architecture.

available templates is displayed as in Fig. 3. The user then selects the type of template to work on, and begins labeling the graph with Rs and Ps. After finishing labeling, he has to choose an item from the following list of choices:

1. Test the feasibility of this design.
2. Let the computer generate automatically different design alternatives within the same chain.
3. Select another six-link or eight-link template.
4. Let the expert system test all the designs selected.

The attributes of all the graphs selected are stored in a file called RETURN.DAT. When the user finishes the selection and labeling process, the expert system starts reading the graph attributes and begins the evaluation process on each graph. The graph being evaluated is displayed again for the user, followed by the expert system's conclusion. At this point the user is in an interactive mode where he can select from a menu to further test the design by changing some attributes or he can verify the rules contributing to that decision. The conclusion consists of a decision to either reject or accept the design, followed by the confidence factor of that decision, and a list of analyses for the design such as the total number of pistons and total number of cranks. The conclusion of the six-link example in Figs. 4 and 5 is shown in Fig. 10.

The result of the expert system shows that the design configuration based on the six-link graph in Fig. 4 is not feasible and should be rejected. The rejection probability (9/10) illustrates the desirability of the design. If the rejection probability is, for example, 3/10, then the design is closer to acceptance than rejection. To understand how the results shown previously were generated, it is important for the user to view the rules used by the expert system in rejecting the design. These rules are displayed if the designer asks for explanation and are shown below for illustration.

| **Results based on 0–10 certainty system** | Value | Certainty |
|---|---|---|
| 1. REJECT | | 9 |
| 2. link number 1 = | GROUND | |
| 3. link number 2 = | CRANK | |
| 4. link number 3 = | link | |
| 5. link number 4 = | PISTON | |
| 6. link number 5 = | link | |
| 7. link number 6 = | PISTON | |
| 8. Total number of links in system = | 6 | |
| 9. Total number of CRANKS in system = | 1 | |
| 10. Total number of SLIDING PAIRS in system = | 2 | |
| 11. Both SLIDING PAIRS are PISTONS | | |

Fig. 10. Results of the evaluation of the graph in Fig. 4.

RULE #4
IF:
(1) [Number of sliding pairs connected to ground] > 1
THEN:
REJECT – Probability = 8/10
"This configuration limits the degree of sliding in the mechanism."

RULE #32
IF:
(1) Link 4 = "PISTON"
and (2) [Link 4 is connected to a number of joints] > 2
THEN:
REJECT – probability = 9/10
"This piston is not binary. This leads to excessive side-thrust and high piston friction."

Rule #4 asserts that there should not be more than one sliding pair connected to the ground link. If a design configuration does not satisfy this condition, then it should be rejected.

Rule #32 says that if a link is considered a piston, then it should be binary (i.e. connected to two joints). Thus if you refer to the matrix in Fig. 5, you will find that link 4 is connected to three joints. This rule also contributes to the rejection of the design.

The user also has access to all the rules in the knowledge base. This can be accomplished by moving the cursor up or down to view other rules used to count the number of cranks, pistons, and so on, or to decide that a certain link is a piston or a crank. The result of the evaluation of the example on the eight-link structure is shown in Fig. 11.

| **Results based on 0–10 certainty system** | Value | Certainty |
|---|---|---|
| 1. REJECT | | 9 |
| 2. link number 1 = | GROUND | |
| 3. link number 2 = | CRANK | |
| 4. link number 3 = | CRANK | |
| 5. link number 4 = | CRANK | |
| 6. link number 5 = | link | |
| 7. link number 6 = | link | |
| 8. link number 7 = | link | |
| 9. link number 8 = | PISTON | |
| 10. Total number of links in system = | 8 | |
| 11. Total number of CRANKS in system = | 3 | |
| 12. Total number of SLIDING PAIRS in system = | 2 | |
| 13. One of the SLIDING PAIRS is a PISTON | | |

Fig. 11. Results of the evaluation of Fig. 7.

The rules which contributed to the result in Fig. 11 are:

RULE #18
IF:
(1) Link 3 = "CRANK"
and (2) [Link 3 is directly connected to a number of sliding pairs] > 0
THEN:
REJECT – Probability = 9/10
"This configuration results in difficulty in varying the stroke."

RULE #35
IF:
(1) The number of cranks in mechanism > 1
THEN:
REJECT – Probability = 9/10
"Multiple cranks result in multiple drive loops. Hence, one of these loops has to be the control loop. Excessive power will flow through it."

Rule #18 states that if a link is a crank, then that link should not be directly connected to a sliding pair to avoid difficulty in varying the stroke of the piston.

Rule #35 states that there should be no more than one crank in the mechanism to avoid having excessive power circulating through the control loop.

The last two examples illustrate some of the advantages of our expert system. The graphic representation not only simplifies the analysis but also provides a good user interface. Additionally, the expert design knowledge is captured in rules and can be easily revised or augmented. The user is never let out of the entire process and every step taken by the expert system to produce results is available to the user for examination. Knowledge is presented by simple rules which make it easy to trace. The user can change some of the rules or data concerning the design, test the design again, and allow the expert system to perform a comparison between the results generated for the original and new set of rules and data. Creative design may result from such experiments.

## 5. LOOKING AHEAD

The current expert system has been implemented as a prototype. For this system, the next step is to enhance its output format and make it even more user-friendly to designers. At this time the system evaluates configurations based only on structural considerations. Further effort will be aimed at including functional considerations in the engine design rules. Some examples of functional considerations are: intended use of the engine, performance issues, dimensions, weight and operating speed.

The design methodology described is not restricted to variable-stroke engines. For example, it is clear that the same approach may be conveniently applied to design other types of mechanisms. Recently, this methodology has been applied to the design of such mechanisms as gears and robot hands.[11] We have also been studying the integration of it into a more general system that can utilize old design cases to help the design process.

## 6. CONCLUSION

Being able to use graphs to represent an otherwise extremely complex engineering design problem allows us to attack this high-level creative task using the expert system approach. This expert system automates a critical phase of a very powerful approach in mechanical engineering design. This methodology uses synthesis techniques to derive large numbers of different designs, then applies analytical and empirical methods to produce results.[10] One of the advantages of such a design approach is that one can synthesize new configurations which could lead to new designs. However, few engineers can afford to manually use this laborious approach to generate and test hundreds, if not thousands, of design alternatives. On the other hand, an expert system such as ours, which can automatically reduce a significant amount of required human effort, will do much to encourage researchers to pursue such a powerful design technique.

The use of an expert system to partially automate the design process has been shown to have many advantages, some of which are:

- Reducing manual work, such as drawing, labeling, and numbering.
- Saving the user's time and effort in the evaluation of design alternatives.
- Generating design alternatives automatically, from which an optimal solution can be found.
- Informing the user of all the steps and rules which contributed to the final decision.

• Providing an environment for easy experiments to derive creative designs.

In addition to the points listed above, one major advantage of this expert system is consistency. When testing a large number of designs, the results are consistent with all the evaluation rules. All design alternatives which violate any of the evaluation rules are rejected. A few of the results in Ref. 7 lacked consistency probably because some rules were not applied to evaluate certain design alternatives. When these designs were tested by our expert system, we were able to detect their inconsistencies.

## ACKNOWLEDGEMENT

The authors are grateful to and wish to acknowledge the support of this investigation by the National Science Foundation through Grant No. MSM-8809198.

## REFERENCES

1. S. J. Fenves and T. Norabhoopipat, "Potential for artificial intelligence applications in structural engineering design and detailing", in *Artificial Intelligence and Pattern Recognition in Computer-Aided Design*, Ed. J. C. Latombe, North-Holland, 1978, pp. 105–119.
2. M. N. Huhns and R. D. Acosta, "Argo: A system for design by analogy", *Proc. 4th Conf. Artificial Intelligence Applications*, Mar. 1988, pp. 146–151.
3. J. Kowalski, "Modeling knowledge-based system for optimum design of machine construction", *Proc. Int. Conf. Engineering Design*, vol. 2, Aug. 1987, pp. 622–630.
4. M. L. Maher and S. J. Fenves, "HI-RISE: An expert system for preliminary structural design of high-rise buildings", *Knowledge Engineering in Computer-Aided Design*, Ed. J. S. Gero, North-Holland, 1985, pp. 125–140.
5. G. E. Nevill and G. H. Paul, Jr., "Automated design of mechanical structure configuration", *Proc. Int. Conf. Engineering Design*, vol. 2, Aug. 1987, pp. 656–664.
6. G. Voland, "Decision strategies for expert systems software in engineering design", *Proc. Int. Conf. Engineering Design*, vol. 2, Aug. 1987, pp. 697–702.
7. D. C. Brown and B. Chandrasekaran, "A class of mechanical design activity", in *Knowledge Engineering in Computer-Aided Design*, Ed. J. S. Gero, North-Holland, 1985, pp. 259–263.
8. F. Freudenstein and E. R. Maki, "Development of an optimum variable-stroke internal combustion engine mechanism from the viewpoint of kinematic structure", *J. Mechanisms, Transmissions, and Automation in Design* **105** (1983) 259–268.
9. *EXSYS Expert System Development Package*, EXSYS, Inc., P.O. Box 75158 Contr. Sta. 14, Albuquerque, NM 87194, 1985.
10. F. Freudenstein and E. R. Maki, "The creation of mechanisms according to kinematic structure and function", *Environment and Planning B* **6** (1979) 375–391.
11. P. Datseris and W. Palm, "Principles on the development of mechanical hands which can manipulate objects by means of active control", *J. Mechanisms, Transmissions, and Automation in Design* **107**, 2 (1985) 148–156.

**Stewart N. T. Shen** is Director of the Center for Artificial Intelligence and a Professor of Computer Science at Old Dominion University. He received the B.S. from Cheng Kung University, the M.A. from the University of Washington, and the Ph.D. from Northwestern University. Dr. Shen previously taught at Virginia Polytechnic Institute and State University and the Rochester Institute of Technology. He has served as a consultant to Xerox Corporation, NASA, Arabian Data Systems, United Nations, and other organizations, in addition to his teaching and research activities at universities. He has published numerous papers in professional journals and conferences. His areas of research include expert systems, knowledge representation, hypertext and hypermedia, databases, user interface management systems, and intelligent tutoring systems. He is a member of ACM, IEEE, and AAAI.

**Meng-Sang Chew** is an Associate Professor of Mechanical Engineering and Mechanics at Old Dominion University. He received the B.S. and M.S. in 1977, the M.Ph. in 1979, and the Ph.D. in 1980, from Columbia University. Dr. Chew has worked as a research engineer at General Motors Corporation for six years, and holds two patents. He has also published several technical articles in professional and technical journals, two of which were Best Paper Awards at the Mechanisms Conferences. In addition to his teaching activities, he has served as a consultant and as an expert witness. His research activities have included work in the area of engines and transmissions, applications of expert systems, synthesis of deployable structures, control of flexible space structures, and the design of superconducting magnets and instrumentation for nuclear physics experiments. He is a member of the American Society of Mechanical Engineers, American Institute of Aeronautics and Astronautics, Tau Beta Pi, Pi Tau Sigma, and Sigma Xi.

**Ghassan F. Issa** is a Ph.D. candidate in computer science and a research assistant at Old Dominion University. He received the B.E.T. from Toledo University, the B.S. from Tri-State University, and the M.S. from Old Dominion University. Previously, he worked as an electronics engineer at Al-Taneeb, Inc. in Kuwait, a computer engineer at Tri-State University, and a teaching assistant at Old Dominion University. He holds memberships with ACM, AAAI, and IEEE.

# A COMPARISON OF TWO NEW TECHNIQUES FOR CONCEPTUAL CLUSTERING

STUART L. CRAWFORD and STEVEN K. SOUDERS

*Advance Decision Systems*
*1500 Plymouth Street*
*Mountain View, CA 94043-1230, USA*
*stuart@ads.com*
*souders@ads.com*

Received 1 April 1990

Clustering, pattern recognition, and classification are important components of many artificial intelligence systems, especially those designed to classify new observations. Often, one has access to a history of old observations that have been previously classified and, under these circumstances, the old data may be used as a training set from which one may obtain rules for the subsequent classification of new data. The techniques used to obtain these rules may be traditional statistical methods or modern computer-intensive techniques. Sometimes, however, the history of old observations has not been previously classified. Under these circumstances, the analyst simply wishes to uncover structure in the data and ascertain whether the structure is apparent or real. When the analyst is searching for clusters, statistical clustering methodologies are often used. Although effective at locating clusters, such approaches leave the interpretation of the clusters as a task for the human analyst. A relatively new class of "conceptual" clustering techniques have emerged from the discipline of machine learning. These techniques attempt to both locate and explain clusters among the data. In this way, the explanations of cluster membership may be used to construct rules for the subsequent classification of new data. The generation of interpretable rules, whether by the use of classification algorithms or conceptual clustering algorithms is of considerable importance in reducing the knowledge acquisition "bottleneck" that often impedes progress towards the building of rule-based systems. In this paper, two new techniques for conceptual clustering are introduced and compared.

*Keywords*: Clustering; Hierarchical clustering; Classification; Structure detection; Conceptual clustering; Exploratory data analysis; Classification trees; CART; MOCA; S.

## 1. INTRODUCTION

Clustering, pattern recognition, and classification are important components of many artificial intelligence systems, especially those designed to classify new observations. Often, one has access to a history of old observations that have been previously classified and, under these circumstances, the old data may be used as a training set from which one may obtain rules for the subsequent classification of new data. The techniques used to obtain these rules may be traditional statistical methods such as discriminant function analysis, logistic regression, kernel function classification, or nearest neighbor classification;[1,2] or modern computer-intensive techniques such as projection pursuit,[3,4] ID3,[5,6] or CART.[7] Sometimes, however, the history of old observations has *not* been previously classified. Under these circumstances, the analyst's goal is, at first, fundamentally exploratory in nature—the analyst simply wishes to uncover structure in the data and ascertain whether the structure is apparent or real. When the analyst is searching for clusters, statistical clustering methodologies such as numerical taxonomy,[8,9] principal components analysis,[10] factor analysis,[11] and projection pursuit[4] may be used. Although often effective at locating clusters, such approaches leave the interpretation of the clusters as a task for the human analyst. A relatively new class of "conceptual" clustering techniques[12,13] have emerged from the discipline of machine learning. These techniques attempt to both locate and explain clusters among the data. In this way, the explanations of cluster membership may be used to construct rules for the subsequent classification of new data. The generation of interpretable rules, whether by the use of classification algorithms or conceptual clustering algorithms, is of considerable importance in reducing the knowledge acquisition "bottleneck"[14] that often impedes progress towards the building of rule-based systems.

In this paper, two new techniques for conceptual clustering are introduced and compared. Both techniques deliver a hierarchical partitioning of the input data in a readily interpretable tree display. One approach makes use of both a numerical taxonomy (NT) algorithm and the Classification And Regression Trees (CART) algorithm[7] and involves two passes through the input data. The other approach uses the Multiply–Overlapping Clustering Algorithm (MOCA)[15] and requires only a single pass through the data. Both techniques are used to locate and explain clusters of employees at Advanced Decision Systems. The data used for the analysis characterizes each employee based upon their newsgroup reading behavior.

This paper is organized as follows: Section 2 defines the clustering problem and briefly describes two new approaches to the problem. Section 3 describes the newsgroups data used in this paper. Section 4 describes the analyses undertaken to explore the capabilities of the two algorithms. Section 5 attempts to informally validate the results. Finally, Section 6 summarizes the results of the study.

## 2. TWO TECHNIQUES FOR CONCEPTUAL CLUSTERING

The clustering problem, in its most fundamental form, is simply stated as follows:

> Given a set of observations, each of which is described by a vector of measurements, generate a candidate clustering such that the intra-cluster observation similarity is maximized, and the inter-cluster similarity is minimized.

The science of statistics has devoted a tremendous amount of effort towards the development of algorithms designed to address the clustering problem described above. Those algorithms, however, are concerned primarily with the generation of the clusters, leaving the burden of interpretation of the clusters up to the ingenuity of the analyst. The machine learning community, on the other hand, has devoted considerable effort towards the development of algorithms that both generate and describe clusters. Clusters are typically described by sets of rules that are collectively known as concepts. As such, the machine learning procedures for clustering are commonly referred to as conceptual clustering algorithms.

This paper is intended as an introduction to a pair of relatively new conceptual clustering techniques. Both methods can be described as ''machine learning'' algorithms, although the CART algorithm, described in detail in Appendix A, was developed by statisticians and, in fact, derives much of its appeal from the statistical rigor that characterizes its approach. The sections below provide brief introductions to these two techniques. More detailed descriptions are included as Appendices A and B.

### 2.1. Conceptual Clustering with CART and Numerical Taxonomy

Since CART requires that the analyst specify known class assignments for each observation in the data set, it is inappropriate for conceptual clustering when used alone. The approach introduced in this paper, however, first uses a numerical taxonomy algorithm (NT) to generate clusters and then uses CART to describe those clusters. The CART and NT algorithms are briefly described below.

**NT**: The particular NT algorithm that was used for the experiments described in this paper is HCLUS. HCLUS is available as part of the S language for data analysis and statistical graphics,[16] and belongs to a class of NT algorithms that generate a disjoint hierarchical clustering of the data set. HCLUS is an *agglomerative* algorithm, since it begins by assigning each datum to a separate cluster, and then merges clusters until all data belong to a single cluster. This contrasts with *divisive* approaches which start with a single cluster and partition into subclusters. For a data set with $N$ entries, NT algorithms usually take as input a half-matrix consisting of $N(N-1)/2$ pairwise distance (or similarity) measurements. The agglomerative hierarchical methods then follow a simple paradigm:

1. Create $N$ clusters, one datum (observation) per cluster.
2. Create a new cluster by merging the two nearest clusters.
3. Compute the distance between the cluster merged in Step 2 and every other cluster.
4. Repeat Steps 2 and 3 until all observations belong in a single cluster.

Variations on this approach are obtained by altering the manner in which clusters are merged in Step 2. If two clusters are compared by computing the similarities of the two *closest* members of each cluster, then the technique is called ''connected'', ''single link'', or ''nearest neighbor'' clustering. If Step 2 is modified so that two clusters are compared by computing the *dissimilarities* between the most remote pair of members of each cluster, then the technique is called ''compact'', ''complete link'', or ''furthest neighbor'' clustering. Some methods merge clusters by computing distances between groups rather than individuals. For example, ''centroid'' clustering involves comparing cluster centroids (mean vectors), and ''average'' clustering compares the average of all pairwise distances between clusters.

The approach to clustering can also be varied by altering the distance measure used for merging clusters. Although simple Euclidean (root mean square) distance is probably used most often, Hamming (binary), Manhattan (city block), and general Minkowski metrics may also be used.

**CART**: The approach we use for cluster description involves use of the CART algorithm.[7,17–20] CART takes as input a collection of examples (the *training set*), each of which consists of a *known* class assignment and a vector of features. The feature values may be Boolean, integer, real, or nominal and, in addition, may be both noisy and incomplete. The output from CART is a binary decision tree that can be used to classify subsequent observations for which the class is not known. When the training set is noisy, trees of maximal size are invariably too large in that a smaller tree will perform better in terms of classification accuracy. CART makes use of tree pruning and error estimation algorithms to locate the "right-sized" tree, ensuring a parsimonious, accurate classifier.

CART has been shown to be useful when one has access to data sets describing known classes of observations and wishes to obtain rules for classifying future observations of unknown class. CART is particularly attractive when the data set is "messy," and thus unsuitable for use by more traditional pattern classification techniques. Similarly, if it is important to specify both misclassification costs and prior probabilities of class membership, then CART is an appealing choice. The flexibility, power, and robustness of the CART algorithm make it an attractive choice for classification problems, and CART has been successfully applied to problems in a wide variety of domains.[18,19,20–24] A more detailed account of the CART algorithm is provided in Appendix A.

## 2.2. Conceptual Clustering with MOCA

MOCA[15] is based on the techniques of conceptual clustering, a type of machine learning known as learning by observation.[13] The goal is to partition a set of observations into clusters without requiring any *a priori* class assignment information. The output is a hierarchical tree whose nodes represent clusters of the data. Clusters are produced by partitioning the data based upon values of a single attribute and are thus monothetic. Monothetic splits are those for which the descendants of a given node are based upon values of a *single* attribute, as opposed to many attributes (*polythetic* splits). In contrast to numerical taxonomy algorithms, MOCA both generates and explains the clusters that are uncovered. The explanation is in the form of textual descriptions or classification rules for the clusters.

The development of MOCA was motivated by perceived shortcomings of existing conceptual clustering algorithms. MOCA does not require the user to supply the number of clusters to be generated, and allows for overlapping clusters. The primary innovation of MOCA is a search that iterates over the attribute space of the data rather than through the set of observations being partitioned. This results in improved computational performance when the size of the attribute space is small in comparison with the number of observations in the data set. Appendix B gives a more detailed description of the algorithm.

## 3. THE NEWSGROUPS DATA

Each employee at Advanced Decision Systems (ADS) has a computer account which allows access to a worldwide network of bulletin boards called the USENET. The bulletin boards on the USENET, commonly referred to as newsgroups, are arranged by topic, as indicated by the prefix of the newsgroup name. For example, recreational newsgroups are prefaced by REC, computer newsgroups by COMP, social newsgroups by SOC, and newsgroups dealing with events in the San Francisco Bay area are prefaced by BA. In addition, there are newsgroups that deal solely with matters concerning ADS staff members, and these newsgroups have the ADS prefix.

In order to keep track of what newsgroups each person is interested in reading and the number of articles that person has currently read in each newsgroup, the news reading program maintains a file (named .newsrc) located in the main directory of each person's computer account. The data set analyzed in this paper was generated by reading the .newsrc file owned by each employee and building from it a data record indicating, for each newsgroup, whether the employee was an *active* reader of the newsgroup, was an *inactive* reader (i.e. subscribed, but an infrequent reader), or was *unsubscribed* to the newsgroup. A newsgroup was considered actively read if the number of the last article read was greater than or equal to half the number of the latest article posted to that newsgroup. In addition, for each employee, the total number of active, inactive, and unsubscribed newsgroups was computed and appended to the data record. The final data set consists of 132 observations (one per employee), each of which contains measurements on 306 newsgroups as well as the three summary statistics.

## 4. CLUSTERING RESULTS

This section examines the results of two methods for generating and describing clusters. The first method uses a two-stage approach: clusters are first generated using a standard NT algorithm; observations in the generated clusters are given a class label based upon cluster membership; and rules describing the classes are then induced via application of the CART classification algorithm. The second method makes use of a conceptual clustering algorithm called MOCA. The results of both methods are described below.

### 4.1. Using Numerical Taxonomy and CART

The data set provided as input to the NT component is the newsgroups data described in Sec. 3. Although the goal is to generate a particular clustering over the data, the immediate problem involves choosing the appropriate number of clusters. There are many obvious ways one can imagine this data being clustered: by sex, age, job title, etc. and so it is unclear *a priori* how many clusters really exist. A straightforward way to assess the correct number of clusters uncovered by NT is to display the hierarchical clustering scheme visually. A visual representation of a hierarchical clustering is called a *dendrogram* and is structured as an inverted tree with individuals forming the leaves. The branching structure of the dendrogram illustrates the clustering hierarchy.

The first decision one must make involves choice of distance metric and linkage scheme, as described in Sec. 2.1. Single-link clustering is often recommended[8] because of its desirable properties of continuity and invariance. Continuity simply means that small perturbations of the data will result in small perturbations in hierarchical structure, and invariance means that the clustering procedure itself is invariant under monotone transformations of the similarity data—important when one is confident in the data only up to a rank ordering. Single-link methods have, however, been criticized[25] because of their susceptibility to ''chaining''—a phenomenon in which clusters are joined too early because of the proximity of a single pair of observations in two clusters (recall that single-link clustering is a ''nearest neighbor'' technique). Also, since clusters are formed based upon single distance values, both single- and complete-link methods have been criticized as being non-robust,[9] and average methods have been recommended instead, despite their lack of the invariance property. For reasons of robustness, we choose to use an average linking method for this analysis. Since our data is categorical rather than numerical, we must first recode our three categories as dummy variables (e.g. unsubscribed ≡ 1, inactive ≡ 2, active ≡ 3). Since the use of a Euclidean metric would make the content of our distance half-matrix dependent upon the particular choice of the encoding scheme, we instead choose a Hamming distance. A Hamming distance is computed by counting the proportion of identical entries in a pair of vectors and is therefore independent of the encoding scheme used.

### 4.1.1. A first level of clustering

**The clustering**: The dendrogram obtained from using a Hamming distance and average linking is shown in Fig. 1. Although three main clusters and a single outlier are clearly visible, the dendrogram alone does not ''explain'' the clusters. Why are the employees within these clusters in some way similar and what makes that single employee somehow different from the rest? We attempt to answer these questions by appending to each employee data record a class label indicating the number of the cluster to which it belongs, and then using the CART algorithm to induce a tree that classifies employees using these labels.

The CART tree shown in Fig. 2 correctly places all but one employee record into the node representing the cluster to which it belongs. This clearly illustrates that this clustering is based upon the total number of newsgroups to which employees have explicitly unsubscribed. The first split identifies members of cluster two as those who unsubscribe to more than 206 newsgroups. The second split identifies members of cluster one as those who unsubscribe to between 113 and 206 newsgroups. The single misclassification in this cluster is that of our outlier. Finally, cluster three is identified as those employees who have unsubscribed to less than 113 newsgroups.

**Cluster three explained**: The CART user interface allows the analyst to display descriptive labels of the observations resident at a node (in this case, employee names)

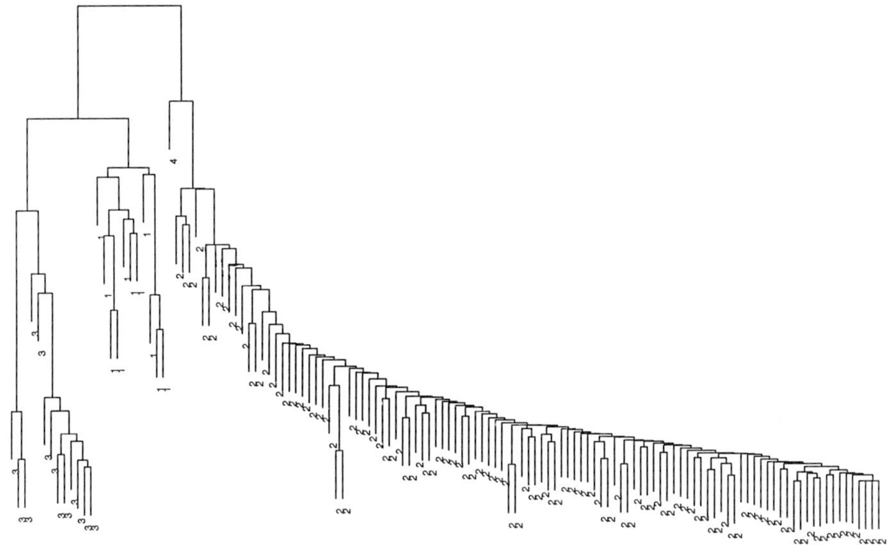

Fig. 1. Clustering of 132 individuals. Note the three main clusters and a single outlier (labeled 4).

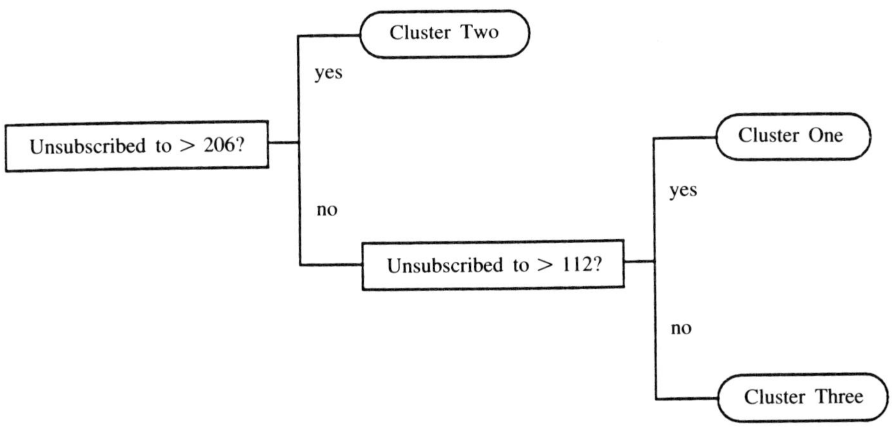


Fig. 2. Classification of 132 individuals based upon three clusters and a single outlier.

and also permits the display of a variety of descriptive statistics at each node. Using these tools, we note that the median number of newsgroups to which the 13 members of cluster three have unsubscribed is only 20—in great contrast to the company-wide median of 292. In addition, the median number of actively read newsgroups is an extraordinarily high 265 (the company-wide median is only 14). How can an employee actively read so many newsgroups? Inspection of the names of these "frequent readers" (not shown here) reveals that all except two are new employees and, as such, have new .newsrc files that, by default, will initially indicate all subscribed newsgroups as active (refer to Sec. 3 for details on how reading behaviors are categorized). Although the median number of actively read newsgroups for cluster three is 265, three members actively read only a few newsgroups. Interviews with these three revealed a rather peculiar news reading behavior—they simply read the few newsgroups of interest then exit from the news reading program without bothering to unsubscribe to those newsgroups of little interest. In summary, cluster three consists of new employees who have yet to unsubscribe to many newsgroups and a few employees with an unusual reading behavior.

**Cluster one explained**: As indicated by the optimal split shown in Fig. 2, cluster one consists of 11 employees who have unsubscribed to between 113 and 206 newsgroups (the median for cluster one is 160—far more than cluster three, but less than the company-wide median of 292). We can begin to explain this cluster by examining the "surrogates" for the optimal split. Surrogate splits are those splits maximally predictive of the optimal split (see Ref. 7 for details) and, for cluster one, we find that 14 other splits partition the data in precisely the same way as the optimal split. These surrogates indicate that cluster one members have unsubscribed to a number of highly technical newsgroups (COMP.SYS.SGI, COMP.SYS.APOLLO, etc.). This suggests that these employees have not taken the time to unsubscribe to a great many newsgroups, but the ones they have unsubscribed to are largely technical in nature. Inspection of the names associated with cluster one show, however, that 50% are non-technical staff (almost twice as many as the company-wide 26% non-technical staff)—indicating that membership in the cluster may be related to job class. As a final note, by forcing an additional split of cluster one, we can classify our outlier appropriately and, in doing so, find that this employee is unusual because he has unsubscribed to ADS.TRASH—an enormously popular ADS-specific newsgroup.

4.1.2. A second level of clustering

**The clustering**: As indicated in Sec. 4.1.1, the first level of clustering essentially partitions individuals based upon general characteristics of news reading behavior (i.e. the way in which the .newsrc file was managed), as opposed to particulars of the specific newsgroups that are actively read. In an effort to uncover subclusters within the 107 members of cluster two, we remove all of the cluster one, three, and four observations, and then re-cluster the remaining data. Since we wish to focus attention on readership of specific newsgroups, we use the data encoding described earlier along with a Euclidean distance measure. In the attribute space, this ensures maximal distance between "active" and "unsubscribed". Furthermore, since we wish to uncover clusters that were not found in the first analysis (at the risk of uncovering spurious clusters), we choose a less robust clustering method—compact (complete-link) clustering. The dendrogram obtained from using Euclidean distance and compact linking is shown in Fig. 3. Inspection of Fig. 3 clearly reveals three main clusters, along with a small group of twelve outliers. As before, we use CART to explain these clusters but, in order to simplify subsequent analysis, we first remove the outliers from the data, leaving a total of 95 employees in three clusters. The CART tree shown in Fig. 4 places 77 of the 95 employees into the correct clusters.

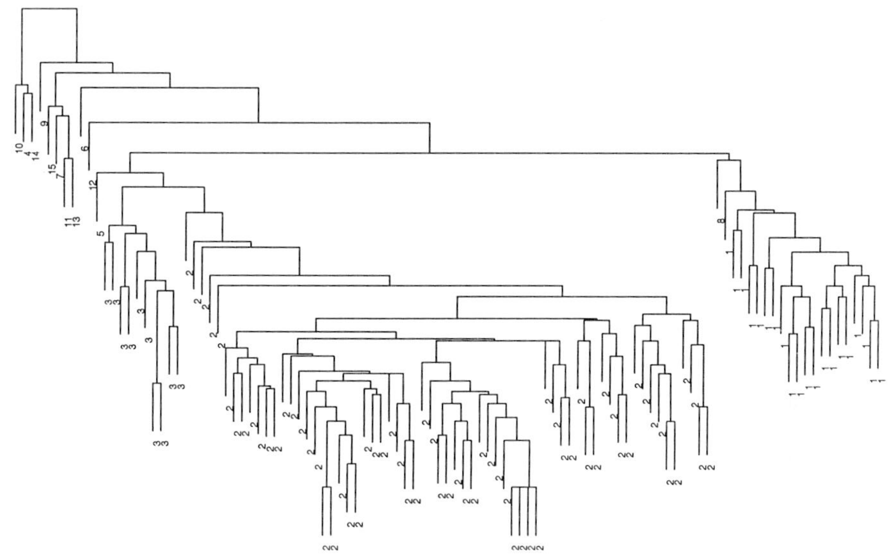

Fig. 3. Clustering 107 individuals. Note the three main clusters and a group of twelve outliers (labeled 4 – 15).

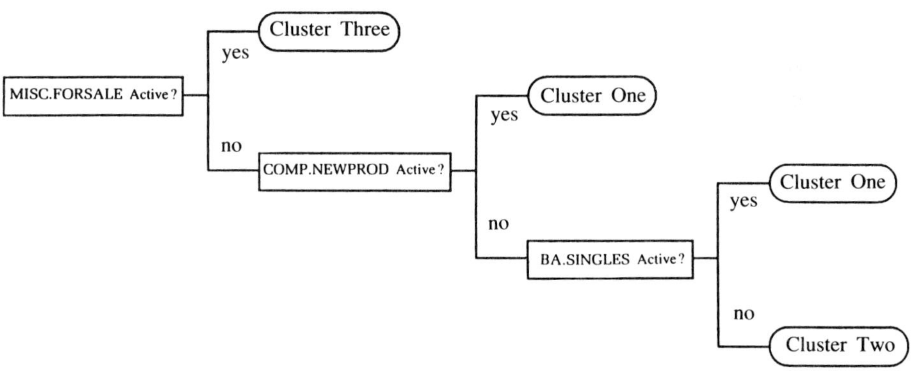


Fig. 4. Classification of 95 individuals based upon three clusters (outliers removed).

**Cluster one explained**: Figure 4 reveals that membership in cluster one is based upon active readership of COMP.NEWPROD or (if that newsgroup is not read) active readership of BA.SINGLES. There are a large number of surrogates for the COMP.NEWPROD split, all dealing with active readership of technical newsgroups most of which are programming related (COMP.SOURCES.X, COMP.SYS.MAC. PROGRAMMER, COMP.LANG.SMALLTALK, REC.GAMES.PROGRAMMER, etc.). In addition, there are a number of surrogates for the BA.SINGLES split, all rather similar in nature (SOC.SINGLES, SOC.WOMEN, REC.NUDE, etc.). CART correctly places 55% of the cluster one members in the appropriately labeled nodes.

Inspection of the names associated with the pair of cluster one nodes shows that the first cluster one node consists exclusively of six technical staff who do a good deal of scientific programming. In addition, all of these technical staff members are married. The second cluster one node contains nine members, six of whom are non-technical staff and all but one of whom are single. These results strongly suggest that cluster one may, in fact, consist of two rather different subclusters—a group of married scientific programmers and a group of single administrative staff members.

**Cluster three explained**: Figure 4 reveals that membership in cluster three is based upon active readership of the newsgroup MISC.FORSALE. Furthermore, perfect surrogates for this split are based upon active readership of seven other non-technical newsgroups (MISC.WANTED, MISC.INVEST, REC.MISC, CA.WANTED, REC.AUTOS, TALK.RELIGION.MISC, and REC.ARTS) and inactive readership of a single technical newsgroup (GNU.EMACS). CART correctly places 60% of the cluster three members in this node. Inspection of the nine names associated with cluster three shows that seven are non-technical staff, with five of those in the accounting and contracts department. These results strongly suggest that this cluster may be interpreted as a clear ''non-technical'' cluster.

#### 4.1.3. Summary

This analysis clearly indicates that use of a readily available NT algorithm to generate the initial clusters, followed by application of the CART algorithm to explain the clusters is a viable approach to conceptual clustering. The initial clustering of the data isolated two small clusters characterized by ''macro-level'' newsgroup reading behavior—that is, clustering is based upon the manner in which staff manage their .newsrc file rather than the specific newsgroups that were read. Once these clusters were removed, a second clustering of the data revealed two additional small clusters characterized by ''micro-level'' newsgroup reading behavior—that is, clustering is based upon the active readership of specific newsgroups. One of these subclusters (cluster three) is clearly administrative in nature, whereas the other (cluster one) seems to consist of both married technical programmers and young, single non-technical staff. The remaining cluster (cluster two) consisted of 75% technical staff and appears to represent the ''core'' technical group at ADS.

### 4.2. Using MOCA

Numerical taxonomy and CART were combined to take a data set with no *a priori* class assignment information and to produce cluster concepts. Since MOCA is explicitly designed for conceptual clustering, it produces similar results in a single pass through the data. The .newsrc data, as described in Sec. 3, contains 132 observations described by 306 categorical attributes that measure newsgroup readership (inactive, active, or unsubscribed) and three attributes that are the total inactive, active, and unsubscribed newsgroups read.

#### 4.2.1. A first level of clustering

**The clustering**: The results of the MOCA analysis are shown in Fig. 5. The first level partitions on the newsgroup COMP.SOURCES.MISC and produces three clusters. Due to the size of the cluster containing all observations that are unsubscribed to this newsgroup (109 observations), it is subjected to a second level of clustering described in Sec. 4.2.2. The other two first level clusters are described below.

**Cluster "noise" explained**: The three observations placed in the cluster labeled "noise" have an inactive value for the COMP.SOURCES.MISC attribute. The cluster description generated by MOCA shows that many newsgroups have an inactive status. The people represented by these three observations (person's names are included in the observations but not shown here) are individuals who are often on travel or work off-site and do not keep their .newsrc file up-to-date, and thus represent unusual or noisy data points. These are the same three unusual individuals identified in cluster three of the CART/NT first level clustering (Sec. 4.1.1).

**Cluster "technical" explained**: The cluster labeled "technical" contains 20 observations that are actively subscribed to the COMP.SOURCES.MISC newsgroup. Review of the names of the employees contained in this cluster reveals that they are primarily technical staff. When we look at the cluster description for the node we see that many technical newsgroups are subscribed to actively. However, many non-technical newsgroups are also actively read. The distribution of newsgroup status shows that 80% of this cluster is in the upper quartile of total active newsgroups (over 40) and in the lower quartile of total unsubscribed newsgroups (less than 250). In summary, these are technical staff members who read a lot of newsgroups. In addition, all but three of the observations from the "noise" and "technical" clusters were identified as outliers and very active readers in the CART/NT approach (Sec. 4.1.1).

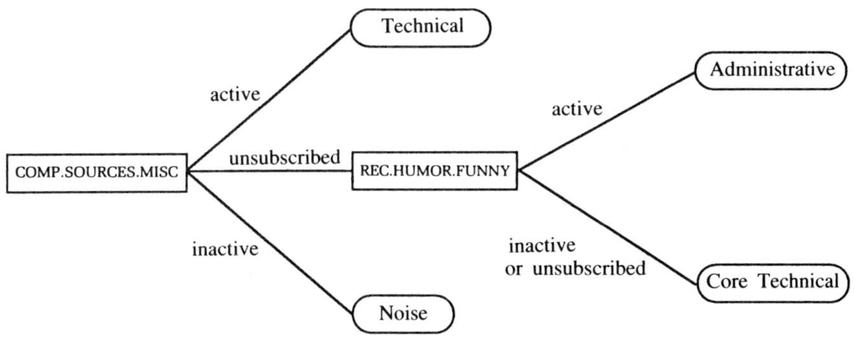


Fig. 5. Hierarchical tree generated by MOCA.

4.2.2. A second level of clustering

**The clustering:** The cluster containing all observations unsubscribed to the COMP.SOURCES.MISC newsgroup identified in the first level partition is subjected to another level of clustering due to its size (109 observations). The two clusters produced based on a split on REC.HUMOR.FUNNY readership are described below.

**Cluster "administrative" described**: Those individuals that have unsubscribed to COMP.SOURCES.MISC and actively subscribed to REC.HUMOR.FUNNY (36 observations in all) are contained in the cluster labeled "administrative". This label is based on 39% of the observations being administrative staff members, which is proportionately higher than the company-wide percentage of 26% administrative staff. Similar to the case with the "technical" cluster, analysis of the cluster description reveals many active newsgroups, both technical and non-technical. This leads to a review of the distribution of active newsgroups (64% of the cluster's observations have more active newsgroups than the company-wide median) and unsubscribed newsgroups (69% are below the company-wide median of unsubscribed newsgroups). This suggests that this is an administrative cluster with an above average amount of newsgroup reading.

**Cluster "core technical" described**: The final cluster contains the individuals that have unsubscribed to COMP.SOURCES.MISC and do not actively read the REC.HUMOR.FUNNY newsgroup (a total of 73 observations). This cluster is made up of 75% technical staff. These individuals exhibit newsgroup readership that is closer to what we might expect. The median for number of active newsgroups is seven and for number of unsubscribed newsgroups is 297, indicating a lower amount of newsgroup reading compared to the "technical" and "administrative" clusters. In addition, 77% of the members of this cluster are contained in the "core technical" cluster found in the CART/NT analysis.

4.2.3. Summary

Four clusters have been identified by MOCA: "noise", "active technical", "active administrative", and "core technical". These clusters support the concepts of trends based upon both readers' newsgroup activity and job description. In summary, given a data set with no *a priori* class assignment information, MOCA has generated clusters that are comparable to the groups that exist within the ADS staff. The most difficult part of this analysis, associating a concept with the clusters produced, is greatly facilitated by the availability of textual class descriptions that can be interpreted with respect to the resulting hierarchical tree. MOCA has been applied with similar success in identifying underlying patterns in other domains including senate voting, criminal and parole records, American universities, business computer sales, and plant and animal taxonomy.

## 5. CLUSTER VALIDATION

As described in Sec. 4, the two clustering approaches produce clusters that reflect patterns in newsgroup readership and job class. The CART/numerical taxonomy

(CART/NT) approach to conceptual clustering appears to partition the data set into three ''macro-level'' clusters and at least three ''micro-level'' clusters. The micro-level clustering appears to partition staff members into ''core-technical'', ''programmer-technical'', ''general-administrative'', and ''single-administrative'' groups. MOCA generates four clusters: ''noise'', ''active technical'', ''active-administrative'' and ''core-technical''. The labels given to these clusters are obtained from analysis of the classification rules or cluster descriptions generated by the algorithms, as well as surrogates of those rules in the case of CART/NT. Examination of the names of the ADS staff populating the clusters lends credence to these labels. Since both the MOCA clustering and NT micro-level clustering appear to group staff based upon their technical orientation, we can take a step towards the validation of this hypothesis by using CART to classify ADS employees based upon each employee's *real* job type. This CART/job-class analysis is described below.

In an effort to evaluate the cluster descriptions generated by the conceptual clustering algorithms, explicit class labels are appended to each observation in the data set. Although staff members of ADS can be loosely described as *technical*, *administrative* or *management*, all management staff maintain a strong technical interest that is likely to be manifested in their choice of newsgroups. As such, all managers are assigned to the *technical* class. Unfortunately, there is no clear job distinction that might separate programmer-oriented technical staff from the remainder of the technical staff, and so the analysis is undertaken with all employees assigned to either the *technical* or *administrative* job class. The question is whether the CART classification based upon known job class is similar to the CART/NT and MOCA clusterings. If so, this supports the hypothesis that the clusters generated by both clustering approaches tend to identify employees by job class. The tree generated by CART based on the job classification rules or cluster descriptions generated by the algorithms, as well as employees according to the job class labels.

Examination of Fig. 6 indicates that a large group (48) of technical staff are characterized by the fact that they are the active readers of the ADS.LISP-MACHINE newsgroup. Since much of the technical work at ADS involves the use of these machines, this newsgroup is likely to be widely read by the technical staff.

The split based upon active readership of the BA.SINGLES newsgroup separates administrative staff from those technical staff that do not read the ADS.LISP-MACHINE newsgroup. The main surrogate for this split is a related newsgroup called SOC.SINGLES. Given that much of the administrative staff is young and single it seems quite reasonable that readership of this newsgroup would be predictive of membership in the administrative staff. Although much of the technical staff is young and single, it may be that the technical staff prefer to invest their time reading the more technically-oriented newsgroup. The fact that SOC.SINGLES characterizes the ''young, single, administrative'' cluster obtained from the CART/NT analysis lends credence to the supposition that the cluster is, in fact, job related.

In summary, comparison of the results of the conceptual clustering analyses with results of the CART/job-class analysis suggests strongly that the micro-level clusters

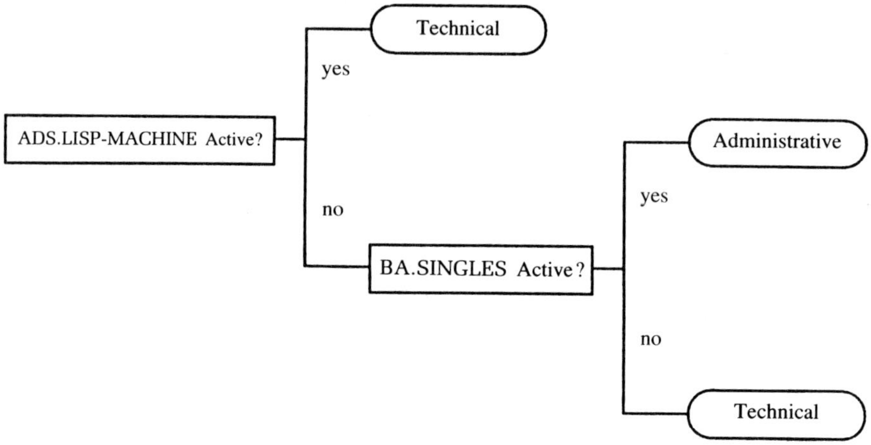


Fig. 6. CART-generated tree for 2 job classes.

generated by NT are indeed based largely upon technical interest. Both analyses reveal partitions composed largely of non-technical (administrative) staff, and technical staff. The CART analysis based upon known job classes tends to separate the technical staff into a large, ''core'' LISP-oriented group and a smaller administrative group. In a similar manner, the analysis based upon the CART descriptions of the NT clusters appears to separate the technical staff into a large ''core'' group, a smaller group interested primarily in programming, and a pair of administrative groups. The MOCA clusters include both small and large technical groups, and an administrative group. The fact that careful analysis of the conceptual clusters generated by both the MOCA and CART/NT approaches yields cluster ''concepts'' that are supported by a subsequent confirmatory CART analysis is strong evidence validating the hypothesis that some of the observed clustering is related to job class.

## 6. CONCLUSIONS

The analyses described in this paper suggest that both the MOCA and CART/NT approaches to conceptual clustering show considerable promise. Each, however, has its own advantages and disadvantages, and these are summarized below.

### 6.1. The CART/NT Approach

This method is appealing largely because NT algorithms like HCLUS are readily available and exhibit well understood characteristics. In addition, the CART algorithm is becoming widely accepted in both the statistics and AI communities. This approach is also attractive because CART's tree pruning capability provides the analyst with insight into the correct number of clusters, since nodes representing spurious, noisy clusters tend to get pruned away. Also, when information regarding the misclassification rate of the cluster description tree is important, CART can provide an unbiased estimate of error rate. Also, CART works well with real-valued variables in the data set. Unfortunately, the CART/NT approach requires *two* separate passes through the data. To summarize, the CART/NT approach is best used when one has a data set that consists of noisy, real-valued observations and/or when an estimate of the misclassification rate of the cluster description tree is important.

## 6.2. The MOCA Approach

Standard numerical taxonomy algorithms are designed primarily to work with real- and integer-valued data sets; nominal-valued variables must be recoded as dummy variables. MOCA, however, is particularly useful in analyzing data sets with nominal-valued variables. Unlike CART/NT, the user is not required to supply the number of clusters when using MOCA, and MOCA requires only one pass through the data set. MOCA can make use of real-valued variables, but only by discretizing the data. Some drawbacks to the use of MOCA for conceptual clustering include the fact that the algorithm is quite new, its characteristics are not well understood, and MOCA is not yet widely available. To summarize, MOCA is best used when the data set consists largely of nominal-valued attributes.

## REFERENCES

1. D. J. Hand, *Discrimination and Classification*, John Wiley & Sons, 1981.
2. D. J. Hand, *Kernel Discriminant Analysis*, John Wiley & Sons, 1982.
3. S. L. Crawford and T. C. Fall, "Projection pursuit: searching for structure in high dimensional space", in *Visualization in Scientific Computing*, Ed. G. M. Nielson, IEEE Computer Society Press, 1990. In press.
4. J. H. Friedman, "Exploratory projection pursuit", *J. Amer. Stat. Assoc.* **82**, 397 (1987) 249–266.
5. J. Ross Quinlan, "Decision trees as probabilistic classifiers", in *Proc. Fourth Int. Workshop on Machine Learning*, Irvine, California, June 1987, Morgan Kaufmann, pp. 31–37.
6. J. Ross Quinlan, "Generating production rules from decision trees", in *Proc. Tenth Int. Joint Conf. Artificial intelligence*, Milan, Italy, Aug. 1987, Morgan Kaufmann, pp. 304–307.
7. L. Breiman, J. H. Friedman, R. A. Olshen and C. J. Stone, *Classification and Regression Trees*, Wadsworth, 1984.
8. N. Jardine and R. Sibson, *Mathematical Taxonomy*, Wiley, 1971.
9. R. R. Sokal and P. H. A. Sneath, *Principles of Numerical Taxonomy*, W. H. Freeman, 1963.
10. D. F. Morrison, *Multivariate Statistical Methods*, McGraw-Hill, 1976.
11. H. H. Harman, *Modern Factor Analysis*, University of Chicago Press, 1967.
12. D. H. Fisher,"Knowledge acquisition via incremental conceptual clustering", *Machine Learning* **2**, 2 (1987) 139–172.
13. R. S. Michalski and R. E. Stepp, "Learning from observation: conceptual clustering", in *Machine Learning: An Artificial Intelligence Approach*, Eds. R. S. Michalski, J. G. Carbonell and T. M. Mitchell, Morgan Kaufman, 1983.
14. E. A. Feigenbaum, "Expert systems in the 1980's", in *State of the Art Report on Machine Intelligence*, Ed. A. Bond, Pergamon-Infotech, 1981.
15. S. K. Souders, "MOCA: The Multiply-Overlapping Clustering Algorithm", Technical Report ADS TR-5926-01, Advanced Decision Systems, 1988.

16. R. A. Becker, J. M. Chambers and A. R. Wilks, *The New S Language: A Programming Environment for Data Analysis and Graphics*, Wadsworth, 1988.
17. S. L. Crawford, "Extensions to the CART algorithm", *Int. J. Man-Mach. Stud.* **31** (1989) 197–217.
18. S. L. Crawford, "Resampling Strategies for Recursive Partitioning Classification with the CART Algorithm", Ph.D. thesis, Stanford University, Stanford, California, 1987.
19. S. L. Crawford and R. M. Fung, "Data-driven assessment and decision making", in *Expert Systems in Economics, Banking and Management*, Eds. L. F. Pau, Y. H. Pao and J. Motiwalla, North-Holland, 1989.
20. R. M. Fung and S. L. Crawford, "Induction, evidential reasoning, and decision theory applied to clinical decision making", in *Proc. AAAI Spring Symposium: Artificial Intelligence in Medicine*, Stanford University, May 1988.
21. R. O. Dillman and J. A. Koziol, "Statistical approach to immunosuppression classification using lymphocyte surface markers and functional assays", *Cancer Research* **43** (1983) 417–421.
22. E. Gilpin, R. Olshen, H. Henning and J. Ross, "Risk prediction after myocardial infarction: comparison of three multivariate methodologies", *Cardiology* **70** (1983) 73–84.
23. L. Goldman, "A computer-derived protocol to aid in the diagnosis of emergency room patients with acute chest pain", *New England J. Medicine* **307** (1982) 588–596.
24. R. Hooper and A. Lucero, "Radar profile classification: a feasibility study", Technical Report, Technology Service Corporation, Santa Monica, CA, 1976.
25. C. Chatfield and A. J. Collins, *Introduction to Multivariate Analysis*, Chapman and Hall, 1980.
26. J. R. Quinlan, "Learning efficient classification procedures and their application to chess end games", in *Machine Learning: An Artificial Intelligence Approach*, Eds. R. S. Michalski, J. G. Carbonell and T. M. Mitchell, Morgan Kaufman, 1983.
27. M. Lebowitz, "Experiments with incremental concept formation: UNIMEM", *Machine Learning* **2**, 2 (1987) 103–138.

## APPENDIX A. THE CART ALGORITHM

CART takes as input a training set $\mathcal{L}$ consisting of $N$ cases, each of which consists of a *known* class $\theta$ and a vector of attribute values. A classification tree $T$ initially consists only of the root node $\tau_1$ containing all of the cases in $\mathcal{L}$. A search is made through the set of possible binary splits of $\tau_1$ until an optimal split $s_{\text{opt}}$ is found. For real-valued attributes $A$, splits take on the form $A \leq r$, where $r$ is the midpoint of any adjacent pair found in the set of unique values attained by $A$. For categorical attributes which can attain possible values $D_1, \ldots, D_M$, splits take on the form $A \in \{D\}$ where $\{D\}$ is one of the subsets of $\{D_1, \ldots, D_M\}$. Once $s_{\text{opt}}$ is located, the root node acquires two descendants, $\tau_L$ and $\tau_R$, each of which now contains a subset of $\mathcal{L}$. Geometrically, $s_{\text{opt}}$ describes a partition orthogonal to one of the coordinates of the measurement space. The partitioning process is applied recursively to each leaf, continuing until all leaves are too small, contain cases from a single class only, or contain identical measurement vectors. When partitioning ends, the initial tree has grown to become a terminal tree $T_{\max}$.

Since, with a noisy domain, $T_{\max}$ almost certainly overfits $\mathcal{L}$, it is pruned backwards, yielding a unique, nested sequence of subtrees $\{T_{\max} \preceq, \ldots,$

$\preceq \tau_2 \preceq \tau_2\}$, and an error estimation procedure is then applied to the sequence in order to select an optimally sized subtree. Subsequent observations are dropped down the selected tree, and classified according to the class membership of the plurality of cases populating the leaf into which they fall.

Since the tree building mechanism attempts to generate a tree with increasingly homogeneous (pure) nodes, a natural splitting criterion is one which tends to maximize some index of purity. For $C$ classes, using an impurity function $\phi$, and defining $p(j\,|\,\tau)$ as the proportion of class $j$ cases at node $\tau$, the impurity of node $\tau$ is defined as: $\iota(\tau) = \phi(p(1\,|\,\tau), \ldots, p(C\,|\,\tau))$. Any split $s$ on $\tau$ sends a proportion $p_L$ of cases to $\tau_L$ and a proportion $p_R$ to $\tau_R$, and the decrease in impurity obtained from splitting $\tau$ by $s$ is defined by $\Delta\iota(s, \tau) = \iota(\tau) - p_R\iota(\tau_R) - p_L\iota(\tau_L)$. The optimal split of node $\tau$ is selected as the split that yields the maximum decrease in impurity as determined by $\Delta\iota(s, \tau)$.

It turns out that the performance of the classification tree algorithm is relatively insensitive to the choice of $\phi$, as long as certain concavity requirements are met. Most commonly used, however, is the *Gini* index, which measures class *diversity* at a node. The Gini index is defined as $\sum_{i=1}^{C} \sum_{j=1}^{C} p(j\,|\,\tau)p(i\,|\,\tau)$, $i \neq j$, where $C$ is the number of classes in the training set and $p(j\,|\,\tau)$ is the proportion of class $j$ cases at node $\tau$.

As described previously, CART avoids the pitfalls of stopping rules by first growing a tree of maximal size, and then pruning backwards in an appropriate manner. The pruning approach is based upon the notion of assigning a *penalty* to the growth of large trees. Defining the cost complexity of tree $T$ as $R_\alpha(T) = \hat{R}(T) + \alpha\mathcal{T}$, where $\alpha$ is a real-valued penalty parameter, $\mathcal{T}$ is the number of leaves in $T$ and $\hat{R}(T)$ is the *resubstitution estimate* (obtained by classifying the cases in $\mathcal{L}$ by the *same* tree generated from $\mathcal{L}$) of the *true* error rate of $T$, it is possible, without exhaustive search, to locate that *unique* smallest subtree $T(\alpha)$ of $T_{\max}$ which minimizes $R_\alpha(T)$ for fixed $\alpha$. Although it is not implemented in this manner, minimal cost-complexity pruning can be thought of as a procedure in which $\alpha$ is steadily increased, with pruning occurring at threshold values $\alpha'$, thus yielding a nested sequence of minimizing subtrees.

Once the sequence of minimizing subtrees has been obtained, a minimum risk subtree, $T_{\text{opt}}$ is sought. If $\hat{R}(T)$ is the criterion used to select $T_{\text{opt}}$ then $T_{\max}$ will always be selected, since $\hat{R}(T)$ decreases with increasing $\mathcal{T}$. However, since $\hat{R}(T)$ is obtained as a result of resubstituting $\mathcal{L}$ into a tree generated from $\mathcal{L}$, $\hat{R}(T)$ is a *downwardly biased* estimate of the true error rate of $T$ and therefore inappropriate.

If an independent test sample (i.e. a set of training cases *not* used in the initial tree growing procedure) is available, then those cases can be used to select $T_{\text{opt}}$ by simply calculating the misclassification rate associated with each subtree in the nested sequence and choosing the subtree with the best performance. Unfortunately, however, such test samples are rarely available and so independent training cases are *simulated* via the statistical error estimation technique of *cross-validation*.

For the definitive description of CART, refer to Ref. 7, and for a complete analysis of alternative procedures for tree error rate estimation, refer to Refs. 17 and 18.

## APPENDIX B. THE MOCA ALGORITHM

MOCA[15] is based on the techniques of conceptual clustering, a type of machine learning known as learning by observation.[13] The goal is to partition a set of observations into clusters without requiring any *a priori* class assignment information. Attributes accepted by MOCA may be Boolean, integer, categorical, or real. The output is a hierarchical tree whose nodes represent clusters of the data. Clusters are produced by partitioning the data based upon values of a single attribute and are thus monothetic. Monothetic splits are those for which the descendants of a given node are based upon values of a *single* attribute, as opposed to many attributes (*polythetic* splits).

Associated with each node in the tree is a class description built from the attribute values of the observations in the node. The operators used in these class descriptions include $=$, $\leq$, $\geq$, *or*, *in-range*, and *member*. The combination of the hierarchical tree and class descriptions show the descriptive information that is typical of conceptual clustering algorithms. Analysts can use the hierarchical tree to gain a high-level interpretation of the clusters produced. An individual node's class description can be viewed to aid in interpreting the concepts or classes represented by the cluster. By representing the results in this hierarchical and symbolic format, analysts can more readily understand and apply the results from MOCA in interpretation of the current data and in classification of future data.

The motivation behind the engineering of the MOCA system is based on perceived shortcomings in existing conceptual clustering and classification algorithms.[12,13,26,27] MOCA does not require the user to supply the number of clusters to be generated, and allows for overlapping clusters. This seems intuitive for various natural domains and facilitates the clustering of data sets that include noisy observations. The primary innovation of MOCA is a search that iterates over the attribute space of the data rather than through the set of observations being partitioned. This results in improved computational performance when the size of the attribute space is small in comparison with the number of observations in the data set.

MOCA begins with a training set $\mathcal{L}$ consisting of $N$ observations described by a set of $k$ attributes $a_1, \ldots, a_k$. An observation is a vector of values, one value per attribute, $[V_{a_1}, \ldots, V_{a_k}]$. A cluster tree $T$ initially consists only of a root node $\tau_1$ containing all of the observations in $\mathcal{L}$. A candidate partitioning is generated for each attribute resulting in the set of candidate trees $T_1, \ldots, T_k$. The candidate tree that maximizes the metrics function (described below) becomes the current classification tree $T'$. The candidate tree for attribute $a_i$ initially consists of a leaf node generated for each possible value of $a_i$. If the cardinality of $a_i$ is $m$, this initial candidate tree will have the leaf nodes $\tau_{21}, \ldots, \tau_{2m}$. For example, the initial tree based on a partitioning of $a_i$, where $a_i$ has a cardinality of $m = 4$, is shown in Fig. 7. All observations having value $V_{a_{i1}}$ for attribute $a_i$ go to node $\tau_{21}$, etc.

All pairwise combinations of the leaf nodes are made and sorted in order of decreasing similarity. An example of such a node combination list is shown at the bottom of Fig. 7. The first node combination in the list is incorporated into the tree

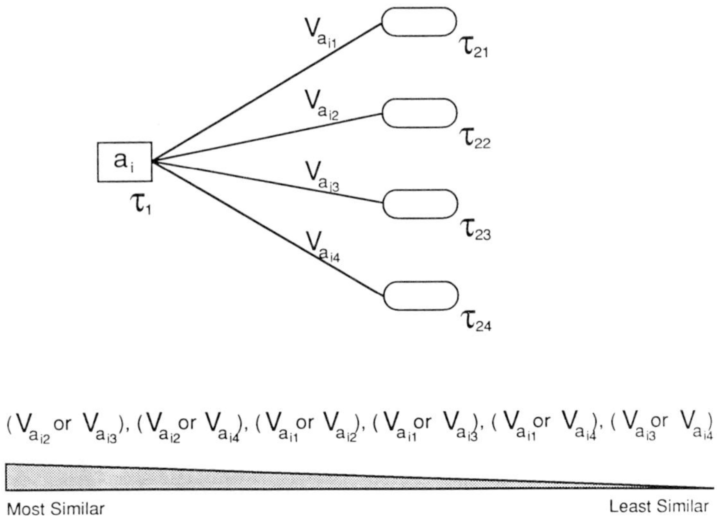


Fig. 7. Initial MOCA tree and node combination list.

(the node combination is added and all subsumed nodes are removed). If the revised tree better maximizes the metrics, it becomes the current working tree, the node combination is removed from the list, the incorporated node is combined with each of the remaining leaf nodes and these combinations are sorted into the node combination list, and the iteration begins again at the beginning of the node combination list. If the revised tree is not better, the next node combination is selected for incorporation. This is repeated until a better tree is generated, the node combination list is empty, the tree contains only two leaf nodes, or a search threshold is reached. In Fig. 8 the tree is shown after successful incorporation of the second element from the node combination list which is the node covering the attribute values $V_{a_{i2}}$ and $V_{a_{i4}}$. In this step nodes $\tau_{22}$ and $\tau_{24}$ are replaced by node $\tau_{22,4}$. Node $\tau_{22,4}$ is combined with the other leaf nodes, $\tau_{21}$ and $\tau_{23}$, and these node combinations are inserted in the node combination list based on their similarity value.

Comparison of the quality of trees is based on three metrics: similarity, lexical simplicity, and sparseness. Similarity is based on a Hamming distance. Simplicity is the negative of the number of operands in a node's class description. Sparseness is the number of data points covered by the class description minus the number of unique observations in the cluster.

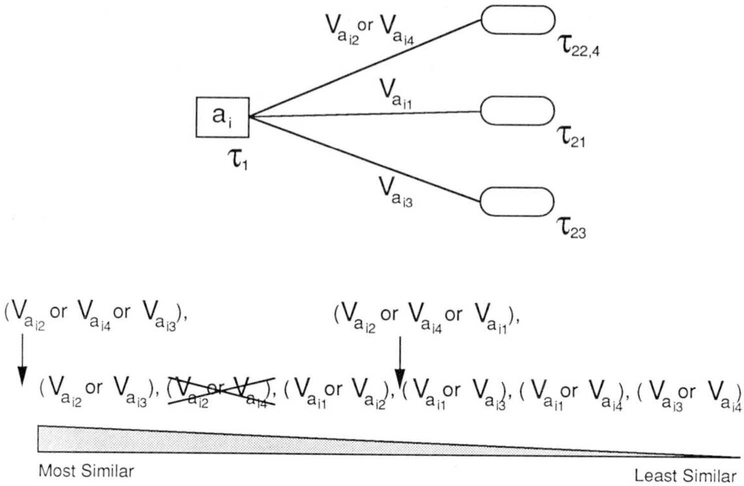


Fig. 8. Revised MOCA tree after incorporation of a combined node.

**Stuart L. Crawford** is a Senior Research Scientist and member of the research department at Advanced Decision Systems. His professional interests include: knowledge induction, classification and conceptual clustering techniques, probabilistic approaches to reasoning under uncertainty, the interactive graphical display of high dimensional computer intensive data analysis techniques, and user interface issues. He is presently working on methods for the induction of Bayesian networks, and on a finely grained parallel implementation of the CART classification algorithm. He obtained his B.Sc. degree from the University of British Columbia, and his M.S. and Ph.D. degrees from Stanford University.

**Steven K. Souders** is a Senior Systems Engineer with Advanced Decision Systems in Mountain View, California. He obtained his B.S. degree in systems engineering from the University of Virginia, and his M.S. degree in engineering–economic systems from Stanford University. Mr. Souders' accomplishments in applied AI research are based on a foundation of experience in large-scale decision support systems. He is currently working in the areas of knowledge acquisition and induction, intelligent data analysis, and knowledge-based development environments in various domains, including defense, intelligence, and criminal investigation.

# QUERYING AN OBJECT-ORIENTED DATABASE USING FREE LANGUAGE

PHILIPPE TRIGANO, JEAN-PAUL BARTHES
CATHERINE GREBOVAL and FRANÇOIS VALLERNAUD

*URA CNRS 817 Heudiasyc*
*Université de Technologie de Compiègne*
*BP 649, 60206 Compiègne Cedex, France*

Received 1 April 1990

A man–machine interface in natural language for a DataBase Management System (DBMS) called VORAS, based upon semantics, is presented. This DBMS can also be used for knowledge representation, and is well-suited to the design of queries in natural language. The system VORAS is an object-oriented DBMS developed from a specific model of representation called the Property Driven Model (PDM). A user may write a query in natural language. Most of the analysis is done at a semantic level. A syntactic level has been added, to improve the performance of the system. However, it is still possible to use a short-hand style.

*Keywords*: Artificial intelligence; Natural language processing; Databases; Object-oriented systems; Knowledge representation.

## 1. INTRODUCTION

One of the most important problems when querying a database is the man–machine interface. Generally people do not like to interact with computer programs through artificial languages. Some databases use a set of menus to synthetise the query. Such a query system may increase the number of questions to an unbearable level, and then may become boring in the case of very large systems which contain a lot of data with very different structures.

A solution is to implement an interface using natural language. Unfortunately, such a system can only have very good performances in a specific and very limited domain, but cannot adapt itself if the database domain changes. Another problem with natural language interfaces is their lack of tolerance of human error. Generally, if the user has a short-hand style, the system does not understand the question.

We have designed a Natural Language Interface for an object-oriented DataBase Management System (DBMS) called VORAS, based upon semantics. VORAS is well-suited for accepting queries in natural language, because the database structure is based on a semantic network. First, an interface where most of the analysis was done only at a semantic level was built;[1] then, a new version containing a syntactic parser was implemented to improve the performance of the system. However, the system is still intolerant of human error.

## 2. DATA REPRESENTATION

The system VORAS is developed from a specific model of representation called the Property Driven Model (PDM) first proposed by Barthes.[2,3] A description of VORAS and PDM can be found in Ref. 1. VORAS allows for the representation of data and knowledge as objects in a very flexible and intuitive fashion, and their manipulation as in a traditional database. An application has been built for the library of the Compiègne University of Technology (BUTC).[3] It is an on-line catalogue FILIBER which is available for consultation, in all the reading rooms, to the one thousand and five hundred users who come to the university every year.

PDM has its roots in Minsky's frame system[4] and in Abrial's data semantic approach.[5] It bears some resemblance to the entity/relationship model.[6] The BUTC application[3] has several objects, such as books, persons, editors, papers, keywords, journals, etc. Each type of object has attributes or properties. For example, a book may be described as:

```
Title     : An Introduction to Database Systems
Editor    : Addison-Wesley
Year      : 1977
Author    : C. J. DATE
Reference : 680.DAT
Language  : English
```

Some of the above properties display "immediate" information, like TITLE or YEAR, and are called *terminal properties*. Others are simply links to other objects, like AUTHOR or EDITOR, and are called *structural properties*. Thus, a book may be described as:

```
%BOOK.5072 is:
    Title     : An Introduction to Database Systems
    Editor    : %company.72
    Year      : 1977
    Author    : %person.4700
    Reference : 680.DAT
    Language  : English
```

While TITLE, YEAR, REFERENCE and LANGUAGE are terminal properties, AUTHOR is a link to a PERSON, and EDITOR is a link to a COMPANY which are described as:

```
%PERSON.4700 is:
Name       : DATE
Initials   : C.J.
Profession : Professor
Author of  : %book.5072

%COMPANY.72 is:
Name      : Addison-Wesley
Activity  : Publishing
Editor of : %book.5072
```

In practice, information is spread among several objects in such a way as to avoid redundancy. In particular, an author is recorded only once, regardless of the number of books and articles he/she may have written. The same is true for editors, keywords, and any other information.

Each structural property is internally represented as a direct and inverse link, so that one can access the authors of a book from its title, or, the books of any author from the author's name. In other words, all links between objects are inverted, as well as any value associated to a terminal property of interest. The latter is left under the control of the user. Hence *entry points* can be created, like for example:

DATE name-of %PERSON.4700

This last mechanism is in essence related to the creation of keys in conventional databases. However, in our case, we must stress that *entry points are not usually unique*, and that one can define as many entry points as desired for a single value, and that entry points are themselves objects. Thus in the example DATE could be the name of a number of persons; alternatively, stating that %PERSON.1000's name is DATE could have created an additional entry point.

Terminal properties are usually associated with a function (called *make-entry*) used to create an entry point to the database. A link associated to the terminal property enables the system to access an entity from the value of this terminal property. Thus, if the attribute NAME (terminal property) of the entity PERSON is an entry point, it is possible to access the entity %PERSON.4700 directly from the value DATE, to get the person's name. It is also possible to know that DATE is a PERSON. So, typing DATE will recover a person whose name is DATE, and who is the author of several books and articles.

The major departures from classical databases are:

- associated values have no type and can be anything including images or programs if needed,
- values not known are not recorded,
- attributes can be added or removed dynamically,
- properties and models are themselves objects, and can be manipulated as such.

The last point is particularly important since it means that we have an integrated dictionary (using the database jargon). The major extensions with respect to the AI representation languages are:

- objects are stored permanently on disc,
- objects have entry ports (keys),
- protection and sharing are implemented.

Models are defined in a bottom-up fashion and as a further convenience to the user. For example, a model of a person is:

| | |
|---|---|
| person-model | |
| entity-name | person |
| terminal property | name, initials, profession |
| structural property | author of |
| required property | name |
| printing function | $$print-person |
| summary print | $$print-person |

Such a model defines a user model that VORAS can interpret for querying the user about corresponding data. Notice that the properties printing function and summary print, both share the function $$print-person which is executed for printing instances of persons. Such a function is called a *procedural attachment*.

A terminal property may have several attributes. The minimum information such a property must have is its property name. For example, the terminal property INITIALS in PERSON is:

Property name : INITIALS
terminal property of: PERSON

A structural property has a somewhat more complicated representation (e.g. AUTHOR):

Property name : AUTHOR
Multiplicity : 5
Successor : PERSON
structural property of: BOOK, ARTICLE

The Successor attribute indicates what kind of entity is linked by the property. Multiplicity in this case is the maximum number of allowed successors for a given book, or article. A model is just a description of an object. For example, a simple model of a BOOK is:

Entity name : BOOK
Terminal properties : Title, Year, Reference, Language
Structural properties: Author, Editor
Required properties : Title, Reference

Finally, models themselves are instances of a meta-model (which is an instance of itself), which allows the user to create models (or schemas) interactively very easily using the same software, as shown in Fig. 1.

It is interesting to note that the models of properties ($EPS, $EPT) are instances of the model of entities ($ENT) and that $ENT is an instance of itself, and is the meta-model. The bottom-up modeling process therefore stops right there. Furthermore,

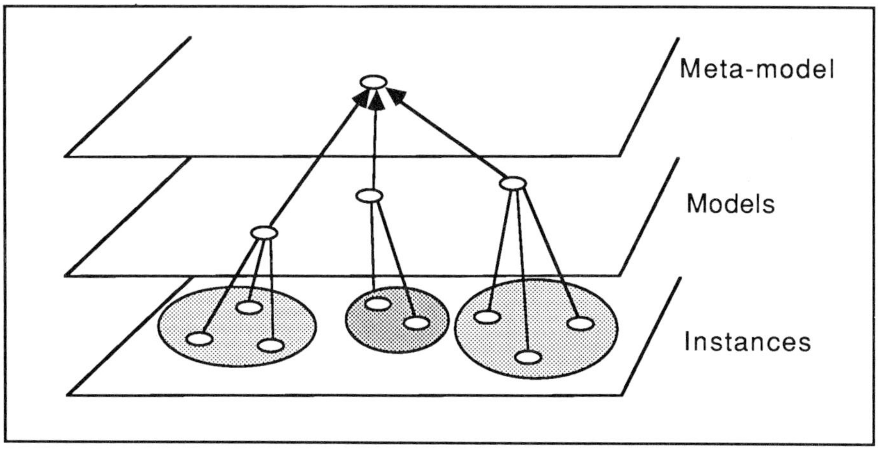


Fig. 1. PDM instance hierarchy.

as in database schema, models in PDM *specify* the structure of instances and *are not prototypes* like in artificial intelligence.

In practice if we detail the exact structure of an example of a book written by a person, we obtain something somewhat more complex, as shown in Fig. 2. The meta-model $ENT specifies the structure of all models, whether system-defined like those of properties ($EPS, $EPT) or user-defined like PERSON or TITLE. Property models $EPS and $EPT specify user-defined properties like AUTHOR or NAME. But since models and properties are objects, the same structural schema applies (Fig. 3).

A set of functions for implementing the PDM was developed in 1978 and has been used ever since. The resulting DBMS is called VORAS. Its current version running under VAX/VMS is 4.2. A commercial version named G-BASE is distributed by GRAPHAEL for workstations. A new version, LOB,[7] has been implemented using object-oriented programming methods (message passing).

## 3. QUERYING THE SYSTEM

VORAS also allows free-style querying, first described in Ref. 8. For any given input sentence, VORAS reconstructs a formal query. Then after rephrasing and user validation, access is done accordingly. It is possible to separate access into two different steps (Fig. 4):
- construction of the formal query from the user's sentence,
- access to the database from the formal query.

The second step has been described in Ref. 8, and is not the subject of this paper. However, we can give some explanations about the formal query. A formal query is a tree, represented as a list. It indicates the path that links together each entity contained in the query. The root of the tree is the entity subject of the request. The leaves of the tree represent values associated to terminal properties. Before giving an example, let us show a schema related to the various entities and relations associated to a database for a library (Fig. 5).

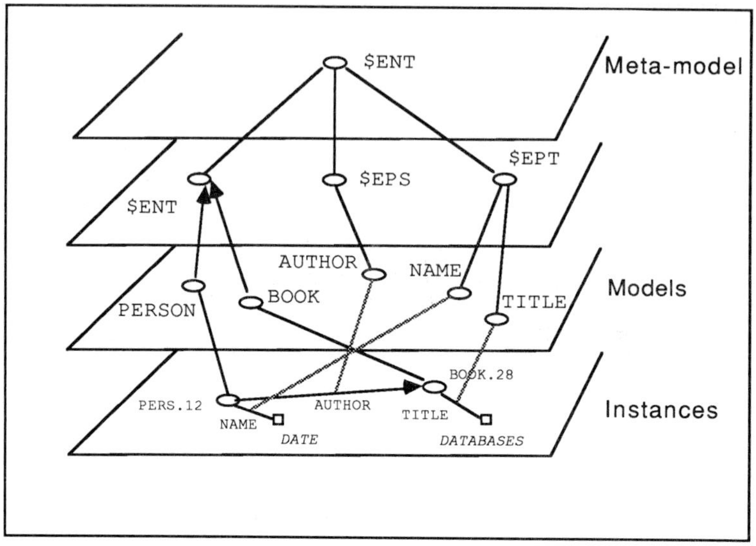


Fig. 2. Example of a book/author/person structure with PDM.

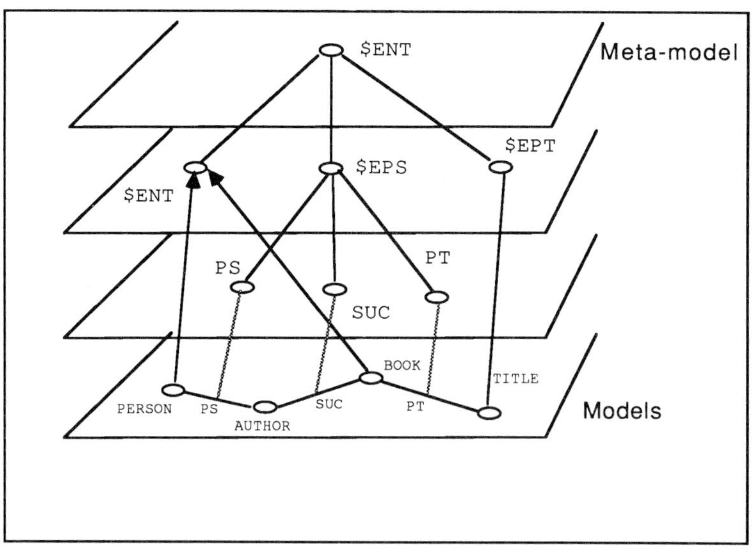


Fig. 3. Structural relations between models.

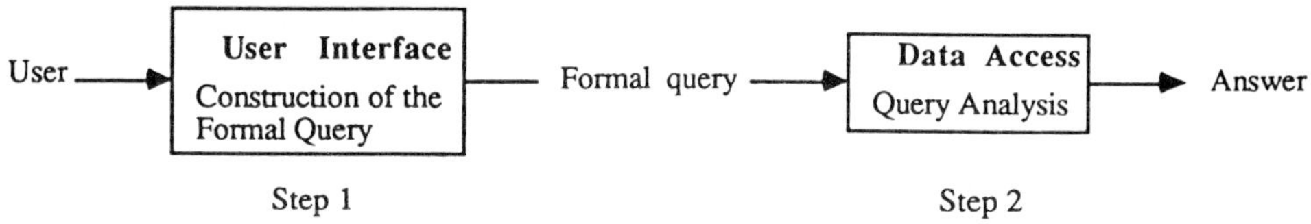


Fig. 4. Access to the database.

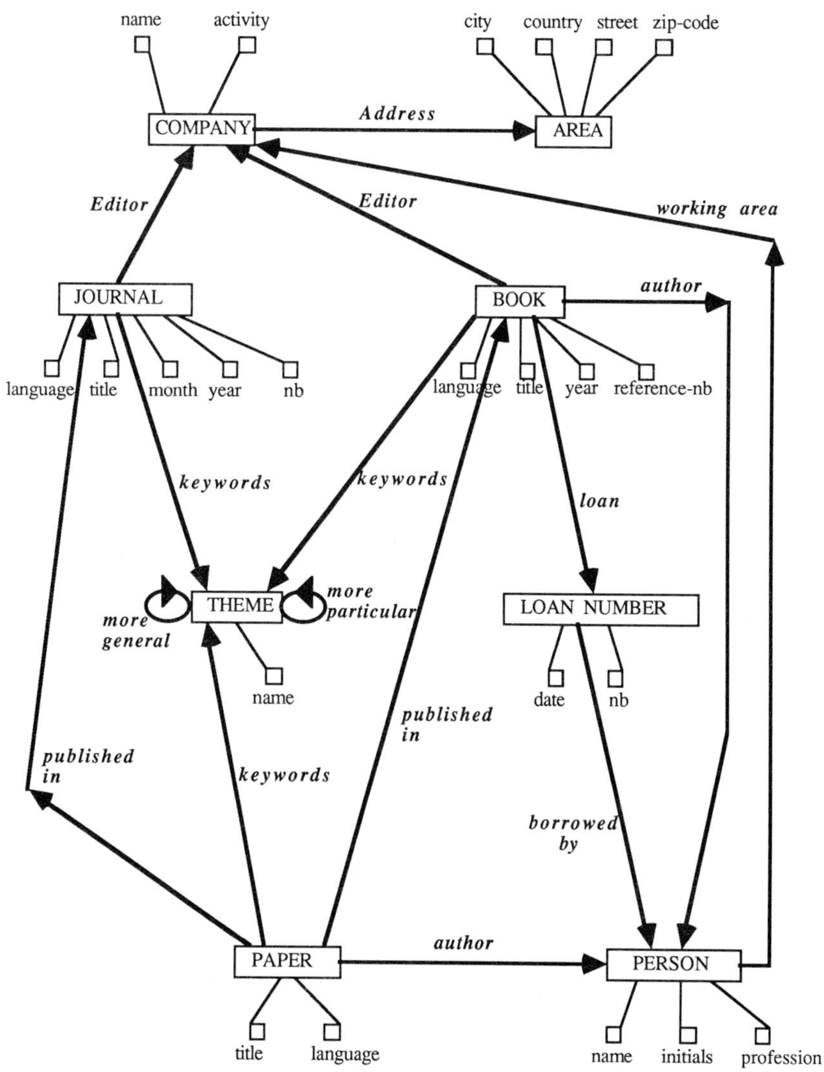


Fig. 5. Example of a database model for a library.

With such a base, if one wants to ask: "*Who works at Compiègne and has written papers in Byte?*", the following formal query will be created:

```
(PERSON (WORKING_AREA
            (COMPANY
                (ADDRESS
                    (AREA (CITY is (Compiegne))))))
        (AUTHOR.OF
            (PAPER
                (PUBLISHED_IN
                    (JOURNAL (TITLE is (Byte)))))))
```

PERSON is the entity looked for. *Byte* and *Compiègne* are entry points. Such a query will be associated to the tree presented in Fig. 6.

Thus, in the user interface, the first step of the access consists in translating a user's sentence written in free-style (natural language) into a formal query. Such a step allows the user to ask questions more easily. The program tries to reshape the sentence, according to the formal query syntax, by using the data given by the user according to the database structure.

First, the system tries to find the words contained in the database (or in its associated dictionary) from the sentence. Then a formal query is built from the entities, properties, and entry points found at the previous step, and a text in free-style is associated to the query. To build the formal query, the system uses a syntactic parser based on the ATN technique.[9] This analysis produces a first tree containing the structure of the natural language sentence. It is thus possible to cut the user sentence into several simple queries, and to know the important elements and operators (AND, OR, NOT, etc.) of this sentence.

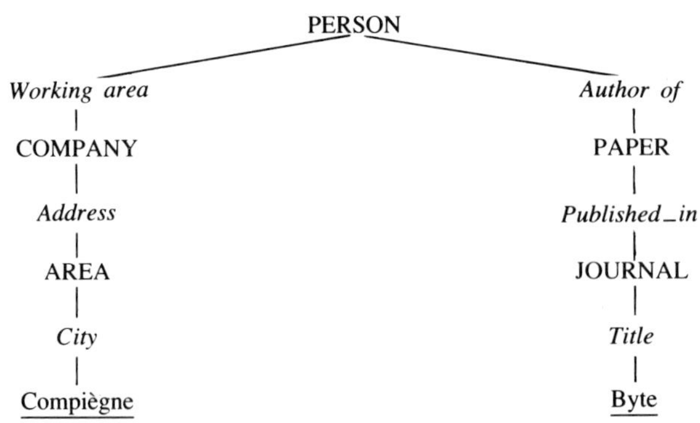


Fig. 6. Tree associated to the formal query.

Then a semantic method is used to better understand what the user wants. The program tries to reshape the sentence, according to the formal query syntax, by using the data given by the user according to the database structure and data (entry points).

If the syntactic analysis has failed, because of a syntax which is different from the grammar known (for example a short-hand style), then only the semantic module is used. Thus, a user's sentence may take any form. No specific syntax is required. In particular, it is possible to have a grammatically incorrect question. However, the system will be more efficient (because of the syntactic analysis) if the user writes correct sentences, because the formal query will be built without any ambiguity.

If only semantic analysis is done, then several interpretations may be possible, and the system could build different formal queries. In that case, the several free-style texts related to such formal queries are presented, and the user must indicate the one he wants. The system then uses the formal query associated to the selected solution, to access the data and to give an answer.

To better understand what is interesting about the syntactic module, we will first describe the lexical and semantic analyses, before the syntactic analysis.

## 3.1. Lexical Analysis

The system uses a dictionary only to store the words of the database model, and their various synonyms. Thus, the whole vocabulary of the model is located at one place. The words associated to the effective data are stored in the database itself. Synonyms are important, because they allow the user to write different words to express the same idea. All the words found will be converted into their representative concept during the lexical analysis.[10] If a word is not present either in the dictionary or in the database, it is then discarded. So, any unknown word is considered as noise, and then filtered out.[10,11] In that case, the syntactic analysis will not be used (because of the unknown words).

To allow more flexibility, we wanted to have the possibility of recognizing misspelled words and orthographic errors. An algorithm comparing unknown words to other words contained in the dictionary or in the database, such as the one presented in Ref. 12, was not well-adapted in such a system, because the database contains too many words. Another method better suited to this problem is described in Ref. 1.

## 3.2. Preparing Data for Semantic Analysis

A list composed of the most important keywords contained in the user's sentence is built, according to the following algorithm:

- If a word is an entity of the database model (e.g. paper, person, book, . . .), it is put into the list.
- If the word is a structural property of the database model (e.g. address), the source entity and the destination entity associated to the structural property, together with the word itself (structural property), are put into the list (for example, ''address'' would give ''company'' ''address'' ''area'').
- If the word is a terminal property, it is discarded.
- Finally, if the word is an entry point (a datum of the database, such as

"compiègne" or "byte"), the entity and the terminal property associated to this entry point and the word itself are put into the list.

For example, if one writes, "*Who works at Compiègne?*" the following list will be built: (PERSON WORKING_AREA COMPANY AREA CITY COMPIEGNE). If one writes, "*Who has written papers in Byte?*" the following list will be built: (PERSON PAPER JOURNAL TITLE BYTE). In both cases, the word "who" is replaced by its synonym (representative concept) "PERSON". The words "has" and "at" have been discarded, because they are neither in the dictionary nor in the database. The word "works" has been replaced with its representative concept "WORKING_AREA". If we assume that the word "written" is unknown, then this word is discarded (and an important piece of information is lost: the concept of writing/author).

So, the sentences could have been: PERSON WORKING_AREA COMPIEGNE and PERSON PAPER BYTE. The entry point "Compiègne" is linked to the entity AREA with the terminal property CITY. Consequently, these two words are added into the first list. The same is true for "Byte" and JOURNAL and TITLE.

### 3.3. Semantic Analysis

At the first step, only the recognised entities are used. Terminal properties, structural properties, and values (entry points) are ignored. They will be used later to link entities together. A tree associated with the formal query is built one branch at a time. Each branch is associated to a clause of the formal query. The system has to find the entities belonging to a similar branch, by using the word order in the sentence. Thus, the order of entities is important, and can provide a lot of information. The sentence is then transformed into a list of entities:

| | | | |
|---|---|---|---|
| question = | separator_1 | entity_11 entity_12 . . . entity_1$n$ | separator_2 |
| | | entity_21 entity_22 . . . entity_2$m$ | separator_3 |
| | | . . . | |
| | | entity_$k$1 entity_$k$2 . . . entity_$kp$ | separator_$k$+1 |

Separator_1 is the entity looked for. It is the subject of the question. Separator_$i$ ($i > 1$) is the entity associated to a clause, and determines the beginning of a new branch. This kind of entity is included before an entry point (a value). Entities inserted between two separators are present in a similar branch. So, entity_11 . . . entity_1$n$ belong to branch_1, and entity_$k$1 . . . entity_$k$1 belong to branch_$k$.

To determine the entity starting a new branch (the root of a new branch), we use the following method:

* Separator_1 is the root of branch_1
* Separator_1 or entity_11 or . . . or entity_1$n$ is the root of branch_2
* Separator_1 or entity_11 or . . . or entity_1$n$ or entity_21 or . . . or entity_2$m$ is the root of branch_3, etc.

Consequently, the root of a given branch may be any entity present in the previous branches. For example: "*Who works at Compiègne and has written papers in Byte?*"

The list created after the lexical analysis is: (PERSON WORKING_AREA COMPANY AREA CITY COMPIEGNE PAPER JOURNAL TITLE BYTE).

In the first step, the system keeps only the entities. Hence, we obtain:

(PERSON COMPANY AREA PAPER JOURNAL)

Separator_1 is PERSON, separator_2 is AREA (inserted before the entry point "Compiègne"), and separator_3 is JOURNAL (inserted before the entry point "Byte"). PERSON, COMPANY and AREA belong to branch_1, PAPER and JOURNAL belong to branch_2.

To build the formal query, the system has to link each entity of a given branch to the next entity of the same branch, using the structural properties contained in the user's sentence, and the entities and structural properties given by the database model. Thus, the first entity of each branch is linked to the second entity, the second one is linked to the third one, and so on, until the end of the clause. The terminal properties and the entry points are then added at the end of each branch. In our previous example, PERSON will be linked to COMPANY, COMPANY to AREA (for the first branch), PERSON, COMPANY or AREA (we do not know, for the moment, which one is the root of branch_2) to PAPER, and PAPER to JOURNAL (for the second branch).

The link between two entities is done by computing the shortest path between them in the database model graph. Each path is memorized, and only the shortest one is proposed for a user's confirmation. All the structural properties found during the lexical analysis are used to orient the research. In the previous example, the link between PERSON and AREA is given by the shortest path between these two entities, that is: PERSON **Working_Area** COMPANY **Address** AREA. The structural property WORKING_AREA found at the lexical analysis step confirms this solution. So, the terminal property CITY and the entry point "Compiègne" are added at the end of this first branch. The clause becomes:

(PERSON (WORKING_AREA (COMPANY (ADDRESS (AREA (CITY
is (Compiegne)))))))

For the second branch, the root may be PERSON, COMPANY or AREA. If the root is PERSON, then the link between PERSON and PAPER is given by the structural property AUTHOR.OF. If the root is COMPANY, then the link between COMPANY and PAPER is given by the structural property EDITOR.OF. Otherwise, there are three different paths between AREA and PAPER:

- AREA **Address** COMPANY **Editor.of** JOURNAL **Published_in.of** PAPER
- AREA **Address** COMPANY **Editor.of** BOOK **Published_in.of** PAPER
- AREA **Address** COMPANY **Working_Area.of** PERSON **Author.of** PAPER

All three paths are longer than the ones found previously. However, the first two paths have the same length. So, the system cannot decide which one between

PERSON and COMPANY is the root of branch_2. Thus, two solutions are proposed:

(PERSON (AUTHOR.OF (PAPER))) or (COMPANY (EDITOR.OF (PAPER)))

The link between PAPER and JOURNAL is given by the structural property PUBLISHED_IN. So, the two possible branches become:

(PERSON (AUTHOR.OF (PAPER (PUBLISHED_IN (JOURNAL (TITLE is (Byte)))))))

or

(COMPANY (EDITOR.OF (PAPER (PUBLISHED_IN (JOURNAL (TITLE is (Byte)))))))

And two possible formal requests are then built.

```
1st solution:  (PERSON
                   (WORKING_AREA
                       (COMPANY
                           (ADDRESS
                               (AREA (CITY is (Compiegne))))))
               (AUTHOR.of
                   (PAPER
                       (PUBLISHED_IN
                           (JOURNAL (TITLE is (Byte)))))))

2nd solution:  (PERSON
                   (WORKING_AREA
                       (COMPANY
                           (ADDRESS
                               (AREA (CITY is (Compiegne))))
                           (EDITOR.of
                               (PAPER
                                   (PUBLISHED_IN
                                       (JOURNAL (TITLE
                                       is (Byte)))))))))
```

The first request is rephrased as: "*Who is a person whose working_area is a company whose address is an area whose city is Compiègne, and is a person author of a paper published_in a journal whose title is Byte?*"

The second request means: "*Who is a person whose working_area is a company whose address is an area whose city is Compiègne, which is company editor of a paper published_in a journal whose title is Byte?*"

To avoid such a problem, a simple solution would be to add in the dictionary the verb "to write" as a synonym of the phrase "author of". Thus, during the lexical analysis, the system would understand the phrase "has written", and would convert it into its synonym concept "author.of". As it is a structural property, the two entities linked by this property would be added to the list (PERSON AUTHOR.OF PAPER). Thus, the lexical analysis would then give: (PERSON WORKING_AREA COMPANY AREA CITY COMPIEGNE PAPER JOURNAL TITLE BYTE). In that case, the entities PERSON, COMPANY and AREA belong to branch_1, and the entities PERSON, PAPER and JOURNAL belong to branch_2.

The problem of the choice of the root for the second branch is easier. We still have three possible roots: PERSON, COMPANY, and AREA. But we have to find a path between the roots and the entity PERSON (and not the entity PAPER as before). So, the shortest path between PERSON and PERSON, COMPANY and PERSON, and AREA and PERSON is the first one (length equal to zero!). Therefore, only the first solution would be proposed to the user.

However, it is sometimes difficult to know if the verb "to write" introduces the concept "author of" or the concept "author". For example, in the sentence "*Who has written a paper?*" the verb "to write" means AUTHOR.OF (person author.of paper), but in the sentence "*Who has borrowed a paper written by Trigano?*" it means AUTHOR (paper whose author is Trigano). We might even have the following case: "*Who has borrowed a paper written in Byte?*", where the verb "to write" means PUBLISHED_IN (paper published_in journal whose title is Byte).

So, it is not so easy to use synonyms. In the above example, we have to consider whether to use "written by" (synonym: person), "written in" (synonym: published_in), or even "written" alone (synonym: author.of). A good solution in such a case is to use syntactic analysis, which will give us information about the various possible forms of the same verb.

### 3.4. Syntactic Analysis

Syntactic parsing is used to detect conjunctions (AND), disjunctions (OR), and negations (NOT), and to simplify the problem of the choice of a root for each branch. It uses a semantic grammar,[13–15] close to the one presented in Ref. 16. It is possible to employ several formulae such as "could you tell me who . . ." or "I want to know who . . ." or even "who . . .". We can have syntactic categories such as NOUN, VERB, VERBAL GROUP, NOMINAL GROUP. But we can also have semantic categories such as OBJECT, ATTRIBUTE, DIRECT_VALUE, etc. close to the notion of "entity", "terminal property", "entry point", etc. The parsing is done by the technique of Augmented Transition Networks (ATN).[9] The implementation of the system is done according to the recommendations of Ref. 17.

This analyser also allows a better use of synonyms, as seen in the previous example ("to write" ⇒ author, author.of, published_in, etc.). Then, it improves the performances of the semantic analysis, by discarding a lot of ambiguities found before.

However, if the user has a style different from the semantic grammar of the knowledge base, then this parsing fails. In that case, only the semantic method (seen before) will be used, and sometimes, several interpretations of the query will be built (as in the previous example "person/society") and proposed to the user.

At the end of the syntactic parsing, each branch of the query (with its root) has been found, and given to the semantic analyser. For example, if the sentence is "*Who works at Compiègne and has written papers in Byte?*", one tree containing two branches is built:

((**Tree 1** (**Branch 1.1** (PERSON WORKING_AREA COMPIEGNE)
(**Branch 1.2** (PERSON AUTHOR.OF PAPER PUBLISHED_IN BYTE))))

In this example, "who" at the beginning of the question is transformed into PERSON. This noun (person) is the subject of the verbs "to work" and "to write". So, the words "to work at" and "to write" are transformed into WORKING_AREA and AUTHOR.OF. The complement "papers" stays the same (PAPER), but the preposition "in" related to the verb "to write" (in fact, "to write in") placed after this complement (PAPER) introduces the property PUBLISHED_IN. As "who"/"person" is the subject of the two verbs, it will be the root of the two branches. The first entity of a branch is the root.

Sometimes, several different trees may be found from a single query, because of the conjunctions. For example, if the sentence is "*Who works at Compiègne and who has written papers in Byte?*", we then obtain:

((**Tree 1** (**Branch 1.1** (PERSON WORKING_AREA COMPIEGNE)))
(**Tree 2** (**Branch 2.1** (PERSON AUTHOR.OF PAPER PUBLISHED_IN BYTE))))

In this example the subject of the two verbs is different, so we obtain two separate trees (queries).

One very important point with the syntactic parser is the possibility of using questions without entry point (not possible with semantic analysis alone). For example, it is possible to write "*Who writes what?*", or "*Who works?*". In that case, a special analysis is directly done, without using the semantic module, because no entry point is detected. The resulting queries are:

((**Tree 1** (**Branch 1.1** (PERSON AUTHOR.OF *X*)))

and

((**Tree 1** (**Branch 1.1** (PERSON WORKING_AREA)))

In such cases, the natural language module (a 'post-parser') directly manages the database. We obtain a list of people who have the structural property

WORKING_AREA (second case), or a list of people who have the structural property AUTHOR.OF. In this first case, for each person, the list of entities related to this person by the relation AUTHOR.OF is also given.

It is also possible to mix the two kinds of queries (with and without entry point), as for example "*Who works and has written papers in Byte?*". The result of the parsing is:

((**Tree 1** (**Branch 1.1** (PERSON WORKING_AREA))
(**Branch 1.2** (PERSON AUTHOR.OF PAPER PUBLISHED_IN BYTE))))

In this example, the natural language module ('post-parser') manages the database access for the first branch (list of PERSON with the structural property WORKING_AREA), and gives the second branch to the semantic module, for a complementary analysis.

As seen before, syntactic analysis may fail. If the failure is at the end of the question, some parts of the tree, or even some trees, may have already been built. So, only the branch containing the error will be analysed by the semantic module. All the other branches already built will be better analysed. For example: "*Who works and has written papers in Byte and who has loaned papers Byte?*". The result of the parsing is:

((**Tree 1** (**Branch 1.1** (PERSON WORKING_AREA))
(**Branch 1.2** (PERSON AUTHOR.OF PAPER PUBLISHED_IN BYTE)))
(**Tree 2** (**Branch 2.1** (PERSON LOAN PAPER * ***Error**** ))))

In that case, the first branch will be directly managed by the post-parser module for the database access, and the second branch will be analysed by the semantic analyser. The second branch contains no ambiguity, because of the good syntactic analysis (the properties AUTHOR.OF and PUBLISHED_IN have been found). But the third branch has not been analysed correctly. Hence, only the keywords will be given to the semantic module: (PERSON LOAN PAPER BYTE).

## 4. CONCLUSION

The new interface in natural language has improved man–machine communication of the VORAS DBMS. The system was first in a prototype stage. It is now being implemented commercially.

It is quite easy to interrogate the system, in a way close to natural language, using synonyms, misspelled words, conjugated verbs or plural forms. The analysis relies upon the semantic network of the database structure itself. Our dictionary can evolve with the database. If one modifies the database model, then the interface in natural language is automatically modified.

It is possible to foresee a strong interest in such a way of communicating with the database, because it is much simpler than with the old interface (using the formal queries). One could guess that the number of users for such a system is going to increase, due to simpler and better man–machine communication.

REFERENCES

1. P. Trigano, J. P. Barthes and F. Vallernaud, "A free query language for an object-oriented DBMS", *Proc. SPIE Conf. Applications in Artificial Intelligence VII*, Orlando, USA, April 1989, pp. 648–660.
2. J. P. Barthes, M. Vayssade and M. Z. Miaczynska, "Property driven databases", *Proc. Int. Joint Conf. Artificial Intelligence*, Tokyo, 1979, pp. 247–249.
3. J. P. Barthes and A. Bertrand, "Semantic representation of objects in the BUTC Library Index", IATUL, Compiègne, 1986.
4. M. Minsky, "A framework for representing knowledge", *The Psychology of Computer Vision*, Ed. P. E. Winston, McGraw Hill, 1975, pp. 211–277.
5. J. R. Abrial, *Date Semantics, Database Management*, Eds. J. W. Klimbie and K. L. Koffeman, North-Holland, 1974, pp. 1–60.
6. P. P. S. Chen, "The entity-relationship model: Toward a unified view of data", *ACM Trans. Database Systems* **1**, 1 (1976) pp. 9–36.
7. J. P. Barthes, "BOSS version 1.1", Memo UTC/GI, Compiègne University, 1987.
8. F. Fodda, "Sur le problème des accès dans les bases de données de type ensembliste", thèse de 3ème cycle, UTC, 1981.
9. W. A. Woods, "Transition networks grammars for natural language analysis", *Commun. ACM* **13**, 10 (1970) 591–606.
10. P. Trigano, P. Morizet and P. Lebeux, "DIALEXP, a man–machine interface in natural language. Application to an expert system", *Proc. 2nd Int. Expert Systems Conf.*, London, Sept. 1986, pp. 391–398.
11. M. Woodyard and B. Hamel, "A natural language interface in a clinical database management system", *Comput. Biomed. Res.* **14** (1981) 41–62.
12. P. Trigano, "Do not hate bad typed data!", *Cognitiva 87*, Paris, May 1987, pp. 395–400.
13. R. Burton, "Semantic Grammars, An Engineering Technique for Constructing Natural Language Understanding Systems", BBN report n°3453, Dec. 1976.
14. A. Bonnet, "Analyse de texte au moyen d'une grammaire sémantique et de schémas", thése de doctorat d'état, université Pierre et Marie Curie, Paris 6, 1980.
15. A. Bonnet, "Les grammaires sémantiques, outil puissant pour interroger les bases de données en language naturel", *RAIRO Informatique*, Paris **14** (1980) 137–148.
16. D. Kayser, "une méthode simple: les ATN sémantiques", 3ème congrès AFCET RDF/IA, journées d'études "le langage naturel", Sept. 1981, pp. 41–63.
17. M. Bates, "The theory and practice of Augmented Transition Network grammars", in *Lecture Notes in Computer Science, Natural Language Communication with Computers*, Ed. Springer Verlag, 1978, pp. 191–260.

**Philippe Trigano** is Assistant Professor in the Computer Science Department at the University of Technology of Compiègne. He obtained his doctorate from the University of Technology of Compiègne in 1985. He works on artificial intelligence projects, especially projects on natural language analysis, expert systems, and databases. The projects, financed by French companies, are directly applied to industrial problems. He is Director of the undergraduate programs in artificial intelligence, for computer science and engineering training. He is a member of the Association for Research in Cognitive Science.

**Jean-Paul Barthes** obtained his Ph.D. from Stanford University in 1973. He is a Professor in the Department of Computer Science at the University of Technology of Compiègne, in charge of the research program in artificial intelligence. His work is related to semantic representations and to the object paradigm as developed in AI, databases, and programming languages. Some results have led to commercial products like the object-oriented database G-BASE. His current work deals with extended semantic representations for implementing very large knowledge bases kept permanently and shared among several users simultaneously. Dr. Barthes is a member of many academic societies and participates in numerous organizing committees.

**Catherine Greboval** is a Ph.D. student in the Department of Computer Science at the University of Technology of Compiègne. She works on knowledge representation in artificial intelligence and expert systems.

**François Vallernaud** was formly a Master's student in the Department of Computer Science at the University of Technology of Compiègne, in 1988.

# ADAPTIVE PLANNING FOR AIR COMBAT MANEUVERING

IRIS COX HAYSLIP
*Ford Aerospace Corporation**
*Colorado Springs, CO 80920, USA*

JEFFREY P. ROSENKING
*Grumman Corporation*
*Data Systems Division, MSA01-26*
*Bethpage, NY 11714, USA*

JAMES EILBERT
*Grumman Corporate Research Center*
*MSA01-26*
*Bethpage, NY 11714, USA*

Received 1 April 1990

This paper describes Grumman's Rapid Expert Assessment to Counter Threats (REACT) project, designed to aid pilots in air combat decision making. We present a hierarchical design for a planning system which addresses some of the real-time aspects of planning for threat response. This paper concentrates on the lowest level of this hierarchy which is responsible for planning combat maneuvers at low altitude over hilly terrain when the enemy is not in sight. REACT's Lost Line of Sight module attempts to maximize the amount and depth of knowledge which can be utilized in the time available before the system must commit to its next action. It utilizes a hybrid architecture for planning decisions which incorporates multiple knowledge representations and planners based on artificial intelligence, neural networks, and decision theory. This architecture allows planning at different degrees of competence to be performed by concurrently operating planners with differing amounts of knowledge. We describe research on the planning issues in REACT as well as the associated knowledge representation and knowledge acquisition issues. In addition, we describe how work on developing terrain reasoning capability in REACT has suggested guidelines for knowledge base design and data management, system and language specifications, and planner architectures pertinent to real-time coupled systems.

*Keywords:* Planning; Terrain reasoning; Knowledge representations; Neural networks.

## 1. INTRODUCTION

This paper describes the Grumman Rapid Expert Assessment to Counter Threats (REACT) project.[1] The project addresses the problem of providing pilots with decision support in the complex situations which arise in combat scenarios. This entails modeling pilot decision making both at the mission planning (global) level, and at the level of avoiding and countering threats in dynamic battle environments (local level). The discussion will focus on one aspect of planning at the local level, i.e. the

* Work performed at Grumman Corporate Research Center.

production of responses at low altitude over hilly terrain when the opponent is not within line of sight. This restricted domain, addressed by the Lost Line of Sight (LLOS) submodule of REACT, provides a rich testbed for ideas in real-time planning, representation of terrain information, and the representation and acquisition of expert pilot knowledge. These issues are interrelated in the sense that for each level of planning, the available time to plan will affect the choice of representation and the type of representation will, in turn, constrain knowledge acquisition techniques.

In this paper, we present a hybrid approach for planning in this domain. We address the problem of real-time planning in REACT by utilizing concurrent planners in a coarse grain parallel architecture, by supplying different planners with different knowledge representations, and by localizing reasoning about time to plan within a special module. The concurrent planners operate at different levels of competence. The solution of the most competent planner which is available in time to act is chosen for execution. Thus, the planners compete for control of the vehicle,[2] in a "racetrack" architecture that results in functional task subsumption.[3]

Knowledge representations are introduced into REACT based on the needs and capabilities of the individual planners. Currently utilized representations include models, frames, production rules, and precompiled procedural knowledge. Each separate planner module may utilize the data and knowledge representation which is most suitable for its task and speed allotment. The module responsible for producing immediate responses uses knowledge stored in neural networks.

This paper is organized as follows. Section 2 provides a domain description, an overview of REACT, and describes where the Local Planner fits into the overall REACT system. Section 3 specifically deals with the design of the local response planner, concentrating on the Lost Line of Sight module. This module contains our principal research interests and results of applied reactive planning methods. Section 4 describes REACT's multiple knowledge representations. Section 5 describes ongoing knowledge acquisition efforts for the REACT project and details the neural network architecture in the quick response module. Section 6 outlines the implementation status and Sec. 7 discusses conclusions and continued research.

## 2. BACKGROUND

REACT is organized within a nested concurrent blackboard architecture.[4] The problem domain necessitates the use of a global database; therefore the speed problems associated with blackboard architectures, even concurrent ones, are being continually addressed. Some of these problems are a result of the prototype system hardware and software development tools and may be avoided in an actual embedded system.

The REACT world model is based on sensed and stored data about the opponent's status, ownship status, and the terrain over which both are flying. In our simulations, we assume that information about the position and motion of the flying vehicles can be sensed in real-time. However, there is no possibility of completely processing sensed air-to-ground imagery in real-time, so REACT includes databases of previously processed terrain maps.

In the REACT architecture (Fig. 1), the "world state" is maintained in the top level blackboard by three cooperating expert modules. The Map Expert maintains REACT's internal representation of the terrain and does the database and memory management associated with multiple representations of terrain maps. The Threat Assessment Expert determines the lethality of the opponent and does situation assessment, while the Ownship Expert computes the ownship status. The information maintained in the blackboard by these experts, plus current objectives and motivations, determines the plan or course of action that REACT will choose.

Two other modules, the Global and Local Planners (Fig.1), are responsible for their respective planning functions based on the current (and possibly extrapolated future) world states. When the ownship is not within the range of any threat the Global Planner selects a route based on the overall mission objectives. The Global Planner is based on the TREK route planner developed by Georgia Tech Research Institute[5]; it provides global route planning and dynamic replanning, when a newly identified threat is encountered. When there is an immediate threat the Local Planner is invoked. Local planning can be broken down further by the status of the complete system, and by the type of planning used. High altitude, low altitude, and lost line of sight encounters are treated by distinct modules (Fig. 2), as detailed below.

## 3. THE LOCAL PLANNER

The Local Planner (Fig. 2) is decomposed into cooperating modules, some of which utilize conventional models embedded in a structure that allows the models to be controlled and adjusted by heuristics. The modules with the task of handling high altitude threats can utilize results from the Tactics Optimization and Combat Analysis Tool (TOPCAT).[6] TOPCAT is a program for determining optimal air combat maneuvers. It generates tables using a stochastic learning algorithm that permits air combat maneuvering strategies to be optimized by simulation of the combat using accurate aircraft models. Three submodules of the Local Planner are tasked with determining maneuvers at low altitude over hilly terrain. When the threat is within line of sight (i.e. not masked by terrain), scoring function techniques modeled after the Automated Maneuvering (AUTOMAN)[7] system can be used. The AUTOMAN program is a real-time maneuvering program which has been developed for use at the

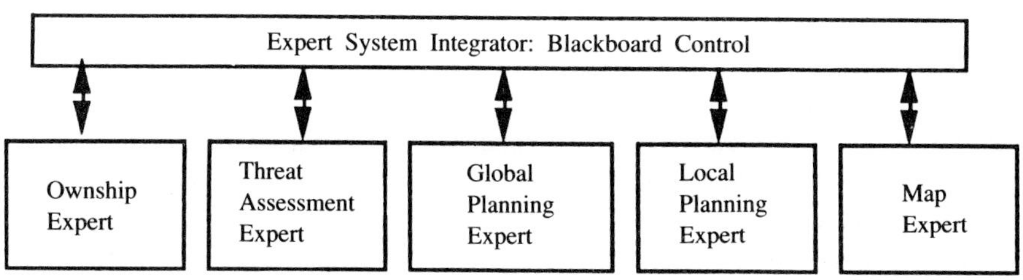


Fig. 1. REACT top level architecture diagram.

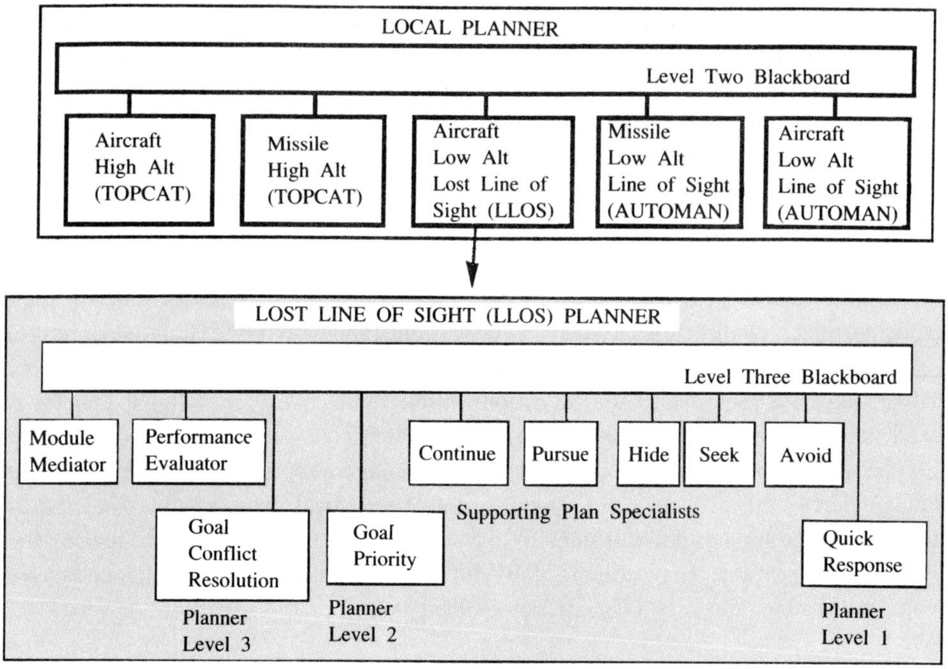


Fig. 2. Submodules of the Local Planner.

NASA Ames Vertical Motion Simulator. We feel that the use of a scoring function tuned by heuristics is a good approach for real-time reaction to visible threats at low altitude. When line of sight to the threat is not available then the LLOS submodule of the Local Planner is in control and is tasked to emulate responses that a pilot would exercise in combat. Therefore, the LLOS module of the Local Planner is the principal research vehicle for techniques in fast planning, and its architecture is detailed in Sec. 3.3.

Within the REACT architecture, the Local Planner and the LLOS module are nested below the top level (Fig. 2). REACT's architecture exemplifies a distributed AI system. Each of the "experts" in the big picture has a complicated function, represented by lower level blackboards. Nested blackboards provide a special method to address the requirement that fast systems be interrupt-driven. If the Local Planner only posts complete sets of data to the higher level blackboard, then the lower level blackboard may be working with a different state of the world than the higher level blackboard. If the operation of the local planner is interrupted, it is easy to find the state before its execution, and consistency management of the high level blackboard is easier. The lower level blackboard serves as a cache for the Local Planner. The blackboard architecture is versatile and if it is kept simple, it is a natural way to think of the Local Planner. Blackboards allow special purpose planners to be patched into the system as knowledge sources. They also support the concurrent processing required for the REACT architecture, although concurrency is presently being simulated.

### 3.1. Interleaving Acting and Planning

A fundamental difficulty of real-time planners is interleaving acting and planning. The real-time requirements are much more stringent in some domains than others. For example, the domain for aircraft planners, such as REACT, is more stringent than the domain for autonomous land vehicles, where most autonomous vehicle architectures have been developed. REACT cannot assume that there is time to stop and think, and rectilinear motion assumptions are out. It is always in the execution phase for some plan or another. A maneuver decision always interrupts a process. This provides a tough constraint on the transition of control from one module to another. There is a significant time lag between a control command and the time at which the commanded heading can be achieved. This system response time (determined by the maneuverability of the vehicle) must be anticipated. There is also a continuum of intermediate states between present aircraft state and planned state.

### 3.2. Modality and Time-To-Plan

The aircraft will always be executing some plan, and top level maneuvers will be prescribed by the Global Planner, AUTOMAN,[7] TOPCAT,[6] or one of the other modules in the Local Planner. The Local Planner modules which are designed to make fast decisions are the reactive elements of the overall planning system. Which module is in control is determined at the top level by a modality operator, with preconditions on each mode described as follows. If there is no local threat, the Global Planner is in control. The Global Planner does replanning for unexpected threats which are not immediate, i.e. far enough away to plan an avoidance path. In the presence of an immediate threat, the Local Planner is in control with modes assigned as follows. If the situation is at high altitude, then terrain is not a factor and TOPCAT is in control. If terrain is a factor, one of two possibilities exists. If there is line of sight between ownship and the threat, then control is relegated to the AUTOMAN module. If the threat is obscured, then the LLOS module is in control.

As with all modality operators there are potential instability problems. For example, suppose the opponent is appearing and disappearing at a fast rate, i.e. just ducking over a ridge and reappearing. In this case, one would not want the system to be undergoing the overhaul of mode changes at every other time step. One can plan for this occurrence by observing that immediately after the opponent disappears, his position is fairly well-known, so AUTOMAN can still be in control. It is only after his positional error is at a certain level that the LLOS module needs to be instituted. In a dynamic environment, the hard test of performance by a system may be in the smoothness of transitions among processes. The best protection against abrupt mode shifts lies in careful design of the separate modules.

Planning with incomplete knowledge and planning under time pressure can sometimes be treated similarly because in the latter, less information/knowledge is used as there is not enough time to process it, and in the former it is not used as it is not there. Therefore, both cases can share some of the same modules. We must not allow our concurrent systems to use blackboard slots which may no longer be pertinent. This is like flagging slots with usefulness coefficients. A better approach is to have concurrently running predictors (e.g. Kalman filter to predict positions) which update slots by prediction until actual information becomes available.

Oddly, in our case, it can be faster to plan with detailed information on the position of the opponent than to plan with approximate guesses. This is because we employ a real-time dogfight algorithm (AUTOMAN) for the case of close-in line-of-sight maneuvering. But more heuristics, planning, and reasoning can come into play at longer ranges and when the opponent is out of sight, i.e. hiding behind a hill. (One could say that an opponent can be out of sight but still nearby and not masked by terrain, i.e. behind or under the aircraft, but we assume the eventual capability to put sensors on aircraft to locate opponents which are within line of sight.)

More complex multi-task behavior may be planned as opposed to simple single behaviors. Sometimes the pilot could plan to do two things at once, such as perform an evasive maneuver and employ a countermeasure, or chart a course to intercept and avoid some obstacles along the way, or deal with multiple opponents such as a launch platform and a missile simultaneously. Whereas there is only time to plan for one goal, such as pursue the target and forget everything else, or evade an obstacle and forget everything else.

### 3.3. A Racetrack Design for the Lost Line of Sight (LLOS) Planner

Acting and planning are simultaneous. Thus, the system is in continuous operation and changes can be in response to quick reactions or longer term planning, but the mode of interruption and change of maneuver method is the same for both. In this sense the system resembles a process control system. One way in which our application differs from previous planners is by the extra complexity resulting from the manipulation of large databases[8] (specifically terrain maps) and the necessity of reducing these databases to usable forms for reasoning systems.

We expect that traditional planning which also utilizes a rich knowledge base and detailed data may never achieve the speed sufficient to make necessary decisions for air combat maneuvering. But not all decisions will be required immediately. Sometimes there will be more time available for detailed planning. Processes must proceed at different speeds, and the architecture must be designed so that various processes are synchronized such that at each stage the system's actions are in accordance with the best possible level of information/knowledge available. Ideally, the processes run concurrently so that if a higher level decision becomes available, the lower level behavior can be pre-empted (subsumed); and if higher level decisions are not ready in time, the lower level behavior is instituted. This is a form of behavioral robustness which in our case includes keeping the aircraft flying and reasonably safe with piecemeal plan macros while comprehensive plans are being formulated. Planning maneuvers for combat aircraft can occur at different levels, where the choice of level is driven by the time available for planning. The effective parameters which determine the time available for planning in this domain include range to target, threat lethality, temporary tactical advantage, and terrain factors.

We consider two separate aspects of multilevel decision making:

(1) depth and detail afforded by the actual form of the data structures and knowledge representation, and
(2) depth and detail afforded by the complexity and thoroughness of the procedures (such as search, contingency planning, etc.) utilizing these structures.

The most reliable plans result from the use of sophisticated planning procedures which utilize detailed data and knowledge. These plans are the ones that are slow to produce. One can speed this up by shortcutting the planning process but still using the detailed knowledge representation, simplifying (or abstracting) the knowledge and data and still using a good planner, or shortcuttng the planning process and simultaneously simplifying the information used (the extreme case of this could be interpreted as a "table look up"). We seek a coherent architecture where any combination of the above can be accomplished as necessary. The abstraction of the data and knowledge is described in Sec. 4.

In the LLOS planner, goals are defined as behaviors, such as hide, seek or pursue, rather than desired world states.[9] (A world state consists of an area of terrain with aircraft and opponent positioned over the terrain with set heading, velocity, and altitude.) Tactical goals generally involve flying while satisfying some set of constraints. The local plans to implement a Pursue behavior are understood and the goal is compatible with one that a pilot might entertain. One cannot specify goals as desired world states, since a goal involves meeting constraints over entire trajectories through state space. There are many ways to pursue an opponent, but there may not be a way to accurately predict where (world state) they might meet.

Potential contentions for control should not be that prevalent for the following reason. The modules are ranked *a priori* by their assigned tasks as to which one uses the deepest knowledge, so the only criterion for gaining control is to have a solution on hand. At each time step each module must respond whether ready or not ready. Opportunistically, at the point where a decision must be made, the highest ranking ready module gets control.

With this assumption we follow a pattern for planning with blackboards. Goals are posted in a stack, and there is a separate knowledge source (plan specialist) assigned to figure out how to accomplish each goal. A knowledge source may not produce complete plans, but may instead post subgoals to the goal stack. The system can choose to act to satisfy a subgoal while still working on plans for other subgoals. By the local nature of the planner, there should not be long chains of subgoals. There is a special Goal Conflict Resolution knowledge source whose purpose is to resolve conflicts in multiple goal situations, where resolve means to compute a solution (plan) which will satisfy all the conjunctive goals simultaneously. If there is no time to resolve the conflict or the conflict has no solution, the Goal Priority knowledge source will have posted which goal gets priority in the current situation. (This specialist essentially replaces the wires and messages of the Brook's design.[2]) If the Conflict Priority specialist has not posted an answer in time, default priorities are arbitrarily set giving preference to conservative strategies. Plans posted by the various specialists are ranked according to merit, i.e. a solution from the Conflict Resolution specialist has priority over a solution from the Goal Priority specialist. Ideally there would be multiple conflict resolution specialists where the "best" looks for optimal paths and the others look for faster compromise solutions. If all of the above are not ready in time, then the precalculated maneuver produced by the Quick Response specialist is chosen. This organization of concurrently operating modules will initially provide three levels of competence:

(1) planning for the conjunctive goals,
(2) planning for the most important goal, or
(3) quick response.

This "racetrack" architecture is designed to be extensible to include other levels of competence. For example, the Conflict Resolution module may become several modules, each serving as a separate contender in the race. The modules find solutions to conjunctive goals, with varying levels of compromise.

We make no claim to completeness of the tactics implemented in REACT, but do claim that the architecture is designed such that many of the key features can be adjusted if needed without requiring a complete system overhaul. The following presents an example of this type of thinking. We assume an approximate estimate on the projected position of the opponent. Once the opponent disappears behind a hill, the area of uncertainty in his position grows as time passes. The size of this area can be estimated based on his velocity, maneuverability limits and other factors. We therefore maintain a blackboard slot with an estimated threat position. If he has not been out of sight for long, then we simply project him linearly down his last observed velocity vector. If we assume a mutually aggressive status, then as time progresses we can estimate his position as a pursuit course subject to terrain. Other prediction strategies may prove to give better results, but changing the prediction strategy should not change the overall architecture. After a certain amount of time has passed we can consider him "lost" and institute other procedures. (In our simulation, we can also fill the estimated position slot with the actual simulated threat position to facilitate comparison of our planner decisions with the maneuvers generated by AUTOMAN. This provides a test format for the planner.)

The LLOS plan specialists currently post their results in the form of a desired point to fly toward, a desired velocity, and desired altitude (terrain clearance). The point produced is a very close (within terrain constraints and aircraft turn radius) point along a path determined by the goals. The aircraft is then "flown" using a guidance routine and integration procedures which are shared with the AUTOMAN program. AUTOMAN chooses maneuvers from a set of seven elemental maneuvers. The LLOS planner can specify maneuvers by point to point directions with execution dependent upon the actual aircraft flight characteristics.

#### 3.3.1. Fundamental behaviors and their associated plan specialists

We now describe the initial set of goal behaviors specified for REACT. These were chosen as a primitive first set and are not assumed to be complete. The set does, however, contain enough possible complexity to include some interesting aspects of planning. In particular, simultaneous goals can be conflicting and the priorities of goals are context-dependent. In the simplest cases the system looks like a production system. The following defines the goal behaviors and their associated plan specialists, and mentions some extensions of the definitions.

The *Continue* behavior is defined to mean "continue on present path, no deviation at present". It is primarily intended for the long range case where one might want to wait before deciding to pursue or avoid. The Continue plan specialist (knowledge source) decides how long to wait before a maneuver is warranted, and posts a flag indicating no change of path direction.

The *Pursue* behavior is defined to mean "steer toward the opponent". Clearly there are many ways to pursue, such as a collision course, pure pursuit, or various lags or leads, but in the current implementation "pursue" means "pure pursuit". The Pursue plan specialist calculates a point which is on the pure pursuit course (direct line) toward the estimated threat position and close to the present ownship position relative to the terrain features and aircraft turn radius. Alternate ways of pursuing are to steer a collision course (steer toward the point of intersection of the two projected paths), which is clearly risky since the whereabouts and path of the opponent is unknown, or to lead the target at varying degrees. It may be that steering a collision course in the early stages and reducing to pure pursuit over time might be a more reasonable approach. Whatever type of pursuit is chosen, the overall design should not change. The default desired altitude command is for terrain following.

*Hide* is a complicated behavior which will eventually mean staying out of line of sight of the opponent. In the short term this is simply interpreted as flying as low as possible. The Hide plan specialist is designed to plot an optimal course taking advantage of terrain characteristics for masking. This might be accomplished in the form of rules which utilize the high level terrain primitives description of the situation, or by a more complicated model. Currently, it is implemented simply as "fly low" and only posts a minimal desired terrain clearance command.

The *Seek* behavior is defined as taking steps to gain line of sight to the target. This is used for several reasons, including reducing the area of uncertainty when it is growing too large, an ownside advantage to be exercised, or for targeting. In its initial implementation Seek is considered as "pop-up" and search. The Seek plan specialist tries to achieve the Seek goal by a choice of maneuvers designed to regain line of sight. (A failed Seek plan may provide valuable negative information to the system, i.e. "know where your target is not".) Complicated plans to achieve the Seek goal may be designed using rules based on the terrain situation. Presently, a simplified Seek implementation is planned which consists of a pop-up and search strategy, namely the posting of a desired altitude representing maximal climb to rise above terrain masking.

*Avoid* means run away. Initially this behavior is reserved for ownside defensive status. However, avoidance might be useful as a temporary retreat strategy associated with an offensive status. The Avoid plan specialist can produce plans by various choices, including following the current course and speeding up, or steering an actual avoidance path. The Avoid specialist is currently not being implemented due to the concentration on the mutually offensive scenario. The Avoid specialist deals with avoiding opponents, not terrain avoidance.

There are obviously ideas which are not covered by these fundamental behaviors. An example of such might be the "lying in wait" or "ambush" behavior. Other behaviors might be sporadic diving, erratic flying, jinks, or other maneuvers designed to confuse the opponent. Though some of these more complicated behaviors are not currently being considered the architecture is designed to be robust enough to be extended to include them as necessary. One additional behavior which is a likely extension will be a Delay behavior, defined as the slowing down of the aircraft in order to provide more computing time.

### 3.3.2. Goal Priority module

The Goal Priority knowledge source looks at the current situation including ground threats, relative weapon strength, mission priority, etc. and prioritizes goals in the goal stack based on context. The results from this knowledge source are not used unless there is a conjunctive goal problem which cannot be solved by the Goal Conflict specialist in time for execution. This is the knowledge source which might allow the aircraft to fly over a surface threat zone in pursuit of an opponent, or to abandon pursuit if surface threats are too great. It would decide which to do if Pursue and Hide could not be accomplished simultaneously. This specialist does no reasoning as to whether the two can be accomplished at once, it only decides which is more important at the moment.

### 3.3.3. Goal Conflict Resolution module

Most of the interesting planning issues are contained here. Certainly some goals may need to be satisfied simultaneously, and occasionally conflicts will occur. For example, a pure pursuit course may require the aircraft to fly up over a hill thereby blocking the Hide goal. But a slight alteration of the path may enable the aircraft to stay hidden longer. A Seek goal may result in a "pop-up" plan which could expose the aircraft to surface search and acquisition radars. These conjunction and constraint problems will have to be accounted for individually. In the first implementation, many of the problems are avoided by simplifying assumptions such as

(1) not putting any surface threat sites in the immediate area,
(2) keeping the terrain fairly simple (smoothing and flying above the rough), and
(3) flying both sides at constant velocities, except for maneuver, etc.

This knowledge will eventually split into several knowledge sources with differing tasks such as

(1) detecting conflicts (like critics),
(2) fixing plans which are blocked by world constraints such as calculating perturbed paths which still partially accomplish goals but satisfy constraints, and
(3) finding an optimal path using a dynamic programming algorithm.

If there is a lot of time available for planning very complicated, many-step paths, then the situation falls under the job description of the Global Planner.

### 3.3.4. Quick Response module

The success of the racetrack architecture depends upon the availability of a default solution whenever one is required, and this is provided by the Quick Response module. Quick Response uses the highest level, least detailed, and most abstracted knowledge representation. It produces solutions by looking up prestored maneuver choices in a special knowledge base which is designed to contain precompiled procedural knowledge and a very simplified representation of terrain. Initially these responses were to be stored in a database and currently a neural network (NN) approach is being investigated (see Sec. 5.3). The Quick Response specialist posts one of eight elemental maneuvers as depicted in Fig. 4. Eventually the format of plan specifications may change, once the quantization errors associated with choosing from a small finite set of maneuvers are studied. Results of work on this representation appear in Ref. 8 and an overview is presented in Sec. 4.

### 3.3.5. Performance Evaluator module

The block in Fig. 2 called the Performance Evaluator is an undeveloped block which is envisioned as an impartial observer intended to assess the effectiveness of the LLOS planner. It will contain a plan evaluator, and a statistics collector to monitor which plans resulted in poor tactical outcome. Results from this endeavor may suggest better plan schema or goal behavior descriptions. This information could also be used to "genetically" optimize the performance of the various expert modules making up REACT.

### 3.3.6. Module Mediator knowledge sources and the controller

The system as it is currently described provides three levels of competence in planning. In other words there are effectively three concurrently operating "planners", each with different capability and operating at a different speed. A Module Mediator (termed meta-level in Ref. 1) knowledge source will be responsible for deciding in the current context when a decision is mandatory. It will then proceed to scan the blackboard to see which of the "planners" is ready with an answer. If the Goal Conflict Resolution module has posted an answer, that maneuver is executed. This corresponds to the highest level of competence. If that module is not ready, the Module Mediator looks for an answer from the Goal Priority module. If that module is ready, its specified top level goal behavior is chosen and if the appropriate plan specialist has computed a plan to accomplish that goal, that plan is executed. This corresponds to the intermediate level of competence. If either the Goal Priority module or the plan specialist it calls is not ready, then the Quick Response module gains control. The Quick Response module is always ready.

The Module Mediator module operates in the same way with a pre-designed list of competence priorities regardless of the number of levels of competence (number of concurrently running planners). It could use contextual information to remove some of the planners from the race. But in general, its job is only to decide when to act and pick the best available answer. This module is the only module which is intended to reason explicitly about time. This was one of the motivations for the architectural design. Assuming that it takes time to track time, the amount of explicit temporal reasoning was minimized.

Other meta-level knowledge sources may eventually be developed. For instance, certain world conditions may trigger an interrupt of the LLOS planner. A meta-level knowledge source could be responsible for polling critical slots on the blackboard to determine if various processes must be interrupted. The controller regulates the concurrent processes, handling contentions for data in the blackboard.

### 3.3.7. Interacting with higher level planners and the world

One interaction of the LLOS planner and the upper levels of the blackboard architecture that makes up REACT is through the goals posted in the LLOS blackboard. We have not yet specified where these goals should come from. Clearly, high level goals should come from the mission objectives, and the more immediate goals should come from the pilot or REACT's model of the pilot's behavior. This leaves open the question of where the goal behaviors (e.g. pursue, hide) are decided. It is within the scope of this architecture for goals to be posted from within the planner (possibly as subgoals generated by planning segments), but goals should come from the pilot. It is at this point that the system design would differ radically in application to an autonomous vehicle or to an embedded decision support system. The best approach for an interactive system is the explicit specification of goals by the pilot. If the pilot was unavailable for explicitly specifying goals, two possible approaches are: (1) inferring the pilot's goals or intentions based on context and his prior actions, and (2) autonomous goal specification by the system.

The first approach essentially describes one component of an intelligent man–machine interface. Inferring the goals of the pilot is essentially a plan recognition process[10,11] whereby his intent is inferred from his actions. This may utilize an explicit internal model of the pilot. Development of a user model and the man–machine interface is not currently being pursued in the REACT project. The second approach, autonomous specification of system goals, may require task modeling whereby goals will be chosen based upon the frequency of their being chosen in like circumstances. Such frequency information may be stored in various structures (e.g. see Ref. 12). Retrieving goals from learned histories may be explored in the NN application within the Quick Response planner (see Sec. 5.3) and extensions to that work are alluded to in Ref. 13.

## 4. KNOWLEDGE REPRESENTATION

The basic strategy for knowledge representation in REACT is to organize all the local planning knowledge with respect to the plan specialists discussed above and their respective goal behaviors. This implies that the pilot's plans (or reactions) are based on his current set of objectives and drives. Candidate structures for representing expert behavior range from simple to complex. Some examples at the simple end are reflexes and fixed action patterns that can be indexed, stored and retrieved from tables (e.g.

TOPCAT[9]) or compiled into neural networks.[14] More complex behaviors can be generated by structures such as decision trees,[15] or production rules that interact through an inference engine. At the top level, there are mental models, plan schema[16] and cognitive maps.[17] These top level structures have no generally accepted form, and none of the current implementations captures the characteristics of the underlying biological models. Any of these representation techniques can be used to store and regenerate a set of responses. The differences lie in the ability to generalize, to detect goal behavior failures, and to compute decisions efficiently. Note that, in an autonomous mode, the system must be able to infer the pilot's current goal behaviors, which requires at least a rudimentary model of the pilot's mental model. However, an adequate representation does not necessarily require duplicating the pilot's mental model.

Real-time planning applications require a method for knowledge organization and distribution which facilitates multi-level reasoning. Planners at different levels of competence require different amounts of knowledge. More time to plan should mean that more detailed information or deeper knowledge can be brought to bear on the problem. Even for the reactive case, where little or no processing can occur, we need as much knowledge as possible to be encoded in a structure with fast retrieval. The REACT knowledge representation hierarchy is being designed to allow the system to take top level approximate solutions in time-critical situations. Figure 3 outlines the levels of the representation hierarchy.

The lowest layer in the knowledge representation hierarchy consists of the unreduced world representation, DMA maps, aircraft positions, velocities, etc. This is the layer where the traditional (numerical) models live. The most complex component of this information is the terrain data maintained by the Map Expert (Fig. 1). In an actual embedded system a Map Expert would serve as a navigation advisor. For our present purposes, we assume that the ownship position is known, and that Map Expert predicts the upcoming terrain, retrieving the pertinent map information, and processing

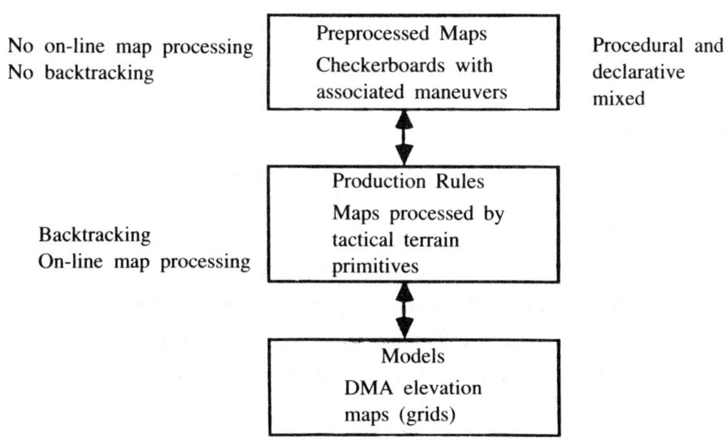


Fig. 3. Knowledge representation hierarchy.

it if required. It is the job of the Map Expert to make the right terrain information immediately accessible in all the forms necessary for utilization by REACT, and to perform consistency management among the levels of the knowledge representation hierarchy. Also, the Map Expert is responsible for reallocating space, i.e. performing memory management if the data becomes obsolete and principally acting as a database and memory manager. One might argue that this layer typifies a database, not a knowledge representation. However, it is possible within REACT to use inference rules at this level to manipulate models by heuristics. It is also possible that detailed DMA maps may require on-line processing in the slower planning modules.

The middle layer of the hierarchy consists of terrain descriptions in terms of tactical terrain primitives[18,19] providing a symbolic description of the lay of the land. At this level, reasoning about the terrain can be accomplished by inference rules. The top level of the hierarchy is the representation where the information available has been filtered and abstracted to the greatest extent. It contains the data structure which is accessed by the Quick Response module in REACT. It is a structure that comprises reduced terrain patterns resembling checkerboards (see Fig. 4) transformed into "small" arrays of numbers with associated maneuver choices (moves in the checkerboard) prestored for various relative opponent placements over the map. Local similarities, and estimated threat placement, as well as matching and generalization schemes reduce the number of possibilities. Details on the development of the REACT knowledge representation hierarchy appear in Ref. 8.

## 5. KNOWLEDGE ACQUISITION

REACT knowledge acquisition is proceeding with two concurrent efforts. The first is traditional knowledge acquisition with the primary tool being the structured interview. The second involves the implementation of an observational or case-based learning system embedded in a full mission simulator. A benefit of this second approach to the acquisition of a pilot's tactical responses is that it eliminates the difficult process of trying to recreate long, detailed reasons for making sensory classifications and selecting sensory guided behavior. Data acquired from running numerous simulations may be utilized by a knowledge engineer to generate rules, by a learning algorithm to infer rules from the results, or stored directly in a database or neural network. The cost of inferring rules from cases is generally very high and a large number of examples may be required to produce even a simple rule base. One advantage of learning responses with an NN is that the response time of the NN system can be very fast. For this reason, the NN approach is being used for the Quick Response module. These approaches to knowledge acquisition are complementary, with each one capturing valued knowledge gleaned from domain experts. In addition, they may be used to verify each other and to measure each one's effectiveness. Over the next year we will be comparing the cost and performance of expert and learning systems.

Our objective is to construct a system that can produce expert performance in the domain of pilot threat response. The following characteristics can be used to identify

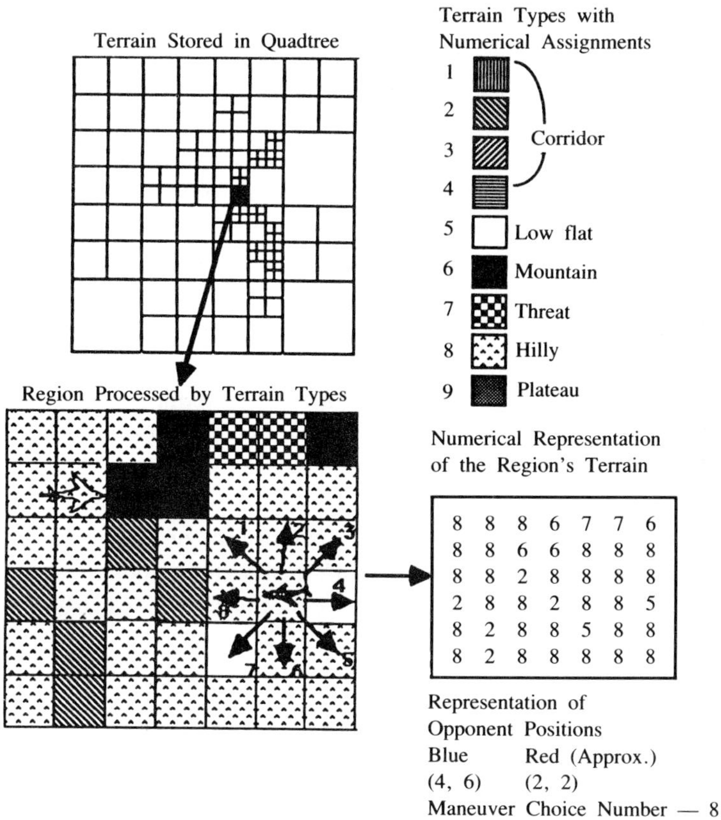


Fig. 4. Processing of terrain data into reduced knowledge representation for the Quick Response planner.

expert performance. Experts can imagine many of the situations that are likely to occur in their domain, even the rare ones. They know procedures, routines, or action sequences that will change the situation in the domain in a specific way. They can also estimate the effect on the domain of actions that they have never observed. The process of building our expert system involves deciding what knowledge acquisition technique to use, what knowledge must actually be stored, and what knowledge representation and retrieval techniques will allow the system to produce expert performance. This selection of techniques is in general an interactive process. The information to be acquired should depend on the representation it is intended to fill out, while the representation must conform to the constraints imposed by the acquisition technique selected.

## 5.1. Traditional Methods

There are a variety of ways in which information can be acquired from experts. We divide these into two main classes: observing the expert's performance, or asking the expert to use introspection and expound on the reasons he is choosing a particular course of action. The information accessible by observing expert performance are the details of the procedures and routines that the expert uses in a given task, and the situations in which those routines are applicable. The situations under which the expert is observed may be uncontrolled (as in task analysis, i.e. watching the expert during normal operations), or controlled (as when the expert goes through an ordered set of test cases). Since the internal states and objectives cannot be observed, it is hard to determine how many behavior modes he can operate in. (Different behavior modes occur when the expert can respond to exactly the same situation in different ways.) In addition, a single observation cannot indicate whether the action sequence executed is fixed, or can branch at various points in the sequence. These issues complicate the process of generalizing the observed routines, which is a fundamental part of building an expert system from observations.

The knowledge acquired by introspection has less information about the details of routines. It is difficult to visualize the components of frequently practiced skills.[20] Again, the situations from which the information is acquired can be structured or unstructured. Knowledge acquired in this way can be encoded into rule-based expert systems in a straightforward manner. The difficult aspects of building an expert system from introspective rules are getting enough information to reproduce the skilled actions that make up a large part of expert behavior, and capturing knowledge about the many special cases that are likely to occur.[21]

The primary traditional method for knowledge acquisition in REACT has been the structured interview. Interviews were organized around scripts, concentrating on eliciting responses to pre-defined scenarios. When used appropriately, the script can be used to guide the interview without forcing adherence to a single theme. A brief description of the interview format appears in Ref. 13. The rules will become part of the Conflict Resolution module in the LLOS blackboard. Currently, we are using raw DMA data as a representation within REACT's rule set, though we plan to shift to a representation with tactical terrain primitives to enhance the scope and efficiency of our system.

### 5.2. Extracting Knowledge from Observations and Case Histories: Skill Acquisition and Learning Mental Models

In machine learning circles, there is a growing realization that two distinctly different types of knowledge contribute to expert behavior. First, there is "automatic behavior" or skills that improve with practice according to the well-known power law, i.e. performance time decreases with number of practice trials to some power.[22] Automatic behaviors require little or no effort, cannot be prevented, and often result in new features that "pop out" of a background.[23,24] These automatic behaviors are only elicited in the proper context. Cognitive maps[17] supply context and organize sets of behaviors. The other type of knowledge needed for expert performance is a mental model of the expert domain. A mental model includes symbolic information about the characteristics and relations of objects and events that occur in the domain. The expert uses the mental model when he wants to reason or internally simulate events that could occur in the domain.[25] We are primarily interested in acquiring skills and the cognitive map that organizes them in the pilot threat response domain.

In skill acquisition, "behavior patterns" with modified perceptual triggers and different chunking of actions are created. When the sensory trigger for a behavior pattern has redundant noticed features, skill acquisition will restrict attention to an adequate subset. In addition, if there is a sequence of behavior patterns that are frequently used together, then the sequence of actions becomes progressively more tightly chunked.[22] Either type of skill learning requires an enormous amount of practice. It also depends on a reasonable level of arousal and attention focused on the right sensations.

The need for skill learning can be justified as an information processing requirement. The longer the sequence of actions a system can perform in response to a single sensation, the smaller the amount of information processing needed to execute a behavior.[26] However, the length of the sequence must be compatible with the variability of the environment, or the system may take action based on conditions that no longer exist. To guarantee that environmental variation is really small over the behavior, many trials are needed and learning should be a slow progressive process.[27]

Conditioning can be thought of as a simple form of skill learning where context is supplied through temporal association. Most of the learning algorithms proposed in the NN literature would fall in the category of conditioning. These include the Hebb rule,[28] the perceptron learning algorithm,[28] Barto and Sutton's[29] associative search elements which use goal information to direct an unsupervised learning algorithm, and the higher order networks of Maxwell *et al.*[30] In each case, there is a finite stimulus pool and a finite response pool; and the learning algorithm attempts to find the best sensation–action primitive pairings for a particular task.

Knowledge acquisition involving the modification of a mental model seems to require a special behavior mode called exploration. Exploration can be used in several different kinds of feature spaces, but in each case there are stereotyped movements through the feature space. In the case of sensory features, say visual, the exploratory mode is differentiated from search by more in-depth analysis of object features, a broader field of view, and longer dwell times between eye movements.[31] Exploratory sequences restrict the type of information that a subject is exposed to during learning. Modification of mental models is a fast process where stable learning may be achieved in just a few trials. The major modifications that can be made are:

(1) recording new nodes when they appear in exploration,
(2) replacing the sensory trigger in a behavior pattern mapping by another,
(3) expanding a node so that it splits into two or more nodes or categories.

These changes are generally triggered by the recognition of novelty failure, or successful behavior.

### 5.3. Neural Network Approach

In the REACT approach to representing pilot threat response, each planning module has a single set of goals and motivations. Within a single module, the selection of maneuvers based on the state of the world can be treated like a basic pattern recognition.[32] It is possible to solve the single module representation problem with a single feedforward NN such as a multi-layer perceptron, Least Mean Squares, RCE, or back-propagation network.[31,33] However, the existence of a network that solves the problem does not generally imply that there is a learning algorithm that can find it. In practice, finding a net that solves the problem requires not only a learning algorithm that converges, but an adequate (but not overly large) set of features and a training set adequate to drive the selected learning rule to the right network. To the authors' knowledge, only the Nestor learning algorithm can guarantee that a representation of any decision surface exists and that its learning algorithm converges. However, Nestor assumes that the right high-level features are available at the outset, and requires very large training sets. Even if an NN converges on a training set, its utility depends on how well it generalizes. Good generalization requires a training set with a broad sampling of the entire domain, and ways of linking features that have a causal relationship or generally appear simultaneously.

We assume that the NN has access to coarse grain features that have tactical significance. To obtain these features, the digital terrain map is transformed into a reduced pattern, or ''checkerboard'' representation resulting in classification of individual regions on the basis of their structural properties (Fig. 4). Five of the nine primary terrain classifications were used (mountain, plateau, hills, flat area, and corridor) in the NN study. (Specifics of the implementation of this terrain data processing appear in Ref. 8. This represents a first choice of feature set, which may be modified pending results of the proof of concept work.) The choice of desired resolution or mesh of each checkerboard is determined *a priori* by the roughness of terrain. Input states are defined as reduced map grids with ownship and opponent positioned on the map, rather like a checkerboard with two positioned players. Only eight maneuvers are currently allowed, i.e. moves into adjacent checks. The default setting for desired altitude is terrain following (this is currently being used to simplify the problem); and desired velocity is constant.

Knowledge acquisition for the Quick Response planner is intended to be accomplished by running a flight simulator over an area for which a checkerboard representation exists. The pilot's response to a (3-D rendering of) terrain would then be recorded together with the checkerboard state. In other words, the pilot sees the ''real'' terrain but his responses are immediately stored in the high level knowledge structure. Proof of concept work has utilized training sets constructed by choosing maneuvers with a simple rule base. The net was implemented using a generalization of back-propagation,[34] called the $L^4$ algorithm. A description of the $L^4$ algorithm is given below.

Our selection of the feedforward NN was based on the potential availability of a large data set of expert pilot responses to different world states, which makes it possible to train the NN. In the first phase of using NNs for Quick Response, a set of rules was encoded in a network[35] where the Quick Response module was restricted to a single behavior mode, i.e. mutually aggressive opponents with the Pursue goal. Continued research on NN approaches to multi-mode systems and other extensions are outlined in Ref. 13.

### 5.4. The $L^4$ Algorithm

A general $n$-layer feedforward network has an input layer, an output layer, and $n - 2$ hidden layers. The activation of the hidden and output layers is given by the equation

$$a_k^{i+1} = F\left[\left(\sum_j w_{jk}^i * a_j^i\right) + b_k^{i+1}\right] \tag{1}$$

where $F$ is the sigmoidal "activation" function, $a_{\langle \text{position } q\rangle}^{\langle \text{layer } m\rangle}$ is the activation of unit $q$ in layer $m$, $b_q^m$ is the bias of unit $q$ in layer $m$, and $w_{qr}^m$ is the weight or connection strength from unit $q$ in layer $m$ to unit $r$ in layer $m + 1$ (see Ref. 28). In general, any number of layers can be skipped, but in this paper we only consider connections to the next higher layer. The activations of units in the input layer, layer 1, are specified by the external input $i_p$, where $p$ is an index on the set of possible inputs:

$$a_j^1(t) = i_{pj} \,. \tag{2}$$

The logistic function was chosen as a "standard" sigmoidal activation function

$$a_i = F(s_i) = \frac{1}{1 + \exp(-s_i)} \,. \tag{3}$$

Learning in virtually all NNs is accomplished through a weight modification scheme. (Here and below, we shall use "weight" to refer to both "weight" and "bias" whenever there is no chance of confusion.) Back-propagation[28] is one such algorithm. The basic form of the back-propagation equations is

$$\Delta_p w_{jk}^i(n + 1) = h * d_{pk}(n) * a_{pj}(n) \tag{4}$$

where $h$ is the learning rate or time step in this discretization.

$$d_{pk} = -\frac{\partial E_p}{\partial \text{net}_{pk}} = (t_{pk} - a_{pk})\, F'(\text{net}_{pk})$$

$$\text{net}_{pk} = \sum_j w_{jk}^i * a_j^i \tag{5}$$

$$E = \sum_p E_p = \sum_p \sum_k (t_{pk} - a_{pk})^2 \,.$$

The worst problems with standard back-propagation, as a learning technique, are that it is slow and that it tends to get stuck in local minima.[28] Arguments about its biological plausibility will be ignored for now. We introduce a set of variations on back-propagation that improves performance in two ways, i.e. convergence occurs more often and faster than in the standard version. In the new algorithm, poorly trained inputs cause large weight changes which improve performance, while well-trained inputs cause no weight change in order to save computational steps. By making large changes, the new algorithm tends to escape many local energy minima.

Our variations on the back-propagation theme derive from the observation that back-propagation involves the minimization of the square of the $L^2$ norm of the difference between the actual and desired outputs summed over all possible inputs. However, correct classification of all inputs requires minimizing the $L^\infty$ norm, which is the supremum of the difference between desired and actual output over all of the $m$ inputs. Unfortunately, the $L^\infty$ norm is computationally impractical for large input sets. The problem arises because one must find the values of $|t_{pk} - a_{pk}|$ for *every* possible input in order to find the maximum. We have found that networks with some relevant inputs and some meaningless inputs can complete their training before all of the possible inputs have even been presented. Thus, calculating the output for every input on every learning cycle would be very inefficient. Another computational problem with the $L^\infty$ norm results from the fact that improvements in the network's performance on one input can make it worse on other inputs.

An $L^n$ norm is a distance measure on an $m$-dimensional space where the distance between $y = (y_1, y_2, \ldots, y_n)$ and $x = (x_1, x_2, \ldots, x_n)$ is defined to be

$$\left( \sum_{k=1}^{m} |x_k - y_k|^n \right)^{1/n} .$$

(Recall that the $L^\infty$ is the limit of the $L^n$ norms.) In other words, standard back-propagation attempts to minimize the energy introduced in Eq. 5. $L^n$ norms with intermediate values of $n$ lead to a more uniform sampling of inputs that generally prevent performance on one input from improving at the expense of performance on other inputs. Thus, there is a trade-off in choosing the size of $n$ that is problem-specific. In simulation experiments, we found good learning performance for $L^n$ norms with $n$ between 4 and 8. Performance varied little over this range.

The definition of energy in these intermediate norms is given by the following generalization of Eq. 5:

$$E = \sum_p E_p = \sum_p \sum_k (t_{pk} - a_{pk})^n . \tag{6}$$

Equation 4 is then modified by using the following $d_{pk}$:

$$d^n{}_{pk} = -\frac{\partial E_p^n}{\partial \mathrm{net}_{pk}} = (t_{pk} - a_{pk})\, |t_{pk} - a_{pk}|^{n-2} F'(\mathrm{net}_{pk}).$$

There are a number of ways to interpret the effect of using $n > 2$. However, all of these are derived from the fact that the size of the weight change for a given input decreases sharply with decreasing output errors $|t_p - a_p|$ for that input. This means that when inputs that are already learned appear, they cause a minimal weight change. In practice, we used a learning algorithm that is intermediate between the $L^n$ and the $L^\infty$ algorithms, i.e. no weight change is made for inputs with very small output errors. Our $L^4$ algorithm has a non-linear relation to $|t_{pk} - a_{pk}|$ that is in sharp contrast to the perceptron and back-propagation learning algorithms, where changes are linearly related to $|t_{pk} - a_{pk}|$. The "$L^n$" variants of back-propagation are discrete approximations of gradient descent algorithms, as is the standard $L^2$ case.

## 6. IMPLEMENTATION STATUS

The REACT prototype system is being developed on the Symbolics™ 3675 computer using the Georgia Tech Generic Expert System Tool (GEST) with specific modules being written in Lisp and numerical procedures (including AUTOMAN and procedures from TOPCAT) being implemented in Fortran and C on a Data General MV/10000. Due to the complexity and scope of the REACT system, implementation efforts have been concentrated on incremental developments designed for maximum flexibility and extendability of the system as a research vehicle. GEST has been extended to accommodate nested blackboards and simulated concurrency. The groundwork and initial stages for coupling the experimental planner have been implemented, including the integration of AUTOMAN and terrain maps. Integrating REACT, the scoring function and game-theoretic approach of AUTOMAN and heuristics in a functionally coupled system allows AUTOMAN routines to be used in the plan executor for the LLOS planner. This will also allow multiple aircraft scenarios to be developed. Another opportunity afforded by the integration of AUTOMAN in REACT is the potential for "flying" the LLOS experimental planner against an AUTOMAN opponent with perfect information, resulting in a test arena for the planner.

Processing of the terrain maps for the high level representation and the rule base for the REACT proof-of-concept neural net training set was completed by Georgia Tech Research Institute. The $L^4$ back-propagation network described above was implemented using PLEXI, a neural network tool from Symbolics™. The network successfully trained on the input/output behavior of the Georgia Tech rule base. Groundwork has begun to enable the embedding of AUTOMAN and the Quick Response planner in the Simulation Systems Development Laboratory full mission simulator. Achievement of this objective will provide automated knowledge acquisition capability and permit empirical comparison of knowledge acquired by traditional means requiring expert introspection and knowledge (compiled behaviors) extracted from simulator runs.

Currently, we are extending REACT's capabilities by utilizing terrain primitives, generated by an associated program, to assist the LLOS planner. The knowledge about the terrain primitives will be combined with the final set of data about the opponent aircraft (obtained before we lost sight of it) and heuristic rules and procedures (obtained from pilot interviews). This information will be used to drive the LLOS planner towards regaining LOS and reinstituting AUTOMAN's control. We have also been experimenting with using LOS calculations to guide the ownship aircraft once an opponent has been lost. This is done by calculating LOS between the ownship's current position and the expected position of the opponent. When LOS between these two points is blocked by terrain we fly our aircraft at a level above that intersecting terrain. This process continues until the opponent is located or the time threshold for searching for the lost enemy has been exceeded.

## 7. CONCLUSIONS AND CONTINUED RESEARCH

The principal concentration of this research is the development of the Lost Line of Sight planner in the REACT system. We feel there are several potential advantages of the ''racetrack'' architecture described in this paper for this fast-moving domain. First, each of the competing planners does not have to reason explicitly about time. Each is designed *a priori* for different time scales. Therefore, the problem of determining the time available for planning is relegated to a higher level expert; this expert uses contextual information to decide when a decision is needed and chooses the best available solution. It is the only module doing explicit reasoning about time-to-plan (deliberation time). The Quick Response module is being designed to provide an approximate solution which is always available. Secondly, the coupling of the ''racetrack'' design with a hierarchy of knowledge representations provides a modular way to develop specialized planners to operate at different time scales.

The real-time planning problem concerns how to accomplish planning such that the process can be pre-empted and an adequate solution at any stage is produced. Various methods have recently been proposed for accomplishing these objectives. One is the discovery and employment of anytime algorithms[36] which can be stopped at any point in execution and yield useful results increasing in utility as planning time increases. Other approaches toward the same objective appear in Refs. 32 and 37. The approach presented in this paper resembles a discretized version of the anytime algorithm, wherein the expected planning time is divided into several intervals and a separate planner is engineered for each time window. Another feature of our approach is the emphasis on integrating modules which essentially do no planning, that is, modules which simply retrieve learned responses.

We plan to combine the introspective and observational approaches to knowledge acquisition in the threat response domain. The natural division is to apply NNs to observed behavior in order to capture the automatic behaviors that the pilot uses. Information about how the pilot selects behavior modes and weighs objectives can be encoded in rules extracted from introspective reports. In the pilot threat response domain, we believe that this division of labor is possible if the division into expert modules described above can be done. We intend to capture a pilot's skilled responses from observations and case histories as a pilot ''flies'' a mission in a simulator. The introspective analysis of the same mission will be captured using protocol analysis or pilot commentary on the tape. We hope to capture enough pilot knowledge in a computer program, which combines NN and expert system methods, to allow it to compete with a human pilot in a simulator. The efficacy of the knowledge acquisition/representation/retrieval techniques will be judged by the system's performance.

## ACKNOWLEDGEMENTS

We would like to thank the following individuals for their efforts in supporting the extension of REACT and in formalizing the ideas presented in this publication: Jay Mendelsohn, John Gilmore, Stefan Roth, Anne Parrish, Fred Austin, and Joe Verzulli.

## REFERENCES

1. I. Hayslip and J. Rosenking, "Adaptive planning for threat response", in *Proc. Artificial Intelligence VII*, SPIE, 1989.
2. L. P. Kaelbling, "An architecture for intelligent reactive systems", in *Proc. Reasoning about Action and Plans Workshop*, Timberline, OR, Eds. M. Georgeff and A. Lansky, Morgan Kaufman, 1986, pp. 395–410.
3. R. A. Brooks, "A robust layered control system for a mobile robot", *IEEE J. Robotics and Automation* **2**, 1 (1986) 14–23.
4. S. Roth, S. Tynor, J. Gilmore and J. Mendelsohn, "GEST development of a blackboard expert system tool", Workshop on Blackboard Systems Implementation Issues, AAAI 87.
5. J. Gilmore and A. Semeco, "Knowledge-based approach toward developing an autonomous helicopter system", *Optical Engineering* **25**, 3 (1986) 415–427.
6. M. Falco, G. Carpenter and A. Kaercher, "The analysis of tactics and system capability", in "Aerial Dogfight Game Models", Grumman Corporate Research Department, Report No. RE474, May 1974.
7. F. Austin, G. Carbone, M. Falco and H. Hinz, "Automated maneuvering decision for air-to-air combat", *Proc. AIAA Guidance, Navigation and Control Conference*, Monterey, CA, 1987, pp. 659–669.
8. I. Hayslip and J. F. Gilmore, "A multi-level knowledge representation for reasoning about terrain", in *Proc. U.S. Army Artificial Intelligence Research for Exploitation of the Battlefield Environment*, Nov. 1988, pp. 123–137.
9. M. Georgeff and A. Lansky, *Reactive Reasoning and Planning*, *Proc. AAAI 87*, pp. 677–682.
10. R. Wilensky, *Planning and Understanding: A Computational Approach to Human Reasoning*, Addison Wesley, 1983.
11. K. Rubin, P. Jones and C. Mitchell, "OFMspert: Inference of operator intentions in supervisory control using a blackboard architecture", *IEEE Trans. Syst. Man Cybern.* **18**, 4 (1988) 618–637.
12. A. Barto, R. Sutton and P. Brouwer, "Associative search network: A reinforcement learning associative memory", *Biol. Cybern.* **40** (1981) 200–211.
13. J. Rosenking, I. Hayslip and J. Eilbert, "Traditional and automated approaches for acquiring expert knowledge", to appear in *Applications of Artificial Intelligence VIII*, SPIE, 1990.
14. S. Grossberg, "How does the brain build a cognitive code?" *Psychol. Rev.* **87** (1980) 1–51.
15. E. A. Feigenbaum, "The simulation of verbal learning behavior", *Proc. of the Western Joint Comp. Conf.* **19** (1961) 121–132.
16. M. A. Arbib, "Brain theory and cooperative computation", *Human Neurobiology* **4** (1985) 201–218.
17. S. Kaplan and R. Kaplan, *Cognition and the Environment*, Praeger, 1982.
18. D. Kuan, "Terrain map knowledge representation for spatial planning", in *Proc. First Conf. Artificial Intelligence Applications*, 1984.
19. D. McDermott and A. Gelsey, "Terrain analysis for tactical situation assessment", in *Proc. 1987 Workshop Spatial Reasoning and Multi-Sensor Fusion*, Morgan Kaufmann, 1987, pp. 420–429.

20. R. E. Nisbett and Wilson, "Telling more than we can know: Verbal reports on mental processes", *Psychol. Rev.* **84** (1977) 231–259.
21. J. H. Holland, "Escaping brittleness", in *Machine Learning Vol. 2*, Eds. R. S. Michalski, J. G. Carbonell and T. M. Mitchell, Morgan Kaufmann, 1986, pp. 593–624.
22. A. Newell and P. S. Rosenbloom, "Mechanisms of skill acquisition and the law of practice", in *Cognitive Skills and Their Acquisition*, Ed. J. R. Anderson, Lawrence Erlbaum Assoc., 1981.
23. D. LaBarge, "Automatic information processing: a review", in *Attention and Performance, Vol. 9*. Ed. S. Dornic, Lawrence Erlbaum Assoc., 1983, pp. 173–186.
24. D. Kahneman and A. Henik, "Perceptual organization and attention", in *Perceptual Organization*, Eds. M. Kubovy and J. R. Pomerantz, Lawrence Erlbaum Assoc., 1981.
25. W. Kintsch and J. G. Greeno, "Understanding and solving word arithmetic problems", *Psychol. Rev.* **92** (1985) 109–129.
26. G. DeJong, "An approach to learning from observation", in *Machine Learning, Vol. 2* Eds. R. S. Michalski, J. G. Carbonell and T. M. Mitchell, Morgan Kaufmann, 1986, pp. 571–589.
27. R. M. Shiffern and S. T. Dumais, "The development of automatism", in *Cognitive Skills and Their Acquisition*, Ed. J. R. Anderson, Lawrence Erlbaum Assoc., 1981, pp. 111–140.
28. D. E. Rumelhart, G. E. Hinton and R. J. Williams, "Learning internal representations by error propagation", in *Parallel Distributed Processing, Vol. 1*, Eds. D. E. Rumelhart and J. L. McClelland, MIT Press, 1986, pp. 318–361.
29. A. G. Barto and R. S. Sutton, "Landmark learning: An illustration of associative search", *Biol. Cybern.* **42** (1981) 1–8.
30. T. Maxwell, C. L. Giles, Y. C. Lee and H. H. Chen, "Non-linear dynamics of artificial neural systems", *Proc. Amer. Inst. of Physics*, Snowbird Utah, ISI, 1986.
31. J. O'Keefe and L. Nadel, *The Hippocampus as a Cognitive Map*, Clarendon Press, 1978.
32. J. L. Eilbert and I. Hayslip, "A mixed neural network/rule-based architecture for air combat planning", *Proc. AIAA Computers in Aerospace VII Conference*, 1989.
33. B. Widrow and S. D. Stearns, *Adaptive Signal Processing*, Prentice Hall, 1985.
35. J. A. Anderson, "Cognitive and psychological computation with neural models", *IEEE Trans. Syst. Man Cybern.* **13**, 5 (1983) 799–814.
36. T. Dean and M. Boddy, "An analysis of time-dependent planning", in *Proc. AAAI*, 1988.
37. B. D'Ambrosio, "Resource bounded agents in an uncertain world", Oregon State University, Dept. of Computer Science Technical Report, 1989.

**Iris Cox Hayslip** holds a Ph.D. (1982) in mathematics from the State University of New York at Stony Brook. She is the principal investigator for the Cooperating Intelligent Systems project at Ford Aerospace Corporation, Colorado Springs Division. Before joining Ford Aerospace, she was a Senior Research Scientist in the Computing Sciences and AI Laboratory of the Grumman Corporate Research Center. While at Grumman, she was the principal investigator for the Rapid Expert Assessment to Counter Threats (REACT) project, and was engaged in research on distributed, coupled AI systems for real-time pilot aids. Previous to her position at Grumman, she was an Operations Research Analyst in the Tactical Air Systems Division of the Naval Air Development Center. Her principal research interests are in fast planning and knowledge representations for tactical reasoning. Her current research emphasis is on cooperative planning with the human in the loop.

**Jeffrey P. Rosenking** is a principal developer on the REACT project. He is a member of the Image Processing and Artificial Intelligence Laboratory in the Grumman Corporate Research Center. Mr. Rosenking is a member of the Artificial Intelligence Technical Committee of the IEEE Computer Society, AAAI, and X3J13, the ANSI Technical Committee for the Standardization of Common Lisp. He received a B.S. in computer science from the State University of New York at Stony Brook, and an M.S. in computer science from the New York Institute of Technology. Mr. Rosenking is currently on a leave of absence from Polytechnic University, where he is enrolled in the Ph.D. program. He has developed expert and knowledge-based systems for manufacturing, training, networking and threat response applications.

**James L. Eilbert** holds a B.S. (1973) in physics from the State University of New York at Stony Brook, an M.S. (1975) in applied mathematics form the Courant Institute at New York University, and a Ph.D. (1980) in Biomathematics from North Carolina State University. Currently, he is a Senior Research Scientist at Grumman Corporate Research Center in Bethpage, New York. He has done work in neural network architectures and in neural network models of attentional mechanisms. His other areas of research include model-based vision and machine learning.

# AM/AG MODEL: A HIERARCHICAL SOCIAL SYSTEM METAPHOR FOR DISTRIBUTED PROBLEM SOLVING

D. G. SHIN and J. LEONE*

*Computer Science and Engineering Department*
*University of Connecticut*
*Storrs, CT 06269-3155, USA*

Received 1 April 1990

This work explores a distributed problem solving (DPS) approach, namely the AM/AG (Amplification/Aggregation) model. The AM/AG model is a hierarchic social system metaphor for DPS based on Mintzberg's model of organizations. At the core of the model are information flow mechanisms, namely, *amplification* and *aggregation*. Amplification is a process of decomposing a given task, called an *agenda*, into a set of subtasks with magnified degree of specificity and distributing them to multiple processing units downward in the hierarchy. Aggregation is a process of combining the results reported from multiple processing units into a unified view, called a *resolution*, and promoting the conclusion upward in the hierarchy.

Amplification is discussed in detail. A set of generative rules is introduced. Each rule specifies a set of actions for transforming an input agenda into other forms with higher specificity. The proposed model can be used to account for the memory recall process which makes associations between vast amounts of related concepts, sorts out the combined results, and promotes the most plausible ones. An example of memory recall is used to illustrate the model.

*Keywords:* Distributed problem solving; Multiagent cooperative computation; Distributed control; Reasoning mechanisms and modes; Memory recall model.

## 1. INTRODUCTION

Many researchers have found natural and social system metaphors useful for creating computational models for solving complex problems. They believe some classes of very complex problems can be tackled by carefully coordinating large numbers of individual problem solvers which possess minimal expertise. Each individual problem solver alone is capable of performing a very simple task; but collectively the effort of a group of problem solvers can yield synergistic effects. For example, Franks investigated how the collaborative efforts of army ants building hills exhibit intelligence.[1] Kornfeld and Hewitt generalized the self-management control behaviors of scientific communities.[2]

* This author is currently with the Electric Boat Division of General Dynamics Corp., Groton, CT 06340-4989, USA.

In this work, we present a hierarchical social system metaphor, based on Mintzberg's model of corporate organizations, for distributed problem solving (DPS). Mintzberg models an organization as a collection of agents forming a hierarchic structure.[3] Each agent carries out a task autonomously and communicates its decisions and corresponding information horizontally as well as vertically within the hierarchy. The power of the organization is derived from the synergistic efforts of the agents, although each agent itself executes only a very simple task. We believe these characteristics of an organization allow the development of the various computational elements involved in DPS, including how each problem solver should communicate with other problem solvers; how a group of problem solvers should be organized; how a task can be divided into multiple subtasks; and how the results of multiple subtasks can be combined into a solution. This understanding of how organizations function allowed us to develop a computational DPS model, called AM/AG (Amplification/Aggregation).

At the core of the AM/AG model are information flow mechanisms, namely, *amplification* and *aggregation*. Amplification is a process of decomposing a given task, called an *agenda*, into a set of subtasks with magnified degree of specificity and distributing them to multiple processing units downward in the hierarchy. Aggregation is a process of combining the results reported from multiple processing units into a unified view, called a *resolution*, and promoting the conclusion upward in the hierarchy.

This work presents only the amplification aspect of the AM/AG model, due to space limitation. Amplification includes the use of a set of generative rules, each of which specifies a set of actions for transforming an input agenda into other forms with higher specificity. The proposed model is used to account for the memory recall process which can be considered as making associations between vast amounts of related concepts, sorting out the combined results, and promoting the most plausible ones. An example of memory recall is used to illustrate the model.

## 2. THE AM/AG MODEL

The goal of this work is to incorporate the view described above on an organization's information flow into a computational cooperative model. The schematic view of the model is shown in Fig. 1. The basic elements of the model are agents, organized in a hierarchical structure. For each agent, say $A$, there exist one or more *immediate subordinate agents*, denoted by $IS(A)$, except the agents at the bottom of the hierarchy, which have no subordinates and are named rank and file. The topmost agent, called the apex manager, communicates with the environment. The behavior of agents is governed by the following rules:

1. An agent $A$ can communicate only with his immediate subordinate agents $IS(A)$.
2. The apex manager has an ability to create his immediate subordinate agents.
3. The agent $A$ can grant to each $A_i \in IS(A)$ an ability to create its own immediate subordinate agents, i.e. $IS(A_i)$.

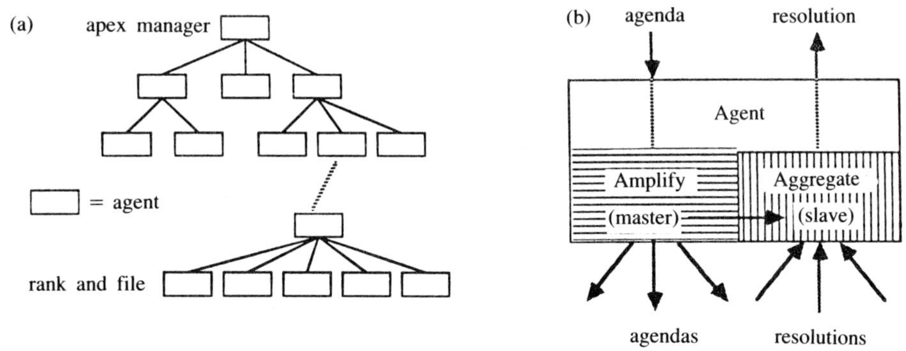


Fig. 1. Description of the AM/AG model.

4. The agent $A$ can revoke from the grantee the privilege of granting an ability to create subordinate agents.
5. The agent $A$ can remove an agent $A_i \in IS(A)$.
6. The agent $A$ can request an agent $A_i \in IS(A)$ to remove an agent in $IS(A_i)$.

The primary function of each agent is to communicate two types of information structures, *agenda* and *resolution*. An agenda is the information each agent receives from its superior as a problem to be resolved, and a resolution is the information each agent provides to its superior as a solution to the presented problem. The apex manager receives an agenda from the environment and provides to the environment a resolution. Both to an agenda and a resolution, say $k$, the notion called *degree of specificity*, denoted by $S(k)$, is applied. Let $k_1$ and $k_2$ be either a pair of agendas or a pair of resolutions. If the information specified in $k_1$ is less stringent than that specified in $k_2$, then $S(k_1)$ is said to be less than $S(k_2)$. This is expressed by $S(k_1) \leq S(k_2)$. For example, if $k_1$ is "There was a car nearby" and $k_2$ is "There was a red car nearby", then it holds that $S(k_1) \leq S(k_2)$. The notion of degree of specificity can be extended to between an agenda and a set of agendas and between a resolution and a set of resolutions.

When an agent $A$ receives an agenda $a_{\text{in}}$, $A$ first converts $a_{\text{in}}$ into an intermediate form, say $a_{\text{out}}$; $A$ then decomposes $a_{\text{out}}$ and distributes the decomposed segments to each $A_i \in IS(A)$ appropriately. Let the notation $\vec{a}_{\text{out}}$ include the status of decomposition as well as distribution of $a_{\text{out}}$. $a_{\text{in}}$ is said to be *amplified* into $\vec{a}_{\text{out}}$ by $A$. Each agenda, received by a member of $IS(A)$, is called *an amplified agenda derived from* $a_{\text{in}}$. The following property holds for agenda amplification:

**Proposition of Amplification:**

$$\text{If } a_{\text{in}} \text{ is amplified into } \vec{a}_{\text{out}} \text{ by an agent } A, \text{ then } S(a_{\text{in}}) \leq S(\vec{a}_{\text{out}}) .$$

During the amplification process, $A$ establishes and stores a policy (scheme) in its local memory for aggregating the results to be reported by $IS(A)$ on the amplified agendas. $A$ makes use of the policy later during the aggregation process. This activity of establishing a policy is indicated in (b) of Fig. 1 as the horizontal arrow representing the master-slave intra-relationship within the agent description.

When an agent $A$ receives one or more resolutions, say $\vec{r}_{in}$, from $IS(A)$, $A$ can modify $\vec{r}_{in}$ into another form, say $r_{out}$, according to the aggregation policy established *a priori* during the course of amplifying the corresponding agenda. The $r_{out}$ becomes $A$'s resolution on the agenda $a_{in}$ which $A$ received previously, and $r_{out}$ is promoted upward in the hierarchy. $\vec{r}_{in}$ is said to be *aggregated* into $r_{out}$ by $A$. An agent aggregates a set of resolutions by applying an appropriate set of aggregation functions. Aggregation does not add any additional information to the collected information. The aggregation process can only eliminate unnecessary information from the collected one. This property is stated in the following form:

**Proposition of Aggregation**

If $\vec{r}_{in}$ is aggregated into $r_{out}$ by an agent $A$, then $S(r_{out}) \leq S(\vec{r}_{in})$.

## 3. AMPLIFICATION WITH GENERATIVE RULES

This section discusses the first computational phase, i.e. amplification, of the AM/AG model. The discussion of the second phase, i.e. aggregation, is deferred elsewhere due to space limitations. (Details of the aggregation process can be found in Ref. 4.)

### 3.1. Generative Rules

The generative rules are the basic set of rules which facilitate transformations of the current agenda into multiple subagendas. Each generative rule is a pair of agenda schema and expansion action, $\langle S, A\rangle$, where $S$ is intended to match the current agenda or its fragment and, if the match is successful, $A$ prescribes possible ways of transforming the current agenda into other forms.

Our development of the generative rules has been inspired by a classic syntactic and semantic analysis of English by Quirk *et al.*,[5] which provided the basis for identifying the 30 types of generative rules. In Ref. 5, Quick *et al.* present 33 different clause patterns each of which intends to signify one meaningful combination between the syntactic constituents (e.g. subject, verb, object, complement, etc.) and their semantic roles (e.g. agent, instrument, locative, etc.). Our approach is to introduce an agenda schema, namely, *a canonical form*, for each clause pattern. This approach is based on the assumption that the canonical forms would match most of the agendas furnished to each processing agent.

#### 3.1.1. Canonical form

Each canonical form conveys information about the possible semantic roles of the participating syntactic constituents. A canonical form can be expressed in many different ways. Nevertheless, one existing knowledge representation work provides a number of built-in mechanisms which are used by the expansion actions to manipulate the canonical forms.

Sowa's *conceptual graph* provides ways of relating the syntactic constituents with their semantic roles.[6] Two basic representation units of the conceptual graph are *concepts*, expressed by [ ], and *conceptual relations*, expressed by ( ). A conceptual relation links two related concepts by specifying the *role* of one concept with respect to the other. Figure 2 shows a few canonical forms expressed using conceptual graph. Here, only three among 30 canonical forms are shown. The rest can be found in Ref. 4.

The first canonical form given in Fig. 2 comprises three concepts and two conceptual relations. Here, the concepts, $c_1$, $c_2$, and $c_3$, are indicative of, respectively, the subject, verb, and direct object participants in the meaning representation. The conceptual relations, AGENT and OBJ, indicate the semantic roles assumed by the participants. Thus, $c_1$ is the agent of the action indicated by the concept $c_2$, and $c_3$ is the recipient of the action indicated by $c_2$. The second canonical form is intended to express the idea that $c_1$ is situated in the physical or abstract place indicated by $c_2$. For example, "The girl is in trouble" can be expressed in conceptual graph as:

$$[\text{girl}] \rightarrow (\text{PLACE.IN}) \rightarrow [\text{trouble}]$$

The third canonical form represents the "is-a-part-of" relationship. For example, both "The sofa is part of the living room furniture" and "A finger is part of your hand" can be expressed using the conceptual relation PART.

1. $[c_1] \leftarrow$ (AGENT) $\leftarrow [c_2] \rightarrow$ (OBJ) $\rightarrow [c_3] \Rightarrow$
   (a) FOCUS ($[c_2] \leftarrow$ (OBJ) $\leftarrow [c_3]$)
   (b) SPECIALIZE ($c_2$, $c_1$) and call the result $r_1$.
   (c) ATTRIBUTIZE ($c_3$) and call the result $r_2$.
   (d) INTERSECT ($r_1$, $r_2$) and call the result $r_3$.
   (e) PRODUCE ($[c_3] \rightarrow$ (ATTR) $\rightarrow [r_3]$)
2. $[c_1] \rightarrow$ (PLACE.IN) $\rightarrow [c_2] \Rightarrow$
   (a) FOCUS ((PLACE.IN) $\leftarrow [c_2]$)
   (b) If $c_2$ is a simple concept, then do
      i. DEFINE ($c_2$) and call the result $r_1$.
      ii. EXPLODE ($r_1$)
      iii. PRODUCE ($c_2$, $r_1$)
   (c) Else do
      i. AMPLIFY ($c_2$) and call the result $r_1$.
      ii. CHARACTERIZE ($c_1$) and call the result $r_2$.
      iii. PROJECT ($r_2$, $r_1$) and call the result $r_3$.
      iv. MAXIMIZE ($c_1$, $r_3$) and call the result $r_4$.
      v. PRODUCE ($r_2$, $r_4$)
3. $[c_1] \rightarrow$ (PART) $\rightarrow [c_2] \Rightarrow$
   (a) FOCUS ($[c_2]$)

Fig. 2. Examples of generative rules.

### 3.1.2. Expansion actions

An expansion action is associated with each canonical form. An expansion action produces a more stringent version of the input agenda which matches the expansion action's corresponding canonical form. Figure 2 shows the expansion actions attached to their corresponding canonical form. Each expansion action is a sequence of graph manipulation operations.

A number of graph manipulation operations have been devised whose functions include finding the relationships (e.g. generalization, specialization) between a pair of conceptual graphs, transforming a graph into new graph(s) (e.g. join), and determining containment relationships between individual concepts (e.g. subtype, supertype). Given below is the set of operations for the expansion actions. Examples of these operations are illustrated in Sec. 4.2.

AMPLIFY ($x$) calls the procedure AMPLIFICATION with the graph $x$. The result of amplifying $x$ is marked with NO-JOIN. This indicates to the procedure AMPLIFICATION that the current result is not to be joined with the input agenda.

ATTRIBUTIZE ($x$) is a form of SPECIALIZE except that the search for the more stringent subtype of the concept $x$ is unconstrained.

CHARACTERIZE ($x$) consults with the background knowledge and generates a set of individual concepts that are commonly related to the meaning representation of graph $x$.

DEFINE ($x$) consults with either the context description or, if that fails, the background knowledge to find the definition of the concept $x$.

EXPLODE ($x$) separates the meaning of the composite graph $x$ into its constituent subgraphs.

FOCUS ($x$) selects a subgraph of the graph $x$ from which the new subagenda is to be derived.

JOIN ($x$, $y$) finds the common overlap $c$ of the two graphs, $x$ and $y$, and attaches the subgraphs $x - c$ and $y - c$ to $c$.

INTERSECT ($x$, $y$) finds the set of concepts which is an overlap of the two different sets of concepts $x$ and $y$.

MAXIMIZE ($x$, $y$) consults with the background knowledge and finds the set of maximal common subtypes of the concepts $x$ and $y$.

PRODUCE ($x$, $y$) is a lexical operation which simply creates a syntactic structure by embedding the concept relation $y$ with the pair of graphs $x$. Example concept relations for $y$ include (→(ATTR)→), (→(PART)→), (→⟨TRANSPOSITION⟩→), and (→⟨ONE-DIGIT-OFF⟩→).

PROJECT ($x$, $y$) compares the set of graphs, $x$, with the graph $y$ and returns each subgraph of $y$ which matches any element graph in $x$.

SPECIALIZE ($x$, $y$) consults with the background knowledge to find a more stringent subtype of the concept $x$. The search for the subtype is constrained by the concept $y$.

### 3.2. Amplification Procedure

Amplification procedure is the control mechanism for applying generative rules. It determines which generative rule should be used, facilitates the execution of the expansion actions, combines, if necessary, the information derived from the expansion actions with the current input agenda, and determines if the newly created subagenda is canonical. This control mechanism is incorporated into the procedure AMPLIFICATION which is given below. This procedure is executed when an agenda, $a_{\text{in}}$, is presented to a middle-line manager or the apex manager.

Procedure AMPLIFICATION ($a_{\text{in}}$)

STEP 1: For the input agenda $a_{\text{in}}$, determine whether $a_{\text{in}}$ can be resolved as it is; for example, if $a_{\text{in}}$ contains a conceptual relation delimited by $\langle\ \rangle$, then $a_{\text{in}}$ is immediately computable. If any resolution can be found, store the resolution locally and exit.

STEP 2: For the input agenda $a_{\text{in}}$, find a generative rule, say $G$, such that the canonical form of $G$ matches some subgraph $\psi$ of $a_{\text{in}}$.

STEP 3: For the rule $G$ and its corresponding matching subgraph $\psi$ of $a_{\text{in}}$, apply the expansion action of $G$ to $\psi$. Let the set of modified subgraphs of $\psi$ be denoted by $\Psi(r)$.

STEP 4: For each modified subgraph $s \in \Psi(r)$, unless $s$ is marked with NO-JOIN, perform JOIN on $s$ and $a_{\text{in}}$ to create an intermediate graph $s'$. Test $s$ and $s'$ against the canonical forms of the generative rules and let $s$ or $s'$ that matches any canonical form be a new valid subagenda. Overall, the collection of all new valid subagendas is denoted by $a_{\text{out}}$. Distribute each new subagenda of $a_{\text{out}}$ downward in the hierarchy.

## 4. APPLICATION TO MEMORY RECALL

Memory recall is one of the most complicated human mental processes. Given an input cue, a person can associate it with some highly related concept among vast amounts of previous experiences or memories. It is speculated that such an intriguing process can only result from the synergistic interaction of as many as 100 billion neurons.[7] This observation suggests that the massive parallelism features in the distributed problem solving (DPS) paradigm may provide a way of balancing operational efficiency against complexity.[8] The effectiveness of our proposed DPS paradigm in tackling complexity is demonstrated by using it to model the memory recall.

### 4.1. Example

The particular memory recall process concerned in this work is illustrated by exemplifying an actual incident that occurred to one of the authors. An incident of this kind can be experienced by anyone, in fact, frequently. This example is also used in the following subsection to illustrate the concepts underlying amplification.

One day Shin ran into his friend who came to Shin's apartment complex. The friend told Shin that residential operations had informed him (the friend) that he could move into the apartment #31 as of 6/15. Shin was puzzled because the tenants of #31 had moved in only two months ago. To clarify this, Shin went to #31 and checked with the occupant, Headly:

**Shin** : Are you moving out?
**Headly**: No.
**Shin** : My friend has been told by residential operations that he can move into apartment #31 on 6/15.
**Headly**: Probably, residential operations made a mistake.
[About three minutes later, on the way to the friend, Shin concluded]
**Shin** : Perhaps the correct apartment number is 91.

After Shin was convinced that there had been some mistake, *to be helpful* to his friend, Shin intentionally started to think about what could have been wrong. It took about three minutes for him to conclude that 31 could have been mistaken for 91. How? Later, after analysis he realised that two factors played important roles in his approximate reasoning: (i) an empirical knowledge that the correct apartment number is more likely to be only one digit different from 31; and (ii) an episodic knowledge that Dan, one of his colleagues who lived at 91, moved out at the beginning of June.

### 4.2. Illustration of Amplification

Each processing unit, i.e. an agent, is featured with the set of generative rules and its control structure, the procedure AMPLIFICATION. In addition to this procedure, two other computational elements are involved in the amplification process. The first element, the context description of the current conversation, provides the global and local foci of the concerned conversation and the logical relationships between the concepts embedded in the utterances. Figure 3 shows the context description which corresponds to the conversation given in Sec. 4.1.

**Context**

Shin : [person: Headly] ← (AGENT) ← [move out: ?]
Headly: [no]
Shin : [residential operation] ← (AGENT) ← [communication] → (RCPT) → [person: friend]
↘
[(PMS) → [[person: friend] ← (AGENT) ← [move into]]] ← (OBJ)
↓ ↘
[number: 31] ← (LOC) ← [apartment] ← (OBJ) (PTIM) → [date: @6/15]
Headly:
(PSBL)
↓
[[residential operation] ← (AGENT) ← [perform] → (OBJ) → [mistake] → (ATTR) → [clerical]]

**Global Focus**

[[number: 31] ← (LOC) ← [apartment]] ← (OBJ) ← [move into]

**Local Focus**

(PSBL) → [[residential operation] ← (AGENT) ← [perform] → (OBJ) → [mistake] → (ATTR) → [clerical]]

Fig. 3. An example of context description.

The second element, the background knowledge, is shared and consulted by each processing unit when applying its generative rules. One way of organizing the background knowledge is to store semantic notions associated with each sense of every word in the English vocabulary. Each word sense stored in the background knowledge is expressed in conceptual graph. A fragment of background knowledge is shown in Fig. 4. Two different word senses, $s_1$ and $s_2$, of "mistake" are given in Fig. 4. In $s_1$, "mistake" means identifying something wrongly and, in $s_2$, "mistake" means doing something wrongly. Specifying different class concepts for each word sense provides a way to enforce the notion called "selectional restrictions".[9] The prototype concept "office" and the schema concept "residential operation" are shown. The use of these concepts during the application of generative rules is explained shortly.

**Concept Definitions**

schema for residential operation is
[schedule: {[maintenance], [assignments]}] ← (PRODUCE) ← [residential operation]
[office] ← (ATTR) ↵

prototype for office is
[office] —
(CHRC) → [loc]
(CHRC) → [employee: {*}] → (QTY) → [number]
← (AGENT) ← [work] → (ATTR) → (clerical)
(CHRC) → [task: {*}]

schema for mistake is
$s_1$: [entity] ← (OBJ) ← [identify] → (STATUS) → [¬ correct]
$s_2$: [animate] ← (AGENT) ← [activity] → (STATUS) → [¬ correct]

schema for clerical is
$s_1$: [activity] → (CHRC) → [[manipulate] → (OBJ) → [symbols: {[number], [letter]}]]
$s_2$: [work] → (CHRC) → [tasks: {[record keeping], [file], [type], [transcribe], [communicate]}]

**Type Hierarchy**

| | | |
|---|---|---|
| activity ≥ play | mistake ≥ offsides | perform ≥ sport |
| activity ≥ perform | mistake ≥ strike out | perform ≥ work |
| activity ≥ mistake | mistake ≥ work | |
| | mistake ≥ clerical | number ≥ ⟨one-digit-off⟩ |
| | mistake ≥ law enforcement | number ≥ ⟨transposition⟩ |
| | mistake ≥ ⟨one-digit-off⟩ | |
| | mistake ≥ ⟨transposition⟩ | play ≥ foul |
| sport ≥ basketball | basketball ≥ foul | soccer ≥ foul |
| sport ≥ tennis | basketball ≥ offsides | soccer ≥ offsides |
| sport ≥ soccer | | |
| sport ≥ baseball | baseball ≥ foul | |
| | baseball ≥ strike out | |
| work ≥ construction | clerical ≥ record keep | communicate ≥ phone |
| work ≥ clerical | clerical ≥ type | communicate ≥ talk |
| work ≥ law enforcement | clerical ≥ communicate | communicate ≥ correspond |
| | clerical ≥ transcrible | |

Fig. 4. A fragment of background knowledge.

In the rest of this section, the amplification of an input agenda into a set of subagendas is illustrated. First, for the sake of clarity, the overall agenda amplification is presented in an abstract form in Fig. 5. Then the conceptual graph representation of the agendas and their intermediate transformations are shown in Fig. 6. Three amplifications are explained below in step by step detail.

#### 4.2.1. Illustration One: Amplification of $a_1$ into $a_2$ in Figures 5 and 6

1. The local focus of Fig. 3 is presented to the apex manager as its agenda (i.e. $a_1$ of Figs. 5 and 6).
2. The following expansion actions of generative rule 1 are performed:
   (a) FOCUS indicates the predicate part expressed in the graph form [perform] → (OBJ) → [mistake] to be amplified.
   (b) SPECIALIZE discovers that "clerical" is an activity of residential operation.
   (c) ATTRIBUTIZE discovers many subtypes of "mistake" including "foul", "offside', "clerical", etc.
   (d) INTERSECT determines what subtype of "mistake" overlaps with the activity of "residential operation".
   (e) PRODUCE creates a subgraph which indicates the meaning representation of the newly introduced information. This result is given as $t_1$ in Fig. 6.
3. By the procedure AMPLIFICATION, JOIN operation is performed on $t_1$ and $a_1$, resulting in $a_2$ in Figs. 5 and 6. □

The agenda $a_2$ contains more stringent predicate information than the agenda $a_1$. One point needs to be made clear: why the amplification of $a_1$ concerns only the predicate part. According to Quirk *et al.*, when an idea is elaborated by a sequence of sentences, in general the predicate of the previous sentence becomes the subject of the following sentence and this pattern repeats.

Now it is assumed that $a_2$ has been amplified accordingly into $a_3$. This amplification illustrates the case when a new subagenda omits some component of the input agenda. A similar argument applies here. When the predicate of the previous sentence becomes the subject of the following sentence, the subject of the previous sentence is omitted.

#### 4.2.2. Illustration Two: Amplification of $a_3$ into $a_4$–$a_7$ in Figures 5 and 6

1. The agenda $a_3$ is presented to the corresponding middle-line manager.
2. The following expansion actions of generative rule 2 are performed:
   (a) FOCUS indicates the predicate (PLACE.IN) →[communication] to be elaborated.
   (b) The expansion actions listed in (b) of generative rule 2 are invoked because [communication] is a simple concept.
      i. DEFINE makes a reference to the context description in Fig. 3 and determines the object of the "communication". The result of this action is the subgraph corresponding to the information communicated, i.e. ". . . friend . . . can move into apartment #31 on 6/15".

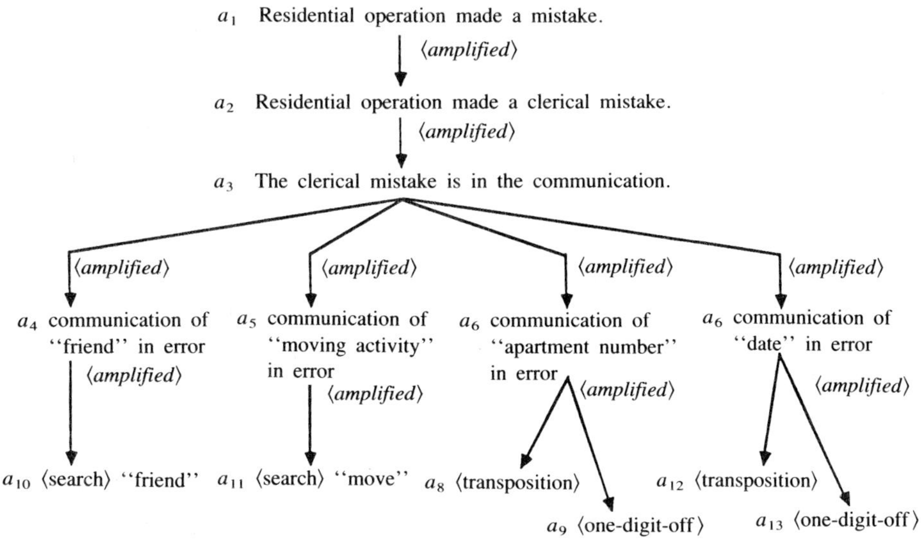


Fig. 5. Amplified agendas.

$a_1$: [residential operation] ← (AGENT) ← [perform] → (OBJ) → [mistake]
  $t_1$: [perform] → (OBJ) → [mistake] → (ATTR) → [clerical]
$a_2$: [residential operation] ← (AGENT) ← [perform] → (OBJ) → [mistake] → (ATTR) → [clerical]
$a_3$: [mistake] → (PLACE.IN) → [communication]
  └→ (ATTR) → [clerical]
  $t_2$: [communication] → (PART) → [person: friend]
  $t_3$: [communication] → (PART) → [move into]
  $t_4$: [communication] → (PART) → [[number: 31] → (LOC) → [apartment]]
  $t_5$: [communication] → (PART) → [[date: @6/15] → (PTIM) → [move into]]
$a_4$: [mistake] → (PLACE.IN) → [communication] → (PART) → [person: friend]
  └→ (ATTR) → [clerical]
$a_5$: [mistake] → (PLACE.IN) → [communication] → (PART) → [move into]
  └→ (ATTR) → [clerical]
$a_6$: [mistake] → (PLACE.IN) → [communication] → (PART) → [[number: 31] → (LOC) → [apartment]]
  └→ (ATTR) → [clerical]
$a_7$: [mistake] → (PLACE.IN) → [communication] → (PART) → [[date: @6/15] → (PTIM) → [move into]]
  └→ (ATTR) → [clerical]
  $t_6$: [number: 31] → (LOC) → [apartment]
  $t_7$: [mistake] → (PLACE.IN) → [[number: 31] → (LOC) → [apartment]]
$a_8$: [number: 31] → ⟨TRANSPOSITION⟩ → [number: ?]
$a_9$: [number: 31] → ⟨ONE-DIGIT-OFF⟩ → [number: ?]

Fig. 6. Illustration of amplification transformations.

ii. EXPLODE fragments the object of communication into several subgraphs.
iii. PRODUCE creates subgraphs consisting of the exploded concept (i.e. "communication") and each of its parts. The results of PRODUCE are the subgraphs $t_2$–$t_5$ in Fig. 6.

3. JOIN operation is performed on $a_3$ and each of $t_2$–$t_5$ resulting in $a_4$–$a_7$, respectively, of Figs. 5 and 6. □

Again, the four output subagendas, $a_4$–$a_7$, are more stringent than the input agenda $a_3$. Each output subagenda can be further amplified. However, because the amplification is constrained by the concept "clerical", some of the amplifications would be useless. For example, concepts such as "number", "date", or "person", may be participants in a meaning representation involving the concept "clerical mistake", but the concept "move into" may not. Below is discussed how the agenda $a_6$ is further amplified.

4.2.3. Illustration Three: Amplification of $a_6$ into $a_8$ and $a_9$ in Figures 5 and 6

1. The agenda $a_6$ is presented to the corresponding middle-line manager.
   (a) FOCUS indicates the predicate (PLACE.IN) → [$c_2$] to be elaborated.
   (b) The expansion actions listed in (c) of generative rule 2 are invoked because [$c_2$] is not a simple concept.
      i. AMPLIFY invokes generative rule 3 because the subgraph corresponding to $c_2$ matches the canonical form of this rule. Thus, the expansion action of rule 3 is to do FOCUS on [[number: 31] →(LOC) → [apartment]]. The result of AMPLIFY, which is given as $t_6$ of Fig. 6, is marked with NO-JOIN.
      ii. CHARACTERIZE is applied to the subgraph [mistake] → (ATTR) → [clerical]. The result is the set of concepts {[number], [letter]}.
      iii. Each concept of {[number], [letter]} is PROJECTed onto $t_6$, resulting in the concept [number: 31].
      iv. MAXIMIZE is applied to [mistake] → (ATTR) → [clerical] and [number] which results in a set of concepts {⟨transposition⟩, ⟨one-digit-off⟩}.
      v. PRODUCE is applied on [number: 31] and each concept of the set {⟨transposition⟩, ⟨one-digit-off⟩} resulting in the set of subagendas $a_8$ and $a_9$ of Figs. 5 and 6.
2. JOIN operation is not performed because the subagendas $a_8$ and $a_9$ are marked with NO-JOIN. □

When a graph contains a conceptual relation delimited by ⟨ ⟩, the graph is in the most primitive form; the meaning associated with the graph is immediately computable without any further amplification. Any conceptual relation expressed with ⟨ ⟩ is processed by the rank and file. The processing is done by the computational procedure attached to the relation itself. Graphs marked with NO-JOIN are not joined with the input agenda in the procedure AMPLIFICATION.

## 5. RELATED WORK

Recently a number of social system metaphors for distributed problem solving (DPS) have been suggested in an attempt to adapt distributed and cooperative social behaviors into decomposing and coordinating complicated AI problems. Minsky's work in *The Society of Mind* illustrates the point of viewing human memory organization as a society of individually specialized agencies each functioning in unison.[10] Chandrasekaran sees social organizations such as honeybee colonies, modern corporations, and medical communities as examples of distributed information processing embodying a variety of decomposition and coordination strategies.[11]

Two representative approaches for organizing cooperative processing units are committees and hierarchies. The differences and similarities between the two approaches are summarized in Table 1 by comparing Smith and Davis' Contract Net model[12] and the AM/AG model. In the committee approach, all the processing units communicate with each other, and in the latter only the adjacent layers of processing units exchange information with each other. The Contract Net model is an example of committee approach in which two forms of cooperation, task sharing and result sharing, are carried out between the processing units via autonomous calls for bids and the making of awards.[12] No predetermined hierarchy is assumed between the processing units. Another example of the committee arrangement, specifically in the parallel problem solving domain, is the scientific community metaphor by Kornfeld and Hewitt.[2] They view scientific communities as a collection of autonomous problem solvers each of which pursues a common goal, generates alternatives, and settles disputes over the alternatives. Kornfeld and Hewitt experimented with the idea of scientific communities using the parallel problem solving language called Ether. In Ether, an object can create another object by instantiating a predefined object schema, adjusting the object's parameters and letting the object function as an individual object participating in the problem solving.

## 6. CONCLUSION

A hierarchic model for distributed problem solving has been presented. This model is based on Mintzberg's model of corporate organizations. Two mechanisms, amplification and aggregation, have been suggested to enable information flow between participating problem solvers. Amplification, employing the generative rules, has been discussed in detail. The concepts underlying the use of generative rules have been illustrated by an example of memory recall.

Chandrasekaran indicates in Ref. 11 that a hierarchical arrangement is favored over the committee approach as the problem environment gets larger and more complex. The illustrated problem, memory recall, is generally known to be an extremely complex, unstructured process which may involve complicated chains of associations among huge amounts of different types of knowledge. Therefore, if Chandrasekaran's position is to be believed, the use of a hierarchic approach, such as the one suggested

Table 1. Comparison between the Contract Net model and the AM/AG model.

| Category | Contract Net | AM/AG |
|---|---|---|
| Generic similarities | • problem decomposition continues until nondecomposable subproblems are generated | • agendas are decomposed during amplification until nondecomposable segments remain |
| Generic differences | • cooperative behavior is between two willing entities | • two entities are not both willing: one entity is the master which creates a second slave entity |
| Structure of interactions | • can broadcast to any entity<br>• point-to-point communication with any entity | • cannot broadcast to any entity<br>• point-to-point communication only with children |
| Workload distribution | **task sharing**<br>• subtasks are created<br>• *negotiation* is the mechanism used to determine which nodes solve the subtasks<br>**result sharing**<br>• implicit form of cooperation<br>• results can be shared with any node | **amplification**<br>• subtasks are created<br>• subtasks are assigned to nodes; no *negotiation* is involved<br>**aggregation**<br>• results shared only with parent node |
| Integration of results | • data arrives from any node in which there is an interaction<br>• integration occurs | • data arrives from the children nodes<br>• suppression occurs |

here, to model the memory recall is justified. Nevertheless, determining the desirability of a model depends more critically on the expected communication modes between the processing units. For example, if an application assumes frequent revisions on the processors' roles of managing or being managed, the committee approach would be more appropriate. In modeling memory recall, no role revision is anticipated while amplification and aggregation occur and, for this reason, we have chosen a hierarchic approach over a committee approach.

REFERENCES

1. N. R. Franks, "Army ants: A collective intelligence", *Amer. Sci.* **77**, 2 (1989) 139–145.
2. W. A. Kornfeld and C. E. Hewitt, "The scientific community metaphor", *IEEE Trans. Syst. Man Cybern.* **11**, 1 (1981) 24–33.
3. H. Mintzberg, *The Structuring of Organizations*, Prentice-Hall, Inc., 1979.
4. J. Leone, "Synergistic Model for Memory Recall", Master's thesis, University of Connecticut, Storrs, CT, Aug. 1989.
5. R. Quirk, S. Greenbaum, G. Leech and J. Svartvik, *A Grammar of Contemporary English*, Longman Group UK Limited, 1987.

6. J. F. Sowa, *Conceptual Structures: Information Processing in Mind and Machine*, Addison-Wesley, 1984.
7. J. A. Feldman, "Connections", *BYTE* **10**, 4 (1985) 277–284.
8. D. E. Rumelhart and J. L. McClelland, *Parallel Distributed Processing: Explorations in the Microstructure of Cognition, Volume 1*, Bradford Books/MIT Press, 1982.
9. J. J. Katz and J. A. Fordor, "The structure of a semantic theory", in *Language* **39** (1963) 170–210.
10. M. Minsky, *The Society of Mind*, Simon and Schuster, 1986.
11. B. Chandrasekaran, "Natural and social system metaphors for distributed problem solving: Introduction to the issue," *IEEE Trans. Syst. Man Cybern.* **11**, 1 (1981) 1–5.
12. R. G. Smith and R. Davis, "Frameworks for cooperation in distributed problem solving", *IEEE Trans. Syst. Man Cybern.* **11**, 1 (1981) 61–70.

**D. G. Shin** received the B.S.E. degree in electronics engineering from Han Yang University, Seoul, Korea, in 1979, and the M.S.E. and Ph.D. degrees in computer science and engineering from the University of Michigan, Ann Arbor, in 1981 and 1985 respectively.

Since 1986, he has been Assistant Professor in the Department of Computer Science and Engineering at the University of Connecticut, Storrs. Before joining the University of Connecticut, he taught briefly at Han Yang University and the Korea Advanced Institute of Science and Technology. His research interests include intelligent database systems, user interface design,and discourse planning.

Dr. Shin is a member of ACM, and the IEEE Computer Society.

**J. Leone** received the B.S. degree in computer science from Central Connecticut State University in 1983, and the M.S. degree in computer science from the University of Connecticut, Storrs, in 1989.

From 1983 to 1985, he worked for Bunker-Ramo Information Systems, where he evaluated modifications to a UNIX kernel and maintained a prepass, assembler, linker, and loader. Currently, he is a member of the Artificial Intelligence group at General Dynamics Electric Boat Division, Groton, Connecticut. His research interests include truth maintenance systems, qualitative physics, distributed artificial intelligence, knowledge-based simulation, and computer security.

Mr. Leone is a member of the IEEE Computer Society.

# CAUSA — A TOOL FOR MODEL-BASED KNOWLEDGE ACQUISITION

WERNER DILGER
*European Business School*
*Schloss Reichartshausen, D-6227 Oestrich-Winkel, F R Germany*

and

JÜRGEN MÖLLER
*Fraunhofer-Institut für Information-und Datenverarbeitung IITB*
*Fraunhoferstrasse 1, D-7500 Karlsruhe 1, F R Germany*

Received 1 April 1990

CAUSA is a knowledge acquisition tool which supports the incremental modeling of complex dynamic systems during the whole knowledge acquisition task. It provides an environment for the modeling and simulation of dynamic systems on a quantitative level. The environment provides a conceptual framework which includes primitives like objects, processes, and causal dependencies, allowing for the modeling of a broad class of complex systems. Simulation allows for the quantitative and qualitative inspection and empirical investigation of the behavior of the modeled system. CAUSA is implemented in Knowledge-Craft and runs on a Symbolics 3640.

*Keywords*: Knowledge acquisition; Modeling environment; Object-oriented modeling; Process-oriented modeling; Causal models; Simulation.

## 1. INTRODUCTION

The increasing number of applications of knowledge-based systems to complex real world problems demands appropriate new tools to support the knowledge acquisition task (analysis task), because the knowledge-based approach differs deeply from the conventional one.

Essentially the knowledge acquisition task is the development of models on some level of abstraction to solve a given problem. The domain of models ranges from abstract mathematical models to 'real world' models which describe the structure and behavior of the investigated system as it appears to the investigator (and users) in terms of properties and functional dependencies. It is a central aspect of expert systems that they include such real world models. The shift from abstract modeling tools like differential equations, queueing theory, finite state machines, etc. to modeling primitives like objects, processes, and causal dependencies which provide means to describe more naturally the system under investigation, should also influence the methods and tools used in the knowledge acquisition task.

Knowledge acquisition should be grounded on a formal model as early as possible. This model should be more than a static description in a formal modeling language—it should allow for the simulation of models under various aspects to make the dynamic behavior of the model explicit, i.e. graspable. A tool for supporting such a model-based knowledge acquisition should satisfy the following requirements:

- The tool must provide an environment in which a knowledge engineer (or designer, or modeler) can incrementally describe, represent, or model (we use all these words interchangeably), all relevant aspects of a broad class of complex systems in an appropriate style. The ability of *incremental modeling* allows for the use of the tool during the whole acquisition task.
- The modeling primitives of the modeling formalism should support the *hierarchical structuring* of the models to overcome the problem of complexity.
- The tool should support the description of only partially known phenomena that can be described using the methods of physics *in principle*, but whose precise physical definition is not yet known. To meet this requirement, CAUSA provides a conceptual framework which includes adequate primitives like objects, processes, and causal dependencies.
- The meaning of the modeling primitives in use must be understandable to the domain experts involved; only in this case can the model serve as a *communication means* between the knowledge engineers and the domain experts. In other words, the modeling primitives should allow a natural (or direct) mapping of real world phenomena into the modeling formalism.
- The tool must include a *simulation facility* to assist the designer in the task of testing and validating models. Simulation allows for the inspection and empirical investigation of the behavior of the described system by making the behavior of the model explicit.
- An easy-to-use *direct manipulation user interface* (based on menus and icons) is needed to support the modeling task and to present the simulation results in various ways.

The design of CAUSA was primarily influenced by these six requirements. In addition, as a tool for the modeling and simulation of dynamic systems on a *quantitative* level, CAUSA was influenced by systems theory[1] and qualitative reasoning (described in Refs. 1 and 2), because an additional aim was to overcome several shortcuts of qualitative reasoning. The application of the qualitative simulation tool CAPAS[3] to some non-trivial case studies in the fields of chemistry and technical engineering has shown the weakness of the proposed methods and furthermore the need for quantitative data in the system under consideration. CAUSA allows for the creation and simulation of quantitative models and assigns some kind of meaning to abstract quantities by means of *qualitative interpretation*. Figure 1 sketches the different approaches.

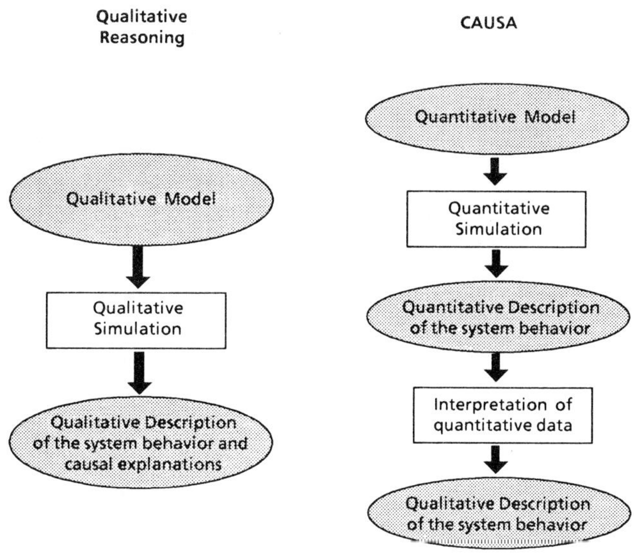


Fig. 1. Contrasting CAUSA with qualitative reasoning.

The result of knowledge acquisition is a model represented in the (internal) CAUSA representation language. In the design phase of the expert system, the CAUSA model can either serve directly as a knowledge base or as a specification of a new knowledge base (the realization can be automated by defining a mapping from the CAUSA representation language onto the target representation language).

Section 2 is the main part of this paper. It contains a description of the concepts like object, process, and others, which constitute the conceptual framework of CAUSA. The simulation is explained in Sec. 3. This is followed by Sec. 4 which describes the interpretation facilities for data. Section 5 gives an overview of the architecture of CAUSA.

## 2. THE ONTOLOGICAL CONCEPTS

CAUSA is best explained by describing the modeling primitives which it provides. These primitives claim a conceptual framework in which the designer can express his or her problems. In this paper we will refer to them as *ontological concepts*. An ontological concept is recursively defined either as an ontological primitive (like property) or as a set of ontological primitives and concepts. For example, the ontological concepts *object* and *process* together with the concept *property identification* constitute the ontological concept *system*. These concepts are the core of the *representation language* and of the *iconographic language* provided by CAUSA for communication and used in this paper. The ontological concepts of CAUSA are properties, objects, constituent-relations, processes, causal dependencies, structural laws, and systems. This is depicted in Fig. 2.

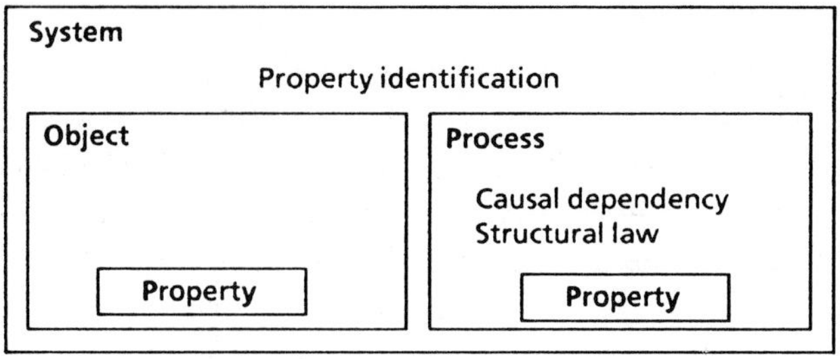


Fig. 2. The ontological concepts.

## 2.1. Properties

Properties are needed to describe phenomena of the real world and abstract entities. In the context of processes the properties are subdivided into exogenous (input) properties and endogenous (output) properties. A property is specified by its *type*, its *domain*, and its *value*. A type of a property is simply a symbol specifying what the property represents, e.g. physical units like m, kg, volt and so on. The value VAL of a property $p$ is restricted to the predefined domain DOM of $p$, i.e. $\mathrm{VAL}(p) \in \mathrm{DOM}(p)$, and is unique at every point in time. The values of properties change in time and these changes are effects of influences. For simplicity we abbreviate $\mathrm{VAL}(p)$ to $p$ in all cases where no confusion can arise. CAUSA contains the three predefined quantitative domains REAL, INT and NAT. REAL denotes the set of real numbers, INT the set of integers and NAT the set of natural numbers. It is also possible to specify an open or closed interval of these sets as a domain:

$$\mathrm{DOM}(p1) = \mathrm{NAT}[10,100]$$
$$\mathrm{DOM}(p2) = \mathrm{REAL}(0, 1)\,.$$

The domain of $p1$ contains all natural numbers between 10 and 100, and the open interval of real numbers between 0 and 1 is the domain of property $p2$. A finite discrete domain is defined by the enumeration of the elements. Every enumeration of a set introduces a total order on the elements. As an example the domain of $p3$ is defined as the (ordered) set of six integers:

$$\mathrm{DOM}(p3) = \{0, 2, 4, 6, 8, 10\}\,.$$

The functions PRED and SUCC are defined in the usual way on all enumerated sets and on every subset of INT and NAT. To make the functions total we define the successor of the greatest element and the predecessor of the smallest element as UNDEFINED.

## 2.2. Objects

Every representation language provides primitives to describe entities. The entities are always represented by a set of characteristic properties (or aspects, or attributes) and some of these languages allow the expression of structural relationships between attributes. In CAUSA the term 'object' denotes any unstructured *set of properties*. Furthermore an object can be constituted using predefined object types. Relationships describing the internal structure of objects are not expressible. Figure 3 shows the graphical representation used in CAUSA of an object type OT2 that consists of two properties P21 and P22 and the subobject C of type OT1.

The object type is defined using the specification language in the following way:

OBJECTTYPE(OT2)
PROPERTY (*p*21 OT2)
PROPERTY (*p*22 OT2)
CONSTITUENT (C OT1 OT2).

## 2.3. Causal Dependencies

A typical relationship between two entities of an observed phenomenon is: "*if the entity A changes in some way then the entity B changes in some way*", or in short, "*A causes B*". The statement in the quoted sentences is known as a *causal dependency* between two events. This kind of relationship is fundamental in describing the *behavior* (or *functionality*) of complex systems. The necessity of causal connections between events is also emphasized in Ref. 4. The fact that the value of a property $p1$ depends on the values of two properties $p2$ and $p3$ (or that $p2$ and $p3$ influence $p1$) is normally written as a functional relation

$$p1 = f(p2\ p3)\ .$$

Such a functional relation *implicitly* contains two causal dependencies which we want to make explicit. For this reason we introduce the predicate *influence* for expressing

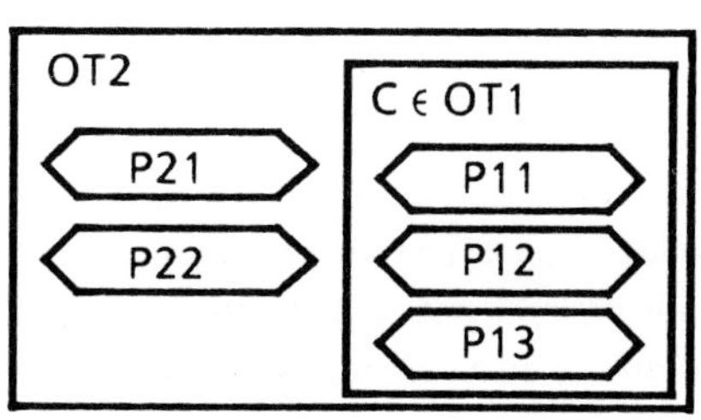


Fig. 3. The graphical representation of an object type.

causal dependencies where the first argument is the influencing property and the second the influenced one:

$$\text{INFLUENCE}(p2\ p1)$$
$$\text{INFLUENCE}(p3\ p1)\ .$$

The causal dependencies between a set of properties restrict the use or interpretation of a functional relation defined on these properties—the functional relation gets a *causal direction*.[4] The *influence set* of a property $p$ is the set of all properties that influence $p$:

$$\text{INFLUENCE-SET}(p) = \{x\text{: INFLUENCE}(x\ p)\}\ .$$

A *causal structure* on a given set $ps$ of properties is the set of all pairs of properties between which the relation INFLUENCE holds:

$$\text{CAUSAL-STRUCTURE}(ps) = \{(x\ y) \in ps \times ps\text{: INFLUENCE}(x\ y)\}\ .$$

The causal structure can be expressed in a *causal graph* where the relation INFLUENCE is denoted by arrows between nodes representing the properties. Causal graphs are used in the graphic interface of CAUSA.

### 2.4. Structural Laws

The value of an influenced property under certain conditions is computed by means of a set of qualified *structural laws*. Such a *structural law set* can be associated with every property. Each qualified structural law for a property $p$ has the form of a logical implication:

$$\textbf{LAW}\ P(p, p1, p2, \ldots, pn)\ \textbf{THEN}\ p := f(p, p1, \ldots, pn)\ .$$

The antecedence of a structural law belonging to a property $p$ of a process is a conjunction of expressions like $p1 > 10$ or $p1 \leq 10 * (p2 - p3)$ where $p1$, $p2$, $p3 \in$ INFLUENCE-SET($p$), and it determines the state in which the law is valid. The consequence of the structural law is an instruction on how to calculate the value of $p$, for example $p := p1 + 2 * p2$. The qualified structural laws associated to a property $p$ must fit the requirements that every name occurring in an antecedence or consequence be the name of either the property $p$ or a property in the influence set of $p$, and that only the value of $p$ be affected (changed).

Structural laws are a more general notion than the structural equations introduced in Ref. 4. The implications allow an easy modeling of states where each state has its own equation. As an example we take an endogenous property $p1$ influenced by two exogenous properties $p2$ and $p3$ (Fig. 4). The value of $p1$ is determined by two structural laws where each law corresponds to a special state. These states are defined in the antecedences of the laws given below.

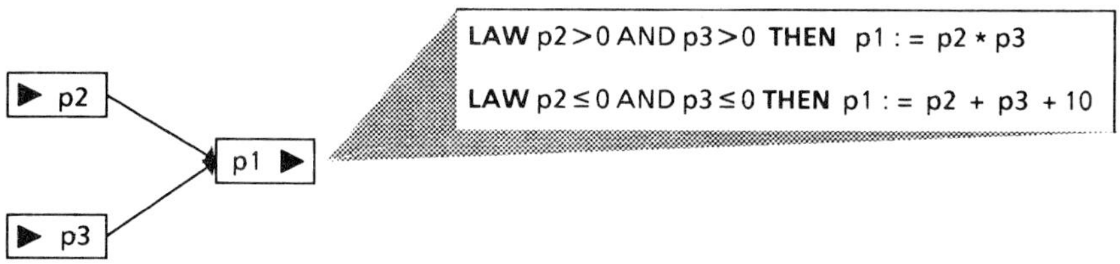


Fig. 4. Example of a causal structure.

The structural law set of a property completely specifies the *structural behavior* of that property relative to the embracing causal structure. It is convenient (and often necessary) to check for undefined property values in the influence set of a property being evaluated. The expression UNDEFINED ($p$) returns 'true' if an assignment to the value of $p$ has been performed, and 'false' if not. The expression can be used in any antecedence.

### 2.4.1. Evidences for values and structural laws

A broad class of problems forces the designer to handle *uncertainty*. In CAUSA property values and structural laws can be augmented with an *evidence value*. The evidence of a law or value $x$ is denoted by $EV(x)$. Under the assumption that the antecedence $Q(p, p1, p2, \ldots, pn)$ of a structural law $L$ of a property $p$ is satisfied, the evidence $EV(p)$ of the new value of $p$ expressed by $B(p, p1, p2, \ldots, pn)$ is a function of the evidences of all properties occurring in the antecedence and the structural law.

$$EV(p) = EF(EV(p), EV(p1), \ldots, EV(pn), EV(L)) .$$

The *evidence function EF* and its range (for example, the interval [0, 1]) can be specified by the user.

### 2.4.2. Evaluation of structural law sets

The value of a property is calculated by evaluation of the structural law set of this property. If there are no evidences, the laws are randomly chosen from the correspondng law set and the first law whose antecedence is evaluated to be true determines the value of the property. If no law is applicable, the property becomes UNDEFINED.

```
EVAL-PROPERTY(PROP);
LAWS: = LAW-SET(PROP);
LAW-APPLIED: = false;
while not LAW-APPLIED and LAWS ≠ ∅
  LAW: = select a law L ∈ LAWS;
  LAWS: = LAWS − {LAW};
```

**if** antecedence of LAW satisfied
**then** VAL(PROP): = result of the consequence of LAW;
LAW-APPLIED: = **true**;
**if not** LAW-APPLIED **then** VAL(PROP): = UNDEFINED.

The evaluation is different if evidences are considered. For every law with a true antecedence the evidence of the obtained result is evaluated by using the function *EF*, and the law which gets the highest evidence value is selected.

EVAL-PROPERTY-WITH-EVIDENCES(PROP);
LAWS: = set of all applicable laws L ∈ LAW-SET(PROP),
**if** LAWS ≠ ∅
**then** LAW: = select the law with the highest E(PROP);
VAL(PROP): = result of the consequence of LAW;
E(PROP): = calculated evidence
**else** VAL(PROP): = UNDEFINED.

2.5. Processes

A *process* is defined as a set of properties with a causal structure and an assignment of structural law sets to some properties. This definition enables us to understand processes as complete descriptions reflecting the behavior of a system with dynamic and interdependent properties. In CAUSA process types can be defined by means of other process types (recursive definitions are not allowed). A process *P*1 embedded in another process *P*2 is a process constituent, or constituent for short, of *P*2. The connections between the properties of *P*1 and *P*2 are established through *identifications*. The definition of a process type introduces a set of property variables or *process variables*. Process variables are described more precisely by the specification of their types and domains. The causal structure is defined by enumerating all causal dependencies between the introduced process variables. Finally the variables are augmented with a set of structural laws.

A process type *PT*1 containing one exogenous property *E*1, some internal properties and two endogenous properties *A*1 and *A*2 is depicted in Fig. 5 The internal property *C* is a *process constant* and it influences property *A*2. This process is a constituent with role name *P* of the comprehensive process type *PT*2. The identifications of properties are indicated by double·lines.

The process type *PT*2 is definable using the graphic interface or the specification language. The specification of process type *PT*1 would have the following form:

PROCESSTYPE(*PT*1)
Declaration of all variables together with their domains:
EXOGENOUS-VARIABLE(*E*1 *PT*1)
INTERNAL-VARIABLE(*I*1 *PT*1)
. . .

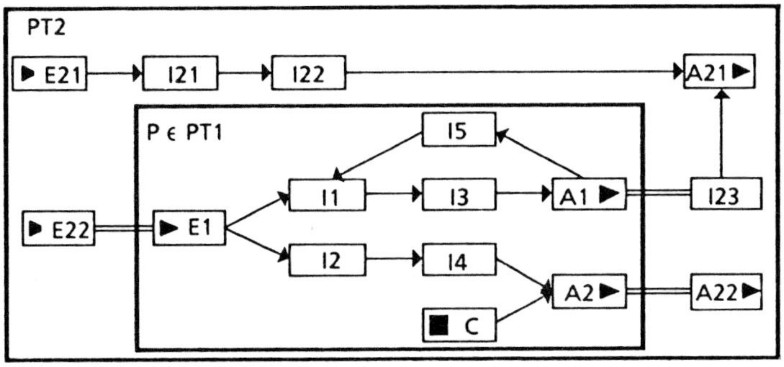


Fig. 5. The graphical representation of a process type.

INTERNAL-VARIABLE(*I5 PT*1)
ENDOGENOUS-VARIABLE(*A*1 *PT*1)

. . .

CONSTANT(*C PT*1)
DOM(*I*1.*PT*1) = REAL[1, 100]

. . .

Definition of all causal dependencies:
INFLUENCE(*E*1.*PT*1 *I*1.*PT*1)

. . .

Next we assign to each influenced variable a structural law set:
LAW-SET(*I*1.*PT*1) = {. . .}

. . .

The type definitions are optionally:
TYPE(*E*1) = *e*

. . .

The process type *PT*2 is specified by:
PROCESSTYPE(*PT*2)
Declaration of variables and causal dependencies analogous to process type *PT*1

. . .

Define the subprocess
CONSTITUENT (*P PT*1 *PT*2)
Make all necessary identifications:
IDENTIFY (*E*22.*PT*2 *E*1.*PT*1)

## 2.6. Systems

A system is a collection of objects and processes organized by means of a set of relations between them. A combination of objects and processes requires the identification of object properties and process properties. Figure 6 shows a system type *ST*1 established by two objects and a single process. The exogenous property *E*1 of the process constituent *P* of type *PT*1 is identified with the properties *P*11 of object *O*1 and the endogenous properties *A*1 and *A*2 are identified with the properties of object

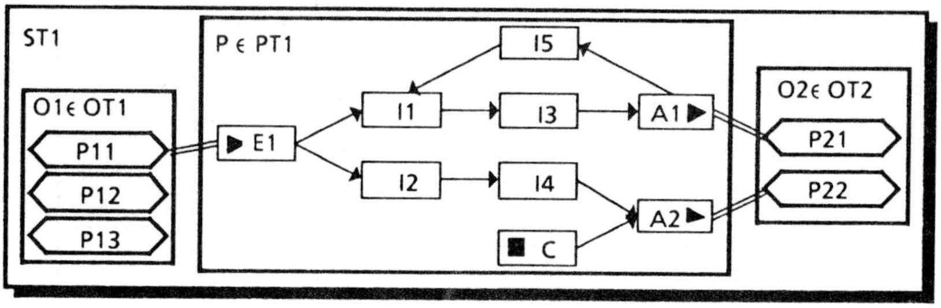


Fig. 6. The graphical representation of a system type.

*O*2, which is indicated by double line connections.
A correct system type must satisfy some constraints:

Each exogenous property is identified with one and only one property of an object or an endogenous property of another process.

Each endogenous property is identified with one and only one object property or an exogenous process property.

From a theoretical point of view the introduction of objects is not necessary. Every theory created by the use of process types and objects can be expressed through a single (concrete) process type. Though both methods provided by CAUSA are equivalent in a formal sense, they are not equal under the aspect of a tool for modeling complex systems. The choice of using either the one or the other is left to the designer (who is aware of the problem) when modeling, and according to individual preference.

## 3. SIMULATION

Simulation is conceived as the computation of a sequence of *states* in which the system can be. A state is a total mapping from the set of the system properties into their respective domains. Thus the value of a property $p$ in the state $s$ should be written as $s(p)$. In what follows it is denoted by an extension of the function VAL as VAL$(ps)$.

### 3.1. Backdrops, Background and Simulation Modes

We assume that the dynamic behavior of a system can be characterized by the values of some of the system properties, usually a small number of them. Such properties, guiding the simulation or observation, are called *backdrops*.[5] Typical backdrops are time and space. All specified backdrops together form the *background* on which a system is inspected.

The simulation environment of CAUSA provides three simulation modes: discrete simulation, event-based simulation and mixed simulation modes. In the case of a *discrete simulation* the background guides the simulation in the following way: For each backdrop a set of values must be given by enumeration or by a function which computes the actual value of the backdrop starting from an initial value. We will refer to both as the *value sequence* to which the functions SUCC and PRED are applicable. In the case of a single backdrop $B$ the value sequence is either enumerated like

$$\text{VALUE-SEQUENCE}(B) = (0, 1, 2, 3, 4, 5, 6, 7, 8, 9, 10)$$

or defined through a function together with an initial value and a termination condition:

$$\text{VALUE-SEQUENCE}(B) = (i = 0, i + 1, i > 10) .$$

The values define points in the $n$-dimensional space of the $n$ backdrops. For each of these points—denoting states of the system—the values of the remaining properties are computed, completing the description of the state. Figure 7 illustrates the discrete simulation.

The background of an *event-based simulation* is restricted to a single backdrop $B$; this backdrop is initiated with a start value. The value sequence of $B$ is dynamically generated during the simulation process by using laws of the form

**LAW** $P(p1, p2, \ldots, pn, B)$ **THEN** OBSERVE $B$ AT $f(B)$ ,

where the consequence inserts an evaluated backdrop value $f(B)$ in the ordered value sequence of $B$. Only if $f(B) > B$, where $B$ is the actual backdrop value, will the system be simulated for the backdrop value $f(B)$. The *mixed simulation mode* has a single backdrop with a specified (non-empty) value sequence, and during the simulation additional backdrop values are generated by the OBSERVE operator.

Any refinement of the value sequence of one backdrop yields additional states. Thus the simulation can be performed on different stages of *granularity* just by refining or coarsening the value sequences of any backdrops. Visually spoken refinement means to look at the simulation through a magnifier.

A simple simulation algorithm for $n$ backdrops ($n \geqslant 1$) follows. Let STARTPOINT-($Bi$) denote the first value of an explicit enumeration or the initial value of backdrop $Bi$, and $bi$ the actual value of $Bi$ in any state.

SIMULATION
$B1$: = STARTPOINT($B1$);
. . .
$Bn$: = STARTPOINT($Bn$);
**while** $b1 \neq$ UNDEFINED **and** . . . **and** $bn \neq$ UNDEFINED
**do** evaluate process;
  $B1$: = SUCC($b1$)
  . . . .

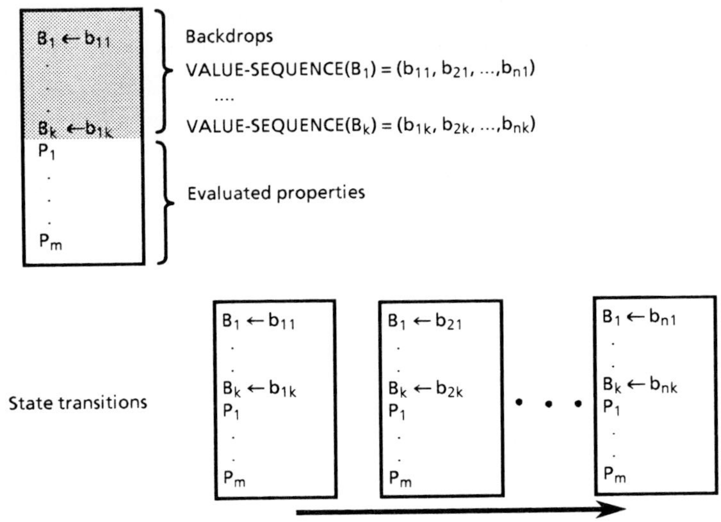


Fig. 7. Illustration of the discrete simulation.

$Bn := \mathrm{SUCC}(bn)$
**endwhile**.

It is convenient to take values of backdrops as *state names*, e.g. as arguments in the function VAL. For example, the expression $\mathrm{VAL}(E(b_1, \ldots, b_n))$ denotes the value of the property $E$ in the state in which the values of the backdrops are equal to $(b_1, \ldots, b_n)$.

3.2. Data Sets

CAUSA provides a facility which allows for a compact recapitulation of a performed simulation. In each state of the simulation the values of some preselected properties are recorded and form a so-called *data set*. A data set is like a protocol generated during a simulation and can be displayed as a table. Its first column contains names of properties and each following column stands for a state occurring in the simulation. The backdrops of a data set are entered in the top rows of the table. If all backdrops are ordered, then the data set is an *ordered data set* (relative to these backdrops).

Table 1 shows data sets in which $B$ is a backdrop and $E1$, $E2$, and $E3$ are selected properties. For example, the third column in this table must be read as "*if B equals 2 then E1 obtains the value 130, E2 the value 50, and E3 the value 24*".

CAUSA is able to derive more information concerning the dynamic aspects from ordered data sets. One piece of derivable information is the value difference of a property between two adjacent states (remember that the values of backdrops are names of states). If there is only one backdrop $B$ we define the differences of the value of a property $E$ between adjacent states $b$ and $\mathrm{PRED}(b)$ (denoted by $\mathrm{PRED}(b) \rightarrow b$) as

Table 1. Example of a simple data set.

| *B* | 1 | 2 | 3 | 4 | 5 |
|---|---|---|---|---|---|
| *E*1 | 140 | 130 | 60 | 90 | 110 |
| *E*2 | 65 | 50 | 20 | 30 | 35 |
| *E*3 | 17 | 24 | 36 | 12 | 6 |

$$\text{DIFF}(E\ \text{PRED}(b) \to b) := \text{VAL}(E\ b) - \text{VAL}(E\ \text{PRED}(b))$$

for every $b$ in VAL-SEQUENCE($B$) where PRED($b$) $\neq$ UNDEFINED. Another piece of derivable information is the change of a property value relative to the change of a specific backdrop $B$. It is defined by the difference quotient for every $b$ in VAL-SEQUENCE($B$):

$$\text{DIFF}Q(E\ \text{PRED}(b) \to b) := (\text{VAL}(E\ b) - \text{VAL}(E\ \text{PRED}(b)))/(b - \text{PRED}(b))$$

where PRED($b$) $\neq$ UNDEFINED. The result is like Table 2.

Data sets can also be displayed as two-dimensional maps where the unique domain is an observation-guiding backdrop and the ranges are the values of the preselected observed properties.

### 3.3. Evaluation Strategies

Evaluation of a process property $p$ means applying a structural law (which is an element of the structural law set of $p$), and this is simply an assignment of a value. For the whole set of properties contained in a process, CAUSA provides two basic *evaluation strategies: Propagate Strategy* and *Equilibrium Strategy*. One of these strategies must be attached to each process. Such an attachment to a process type $P$ is expressed in sentences like

$$\text{EVAL-STRATEGY}(P) = \text{PROPAGATE-STRATEGY}$$

or

$$\text{EVAL-STRATEGY}(P) = \text{EQUILIBRIUM-STRATEGY}$$

An evaluation of a process type or process instance can only be performed if all exogenous properties and all process constants are initialized.

#### 3.3.1. The propagate strategy

This strategy evaluates the process properties in a simple forward propagation of property values. Based on the precondition that all exogenous properties and process constants are evaluated (simply by an initialization) the strategy selects a property for

Table 2. Quantitative data about system changes.

| $B$ | $1 \rightarrow 2$ | $2 \rightarrow 3$ | $3 \rightarrow 4$ | $4 \rightarrow 5$ |
|---|---|---|---|---|
| DIFFQ($E1$, $B$) | −10 | −70 | 30 | 20 |
| DIFFQ($E2$, $B$) | −15 | −30 | 10 | 5 |
| DIFFQ($E3$, $B$) | 7 | 12 | −24 | −6 |

evaluation randomly if all of its influencing properties have been evaluated. At first sight this strategy is applicable only when the causal structure includes no feedback loops. But the propagation strategy allows the stepwise inspection of feedback structures if the structural laws are formulated in an appropriate way.

EVAL-PROPAGATE-STRATEGY(PROC);
EVALUATED: = the set of all process constants and backdrops;
NOT-EVALUATED: = PROCESS-VARIABLES(PROC) − EVALUATED;
**while** NOT-EVALUATED $\neq \emptyset$
  select a property $p \in$ NOT-EVALUATED with
  $\forall x \in$ INFLUENCE-SET($p$): $x \in$ EVALUATED;
  EVALUATE($p$);
  remove $p$ from NOT-EVALUATED;
  insert $p$ into EVALUATED.

3.3.2. The equilibrium strategy

Dealing with feedback loops requires a more sophisticated evaluation strategy. In opposition to the propagate strategy, which assures that every property is evaluated only once, the equilibrium strategy proceeds until no change in any value of the involved properties occurs. A more detailed description of the strategy follows:

EVAL-EQUILIBRIUM-STRATEGY(PROC);
EVAL-SET: = PROCESS-VARIABLES(PROC);
remove all initialized properties from the set EVAL-SET;
**while** EVAL-SET $\neq \emptyset$
**if** there is a $p1$ from EVAL-SET satisfying
  $\forall x \in$ INFLUENCE-SET($p1$): $x \notin$ EVAL-SET
**then** EVAL-PROP: = $p1$
**elseif** there is a $p2$ with an applicable law containing the term UNDEFINED
**then** EVAL-PROP: = $p2$
**else** abort the evaluation;
    remove EVAL-PROP from EVAL-SET;
    EVALUATE(EVAL-PROP);
**if** the evaluation assigns a value different from the previous one
  **then** EVAL-SET: = EVAL-SET $\cup$ $\{x$: INFLUENCE(EVAL-PROP $x)\}$.

The designer working in the CAUSA environment can write his or her own evaluation strategies if the predefined strategies are not appropriate for his or her task.

### 3.4. An Example

A simple scenario to model is the flow of water at a constant rate into a vessel with known dimensions, as depicted in Fig. 8.

The process flow is defined by the following statements:

PROCESSTYPE (INFLOW)
EXOGENOUS-VARIABLE (*R* INFLOW)
EXOGENOUS-VARIABLE (*T* INFLOW)
INTERNAL-VARIABLE (*M* INFLOW)
ENDOGENOUS-VARIABLE (*F* INFLOW)
CONSTANT (*A* INFLOW)
DOM(*A*.INFLOW) = REAL[0, ∞]
DOM(*M*.INFLOW) = REAL[0, ∞]
DOM(*F*.INFLOW) = REAL[0, ∞]
DOM(*R*.INFLOW) = REAL[0, ∞]
INFLUENCES (*A*.INFLOW *F*.INFLOW)
INFLUENCES(*M*.INFLOW *F*.INFLOW)
INFLUENCES(*R*.INFLOW *M*.INFLOW)
INFLUENCES (*T*.INFLOW *M*.INFLOW)
LAW-SET(*F*.INFLOW) = {LAW TRUE THEN $F := M/A$}
LAW-SET(*M*.INFLOW) = {LAW TRUE THEN $M := M + R * \text{DIFF}(T)$}
EVAL-STRATEGY(INFLOW) = PROPAGATE-STRATEGY.

We select *T* as a backdrop with

$$\text{VALUE-SEQUENCE}(T) = (0, 1, 2, 3, 4, 5)$$

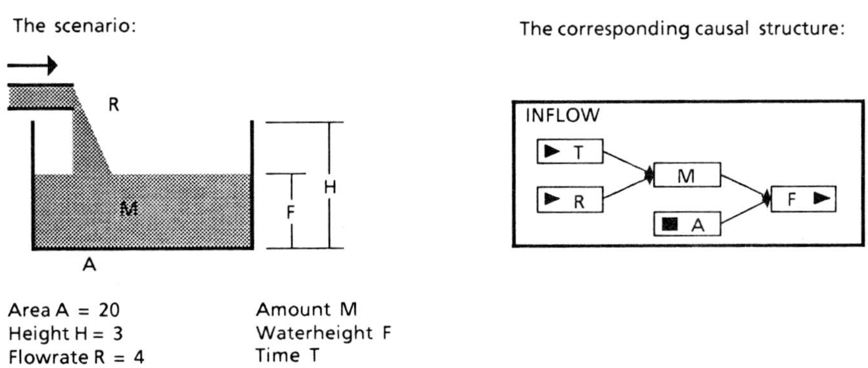


Fig. 8. A modeling example.

and make the following initializations:

$$A:=20$$
$$H:=3$$
$$R:=4.$$

The height of water in the vessel is a function of the flow rate, the area of the vessel, and time. A simulation would generate the ordered data set of Table 3.

If we change the height of the vessel to 0.9 and start the simulation as described above, we obtain again the same data set, but now the last column in the table refers to an impossible state—the height of the water in the vessel exceeds the height of the vessel. To handle this case we must introduce a special operator ABORT to stop a simulation run. We introduce a new constant $H$, which influences the property $F$, and add a new law to the lawset of $F$:

$$\textbf{LAW } F > H \textbf{ THEN } \text{ABORT}.$$

This law avoids the generation of invalid states. The assignment $F:=1.0$ during the simulation causes the activation of that constraint and aborts the simulation. Under the assumption that the flowrate $R$ is a constant or null we can avoid such impossible states by replacing the single law of property $M$ with the following laws; the first law generates the point of time at which the vessel is full and the third law informs the user via the operator NOTIFY that an overflow is occurring:

$$\textbf{LAW } M = 0 \wedge R > 0 \textbf{ THEN } M := M + R * \text{DIFF}(T); \quad \text{OBSERVE } T \text{ AT } T + A * H/R$$

$$\textbf{LAW } M <> 0 \wedge R > 0 \textbf{ THEN } M := M + R * \text{DIFF}(T)$$

$$\textbf{LAW } M = A * H \wedge R > 0 \textbf{ THEN } \text{NOTIFY(‘overflow of vessel’)}.$$

## 4. INTERPRETATIONS

The values of properties are normally interpreted in a given problem context, and sometimes a qualitative description of the behavior is sufficient. An *interpretation* of a property $p$ is a total mapping from the domain of the property into a set of qualitative values QDOM($p$). More generally an interpretation INT is a mapping from a set of quantitative values into a set of qualitative values (symbols):

$$\text{INT}(p): \text{DOM}(p) \rightarrow \text{QDOM}(p).$$

It is possible in CAUSA to associate two interpretations QVAL and QDIFF with every property. One interprets the value of the property, and the other the changes of value. As an example we take the usual qualitative interpretation of the variation of a

Table 3. The data set obtained by simulation.

| $T$ | 0 | 1 | 2 | 3 | 4 | 5 |
|---|---|---|---|---|---|---|
| $M$ | 0 | 4 | 8 | 12 | 16 | 20 |
| $F$ | 0 | 0.2 | 0.4 | 0.6 | 0.8 | 1.0 |

quantitative property $p$, e.g. the mapping from the first derivation into the set of qualitative values INC, DEC, and STEADY. An increasing value of $p$ corresponds to the qualitative value INC, a decreasing value to DEC and a non-changing value to STEADY. The corresponding interpretation for a property $p$ is expressible through a set of *interpretation laws*:

$$\text{INTERPRETATION-LAWS}(p) = \{\textbf{LAW}\ \text{diff}(p) = 0\ \textbf{THEN}\ \text{qdiff:} = \text{steady}, \quad \textbf{LAW}\ \text{diff}(p) < 0\ \textbf{THEN}\ \text{qdiff:} = \text{dec}, \quad \textbf{LAW}\ \text{diff}(p) > 0\ \textbf{THEN}\ \text{qdiff:} = \text{inc}\}.$$

The application of this interpretation to every property in the data set shown in Table 2 would yield a data set like the one shown in Table 4. Note that the transitions of the backdrop $B$ from 1 to 2 and from 2 to 3 are qualitatively equal and collapsed into one transition (indicated by two arrows).

The qualitative interpretation extracts the meaning imposed on the values and changes the properties under consideration. The obtained qualitative description often seems to be more adequate in a cognitive sense, because such a description is easier to understand than the quantitative one.

Theories about pure qualitative modeling have been developed by DeKleer[2] and Forbus.[6] Each of these theories contains a calculus tailored for qualitative values. But a lot of problems arise in this field and therefore we propose another way: whenever we are forced to calculate we go back to the quantitative model and interpret the obtained result qualitatively.

## 5. THE ARCHITECTURE OF CAUSA

CAUSA provides two interfaces for communication. The *specification language interface* allows for the modeling by using single statements as shown in the above

Table 4. Qualitative data about system changes.

| $B$ | $1 \rightarrow\rightarrow 3$ | $3 \rightarrow 4$ | $4 \rightarrow 5$ |
|---|---|---|---|
| DERIV(DIFFQ($E1$, $B$)) | dec | inc | inc |
| DERIV(DIFFQ($E2$, $B$)) | dec | inc | inc |
| DERIV(DIFFQ($E3$, $B$)) | inc | dec | dec |

examples. The *graphic menu-driven interface* provides a comfortable way to interact with CAUSA. This interface consists of three editors for the creation and modification of either object types, process types, or system types. The fourth part is the simulation environment in which the created processes and systems can be inspected through simulation (cf. Fig. 9).

## 6. CONCLUSIONS

This paper presents an overview of the knowledge acquisition tool CAUSA and relates it to the current work in the field of qualitative reasoning. CAUSA was used during the analysis task of a hot-rolling mill to evaluate the possible increase of productivity and the requirements of a knowledge-based control system for evaluation of modeling concepts. During the analysis a complex model of the manufacture including furnaces, roughing train, finish train, cooling system and other system parts was created.

With CAUSA, a broad class of dynamic systems can be modeled more adequately and more precisely in comparison to pure qualitative modeling, but on the other hand, CAUSA lacks expressive power which the QR-tools provide. Our future research will be concentrated on an integration of the qualitative and the quantitative concepts to get the best of both worlds.

## ACKNOWLEDGEMENT

The work has been supported by the BMFT (Ministry of Research and Technology of the Federal Republic of Germany) as part of the project TEX-B (Technical EXpertsystemsBasis).

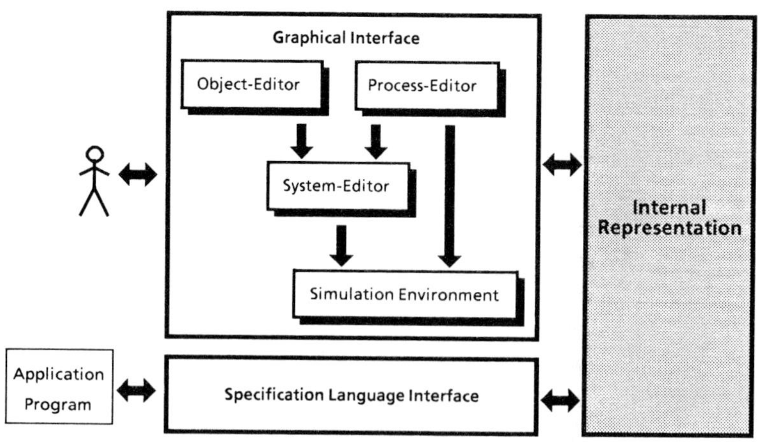


Fig. 9. The architecture of CAUSA.

REFERENCES

1. L. von Bertalanffy, *General System Theory*, George Braziller, 1968.
2. J. DeKleer and J. S. Brown, "A qualitative physics based on confluences", *Artif. Intell.* **24** (1984) 7–83.
3. A. Janson-Fleischmann and G. Sutschet, "CAPAS: A process oriented approach for qualitative analysis and simulation of dynamical systems", in *Technische Expertensysteme: Wissensrepräsentation und Schlußfolgerungsverfahren*, Eds. H. W. Früchtenicht *et al.*, Oldenbourg Verlag, 1988, pp. 227–247.
4. Y. Iwasaki and H. A. Simon, "Causality in device behavior", *Artif. Intell.* **29** (1986) 3–32.
5. G. J. Klir, *Architecture Of Systems Problem Solving*, Plenum Press, 1985.
6. K. D. Forbus, "Qualitative process theory", *Artif. Intell.* **24** (1984) 85–168.

**Werner Dilger** received the M.Sc. and the Ph.D. both in computer science from the University of Karlsruhe in 1974 and the University of Kaiserslautern in 1982, respectively. He has held research positions at the University of Konstanz, the Institute for German Language in Mannheim, the University of Kaiserslautern, and the Fraunhofer Institute for Information and Data Processing in Karlsruhe. Since 1985 he has been a lecturer in Computer Science at the University of Kaiserslautern, and since 1986 he has been heading the research group for knowledge processing at the Fraunhofer Institute for Information and Data Processing. He is now a Professor of Computer Science at the European Business School in Schloss Reichartshausen, Rheingau.

**Jürgen Möller** received his Master's degree in computer science from the University of Darmstadt, Germany, in 1985. Subsequently, he joined the KI research group of Triumph-Adler in Nuernberg, Germany. Since 1986 he has been a member of the expert systems research group at the Fraunhofer Institute for Information and Data Processing in Karlsruhe.

His research interests include modeling-paradigmata, knowledge-based simulation, and the domain of knowledge and software engineering.

REFERENCES

1. [illegible]

2. [illegible]

3. [illegible]

# PRIOPS: A REAL-TIME PRODUCTION SYSTEM ARCHITECTURE FOR PROGRAMMING AND LEARNING IN EMBEDDED SYSTEMS

DALE E. PARSON and GLENN D. BLANK

*Lehigh University*

*Department of Computer Science and Electrical Engineering*

*Bethlehem, Pennsylvania 18015, USA*

Received 1 April 1990

The Prioritized Production System (PRIOPS) is an architecture that supports time-constrained, knowledge-based embedded system programming and learning. Inspired by the theory of automatic and controlled human information processing in cognitive psychology, PRIOPS supports a two-tiered processing approach. The automatic partition provides for compilation of productions into constant-time-constrained processes for reaction to environmental conditions. The notion of a habit in humans approximates the concept of automatic processing trading flexibility and generality for efficiency and predictability in dealing with expected environmental situations. Explicit priorities allow critical automatic activities to pre-empt and defer execution of lower priority processing. An augmented version of the Rete match algorithm implements $O(1)$, priority-scheduled automatic matching. The controlled partition supports more complex, less predictable activities such as problem solving, planning, and learning that apply in novel situations for which automatic reactions do not exist. The PRIOPS notation allows the programmer of knowledge-based embedded systems to work at a more appropriate level of abstraction than is provided by conventional embedded system programming techniques. This paper explores programming and learning in PRIOPS in the context of a maze traversal program.

*Keywords*: Real-time; Embedded system; Production system; Rete algorithm; Reactive processing; Chunking.

## 1. INTRODUCTION

Embedded computing systems do more than consume and produce symbolic text and graphics for direct human interaction. These systems deal with physical phenomena such as visual images, sound, motion, pressure, and temperature. Measurements enter the computing systems through transducers and sensors. These systems use effectors and generators, such as robotic arms and lasers, to produce changes in the sensed phenomena. While symbolic information may appear at the input and output ports of these systems, it usually does so alongside more critical signals and actions that constitute direct interactions with external environments.

A typical embedded computing system must react to important environmental conditions in predictable time. The system must recognize an important external situation in limited time, and then respond in limited time. The higher priority work of an embedded system—reading critical sensors, generating effector control signals, sounding alarms—exhibits this stimulus-response organization. Lower priority activities, such as accounting and routine report generation, execute in the background during lulls in environmental interaction. These processes do not have strict time requirements.

Interrupt-driven event interpretation and reaction have traditionally used assembly language programming. Subsequent work applied the improved constructs of procedural[1] and object-oriented[2] languages to the problems of time-constrained programming. Recently work has begun on adapting the notations and architectures of knowledge-based systems for use in real-time embedded applications.[3]

The Prioritized Production System (PRIOPS) is an architecture that supports the programming and learning of event-driven, constant-time-constrained, pre-emptive stimulus-response processes. The PRIOPS notation is a derivative of OPS5.[4,5] In PRIOPS, pattern matching uses an augmented version of OPS5's Rete matcher to select productions for execution.[6,7] In earlier papers we reported on the PRIOPS architecture and matching algorithm,[8,9] relating key aspects of this two-tiered architecture to the concepts of *controlled* and *automatic* human information processing[10–12] in cognitive psychology. Here we use an example PRIOPS program to explore application of the architecture. The example, which searches a maze for its exit while avoiding dangerous obstacles, presents a method for learning PRIOPS' real-time processes.

## 2. EMBEDDED REAL-TIME COMPUTING

The expression *embedded computing system* identifies a computer that is part of an encompassing piece of machinery or a larger physical system. Popular definitions of an embedded system do not address questions of time or space locality, so for precision we enumerate the properties of an embedded system:

(1) The processing system is embedded in a discrete, functioning physical system.
(2) The discrete, functioning system is embedded in an environment.
(3) Sensors describe the environment to the processing system.
(4) Effectors convey the processing system's reactions to the environment.
(5) The intersection of the current environmental state and the current processing state is non-empty.
(6) Physical localization of the system is important. A restriction on distribution of the embedded system in space and time, the *body concept*, is characterized by the remaining constraints.
(7) Intra-system communication speeds for multiple-processor systems are of the same magnitude as processor speeds. The presence of multiple processors does not necessitate internal communication queuing delays.
(8) A single system clock/time is accurate for all processors within acceptable error. An embedded system does not require the notion of relativistic, partially ordered time found in distributed systems.[13]

(9) The system's physical boundary describes an abstract interface to the environment. The interface is abstract because the sensors do not (normally) exhaustively describe conditions at the boundary. Sensors supply partial information.

*Real-time processing* in PRIOPS is equivalent to *constant-time-constrained* or $O(1)$ processing. The production compiler can determine the worst-case execution time for real-time processes.

## 3. THE TWO-TIERED PRIOPS ARCHITECTURE

A PRIOPS programmer partitions the program problem space in two. Problems amenable to solution using recognition and reaction processes with $O(1)$ time and space requirements go in the *automatic partition* (AP). All other problems go in the *controlled partition* (CP).

The concepts of automatic and controlled human information processing in cognitive psychology inspired the PRIOPS architecture.[10–12] Automatic productions are like habits. Habits are akin to reflexes or instincts, except that they are learned, through practice. They develop in response to repetitive, consistent patterns of interaction with one's environment. Habits trade flexibility for predictability and efficiency. Habits trigger in response to familiar conditions, and produce effective responses to conditions while placing minimal load on the resources of attention and short-term memory. An automatic process may execute without the conscious awareness of the person, and is difficult to avoid or pre-empt. Human controlled processing, in contrast, is thought- and memory-intensive. Controlled processing is appropriate for novel situations requiring complicated activities such as planning and learning. This processing is far more complex, and therefore less efficient and predictable, than automatic processing. The goal-directed, computation-bound processing typical of artificial intelligence architectures corresponds to controlled processing.

### 3.1. Data Flow in the Automatic Partition

Figure 1 illustrates data flow in the PRIOPS architecture. Sensors provide information about the environment to the system. The system manipulates the environment through its effectors. *Reactive processing* stimulus-response production chains guarantee real-time responses to external triggers. Reactive productions lie wholly within the AP. Reaction processing flows from sensors through automatic detection to generated actions. There are no unbounded loops in purely automatic data flow, since a loop implies time indeterminacy. The only feedback loop in the AP is an inherent one, mediated by the external world. It goes from the effectors through the environment to the sensors. (Internal feedback loops are possible in the CP.)

The AP handles time-critical input-output, recognition, and reaction. Being composed primarily of PRIOPS productions, it is in effect a symbol-based interrupt handler and device driver. A small amount of procedural code in a language such as C or Modula-2 may appear for portions of the automatic problem space readily handled by such code. Simple *decoding* activities extract some important environmental

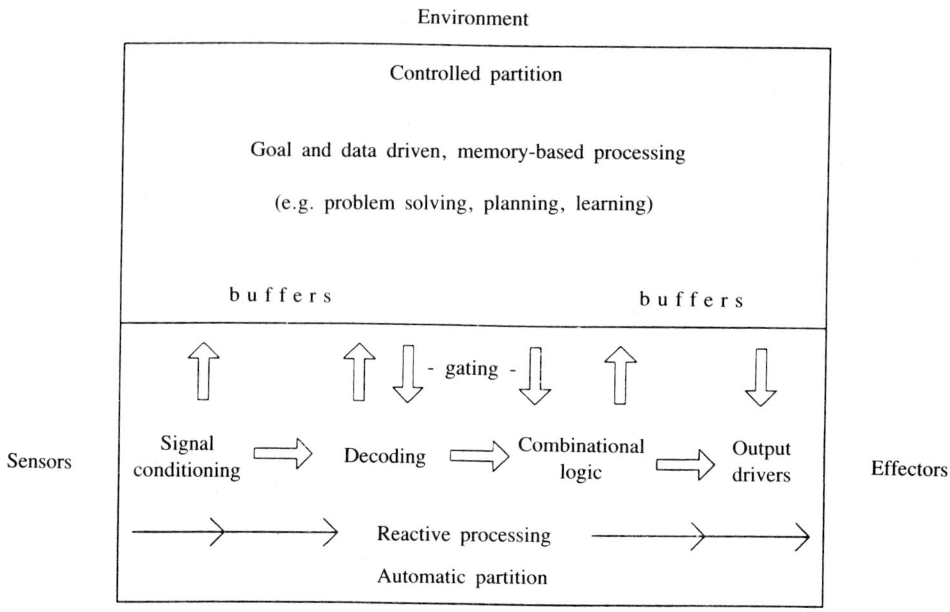


Fig. 1. The two-tiered, controlled-automatic architecture.

information from an individual sensor's data messages. Combining sensed data through *sensor fusion* is necessary for more complex phenomena.

Production systems spend most of their time matching data to conditions (rule left-hand-sides).[7] PRIOPS' augmented Rete matcher assures that automatic match time is constant. Automatic conflict resolution and right-hand side actions also run in constant time.

Automatic productions show *constant-bound space complexity* as well. Variable length data buffering is a means for lowering responsiveness requirements by storing incoming information until the system has time to attend. PRIOPS assumes a constant-bound responsiveness requirement on each reaction to incoming information, measured from the instant that a stimulus arrives until the instant that a response proceeds. Reactive processing must satisfy *instantaneous real-time* requirements. There is no degradation of responsiveness through arbitrary-length buffering in the AP. Furthermore, incoming information on a sensory channel supersedes any earlier information from that channel. Variable-length buffering of sensory data is again inappropriate, since the AP reacts to the immediate environmental situation.

### 3.2. The Controlled-Automatic Interface

The automatic productions of Fig. 1 trigger not only from sensory input, but also from enabling information advanced from the CP. Where short-term memory of stimuli and strategy information is necessary, the CP performs buffering. The controlled portion of such processing does not guarantee $O(1)$ responsiveness.

Buffering at the automatic-controlled interface delays lower-priority controlled computation without losing information. PRIOPS places a constant bound on the length of these buffers, and allocates their space during controlled processing intervals. Automatic processing does not perform memory management, since the complexity of memory management is normally greater than $O(1)$. Control processes draining the buffers cannot react to a particular buffered datum within a constant time limit, but these processes must drain the buffers at a rate that will keep buffer space from becoming exhausted. Therefore control processes must drain the buffers at the same average rate at which automatic processes load them. Interface control processes must satisfy *average real-time* requirements.

### 3.3. Explicit Production Priorities

We have not yet addressed the issue of sharing central processor time among enabled constant-time processes in the AP. (The current PRIOPS implementation is for a uniprocessor machine, although work on multiprocessor production systems[14,15] might be adaptable to the needs of PRIOPS.) If a ready process must wait for computing resources, then its worst-case response time is the sum of its inherent worst-case response time and the total worst-case time it has to wait for other processes to release resources that it needs. Given the difficulties in sharing a single processor among multiple, time-constrained tasks, *explicit pre-emptive priorities* determine the order in which automatic PRIOPS productions get the processor. Priority levels vary from 1 to 127 for automatic productions, and from 0 to $-128$ for controlled productions. Critical tasks and automatic tasks with quick response requirements share the highest priority levels. Worst-case response time for a process of a given priority is the sum of the inherent process time plus the times for all other processes of equal or greater priority plus context switching time, over some encompassing time period in which all of these processes may run. Any time spent servicing hardware interrupts and direct memory access transfers counts as high priority processing. The danger of losing low priority responses is not a weakness in PRIOPS, but is rather a weakness of processor sharing. Priorities allow an embedded system designer to identify the processes that must be guaranteed processor availability. PRIOPS is not unique in applying pre-emptive scheduling priorities to a collection of time-constrained tasks. It *is* unique, however, in applying pre-emptive priorities to Rete matching steps.

### 3.4. Controlled Partition Activities

The CP performs the higher order tasks typical of artificial intelligence architectures. Like controlled processing in humans, the activities of this partition are complex and adaptable, dealing with unexpected or uncertain conditions. Search-based, goal- and data-driven inference can drive CP activities. Problem solving, planning, and learning occur in the controlled domain. Because controlled processing deals with the unknown, and because it requires use of memory and other resources to dynamically varying degrees, we cannot determine *a priori* constant time and space bounds for control processes. All long-term information storage resides in the CP.

In a planning or learning system, the CP will generate some of the automatic code. During planning, rough automatic reactions can be designed that are refined through practice. This paper gives one example of a means for generating automatic reactions from the results of controlled search activity.

## 4. THE MAZE DEMONSTRATION PROGRAM

In the spirit of Pavlov, we shall observe the behavior of a PRIOPS program in a simulated maze. Figure 2 shows an example maze as displayed on a PC monitor. Walls are shaded and tunnels unshaded; the EXIT appears near the upper right corner. Within the maze we shall place two mobile entities: the PRIOPS PROGRAM and the HUMAN (letters P and H in Fig. 2 denote the respective starting positions of these two entities). The PROGRAM wants *a priori* to locate and reach the EXIT. The HUMAN, under keyboard control, is dangerous to the PROGRAM. It will destroy the PROGRAM upon contact. So the PROGRAM instinctively avoids the HUMAN.

Though a toy problem, the maze is rich enough to demonstrate several key ideas of PRIOPS:

- sensor monitoring—responding to obstacles in the maze;
- controlled behaviors—notably searching for the EXIT;
- automatic behaviors—such as fleeing from the HUMAN;
- garbage collection—at the automatic-controlled interface;
- learning—finding a successful path to the EXIT;
- improved behavior—once learning becomes automatic.

The maze, the keyboard-to-maze interface, and the simulated sensors are implemented in C. The PROGRAM itself is a set of PRIOPS productions. The PROGRAM receives sensory input upon beginning execution, upon movement of the PROGRAM, and upon movement of the HUMAN when this movement reaches the PROGRAM's sensors. This input comes from the C functions of the maze. A *sensors* record reports the identity and distance of the nearest obstacle to the '*left*', '*right*', '*up*' and '*down*'. Potential obstacles include a WALL, the HUMAN opponent, and the sought-after EXIT.

### 4.1. An Overview of Maze Processing

Figure 3 shows data flow for the PROGRAM during maze traversal. All automatic operations trigger on immediate sensory information. These productions act during an emergency to move the PROGRAM within constant-bound time, pre-empting lower priority tasks. Automatic maze productions come in three varieties:

(1) EXIT detectors. They become excited when a sensor detects the EXIT. They pre-empt all other productions and lunge out of the maze.
(2) HUMAN detectors. They are triggered when a sensor detects the HUMAN, and they then flee. The PROGRAM prefers to escape at right-angles to the HUMAN whenever possible.
(3) Learned productions that direct the PROGRAM down the path of escape.

Fig. 2. The maze.

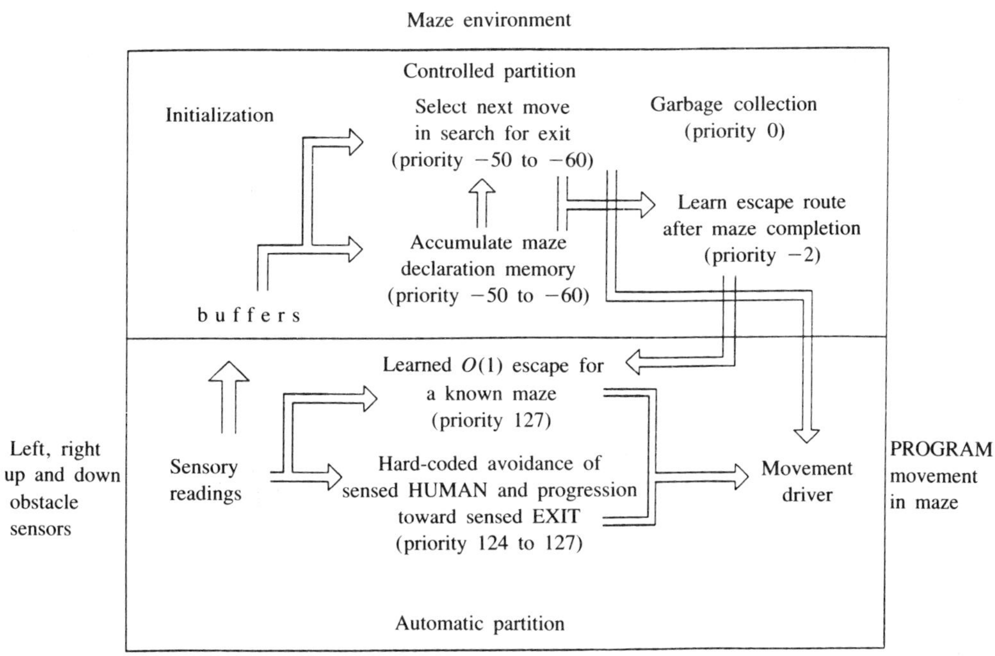


Fig. 3. PROGRAM data flow during maze traversal.

Controlled productions maintain memory of visited maze locations. PRIOPS does not use controlled priorities (0 to −128) for pre-emption, so in the absence of automatic activity, all controlled matching completes before controlled conflict resolution selects a controlled production instantiation to fire. Controlled maze productions come in five flavors:

(1) Initialization—setting up the maze and PROGRAM for execution.
(2) Heuristic search—selecting the next move in search of the EXIT.
(3) Record-keeping—accumulating declarative knowledge about the maze in working memory.
(4) Garbage collection—garbage can include outdated and redundant information in CP buffers.
(5) Learning.

The overall flow of the maze program as seen in Fig. 3 typifies the flow and interaction of automatic and controlled processing in PRIOPS. During the search phase of the problem, controlled productions guide the search and collect declarative information. Initial hand-coded automatic productions deal with time-critical situations by changing the immediate relationship of the embedded system to other entities in the environment. Garbage collection at the controlled-automatic interface performs resource reclamation without slowing automatic reactions. Learning takes the results of controlled search and builds them into reactive automatic productions. The following subsections will examine productions from each part of Fig. 3, from sensory readings and memory, to search behaviors in the CP, to instinctual behaviors in the AP, to garbage collection at the controlled-automatic interface, to learning in the CP, and finally to resulting learned behaviors in the AP. The final subsection discusses execution results for the maze of Fig. 2.

### 4.2. Sensing, Memory, and Search in the Controlled Partition

At the top of Listing 1 are three declarations for working memory element classes. Structures are similar to literals in OPS5. Unlike OPS5, though, PRIOPS is strongly typed. Fields of working memory elements may be of type *int*, *float*, *symbol*, or a *set of symbols*. Strong typing avoids run-time type testing and conversions, which are particularly important for automatic productions. A symbol is similar to a LISP symbol, and is loosely comparable to a string type in other languages. Each distinct symbol is stored uniquely and referenced via a unique pointer. Symbol comparisons, like integer and floating point comparisons, occur using basic machine operations. Consequently symbol tests are $O(1)$ operations and do not depend on symbol lengths. The CP alone acquires new symbols, but both partitions can use them.

The current *sensors* element registers objects in the maze (WALL, HUMAN or EXIT) and their location relative to the PROGRAM. Each *visited* element records how often the PROGRAM has visited its location. Maze search rules and learning rules examine visited memory. Finally, *inspect* elements direct the immediate search from the PROGRAM's current location.

```
(structure sensors          ; 4 pseudo-sensors of program
    symbol  left-sense      ; object-to-left: WALL or HUMAN or EXIT
    int     left-distance
    symbol  right-sense  int  right-distance
    symbol  up-sense     int  up-distance
    symbol  down-sense   int  down-distance
    int     x            int  y; current PROGRAM x,y location
)
(structure visited          ; remembered history of a location
    int x int y             ; location
    int visits              ; number of visits to here
)
(structure inspect          ; possible single move destination
    int x int y             ; location of proposed move
    symbol direction        ; direction from current sensor
)
(p newly-arrived −60
    (sensors ^x ⟨myx⟩ ^y ⟨myy⟩)
    − (visited ^x ⟨myx⟩ ^y ⟨myy⟩)
    →
    (make visited ^x ⟨myx⟩ ^y ⟨myy⟩ ^visits 0)
)
(p look-out −60
    (sensor ^x ⟨myx⟩ ^y ⟨myy⟩)
    {(visited ^x ⟨myx⟩ ^y ⟨myy⟩ ^visits ⟨seen⟩) ⟨books⟩}
    − (inspect)
    →
    (make sequence ^current eliminate-impossible); 1st step of search
    (bind ⟨newseen⟩ (compute ⟨seen⟩ + 1))
    (modify ⟨books⟩ ^visits ⟨newseen⟩); update memory of loc. myx,myy
    (bind ⟨left⟩ (compute ⟨myx⟩ − 1))
    (bind ⟨right⟩ (compute ⟨myx⟩ + 1))
    (bind ⟨up⟩ (compute ⟨myy⟩ − 1))
    (bind ⟨down⟩ (compute ⟨myy⟩ + 1))
    (make inspect ^x ⟨left⟩ ^y ⟨myy⟩ ^direction left); init. the search
    (make inspect ^x ⟨myx⟩ ^y ⟨up⟩ ^direction up)
    (make inspect ^x ⟨right⟩ ^y ⟨myy⟩ ^direction right)
    (make inspect ^x ⟨myx⟩ ^y ⟨down⟩ ^direction down)
)
```

Listing 1. Declarations and controled productions for a new maze location.

The rest of Listing 1 shows two controlled productions that help determine the PROGRAM's next move. They use both immediate sensory information (giving the current location of the PROGRAM) and accumulated memories. They trigger additional productions (not shown), implementing a heuristic strategy. First the PROGRAM rules out such undesirable moves as bumping into WALLS, heading down known dead ends, or reversing its walk. Then it prefers less visited locations and more distant walls. Finally it makes an arbitrary pick from remaining possible moves. Priority values in the controlled range order these heuristics sequentially.

Production '*newly-arrived*' initializes a visited record. Its left-hand side determines that there is no visited record for the current location of the sensors, so its right-hand side action creates a visited record with a '*visits*' count of zero.

Production '*look-out*' triggers when a new sensors element is made at some visited location. Each line of tests on the left-hand side ,of 'look-out' is called a *condition element*. PRIOPS compiles condition elements for use by the Rete pattern matcher. When the matcher finds a visited element for the current sensors location, and finds that there are *no* inspect records (the third condition element is *negated*, signifying a successful match only in the *absence* of any memory elements matching this condition element), the matcher adds an executable instance of this production to the *conflict set*. (Existing inspect records would be left over from search preceding the most recent move; 'look-out' must not trigger until garbage collection productions remove these inspect directives, hence the negated condition element.) Explicit priority and other criteria such as recency and specificity of matched memory elements identify a triggered production to execute. (Readers should consult Ref. 4 for more information on the OPS-based production inference cycle and conflict resolution strategies.) The right-hand side of 'look-out' first makes a *sequence* element (declaration not shown) to serialize the upcoming search. The next two actions compute and store an incremented visits count. The *bind* operations compute locations for the four adjoining spaces, and the *make* operations assert inspect elements. These elements direct upcoming search productions to inspect the adjoining spaces. The sequence element advances from value '*eliminate-impossible*' of Fig. 1 through values '*eliminate-deadends*', '*eliminate-loops*', '*eliminate-visited*', '*eliminate-old*', '*prefer-long*', and '*ready-move*', firing productions that eliminate inspect proposals as it goes along. Sequencing productions modify the sequence element as it completes its work at each stage. When only equally preferable inspect directives remain, an arbitrary one triggers controlled movement. After movement, controlled garbage collection productions remove the outdated sequence and remaining inspect records. The cycle beginning at 'newly-arrived' and 'look-out' of Fig. 1 then runs again.

The majority of production processing time is spent matching memory elements to left-hand side tests. Condition element tests come in two varieties. The first, *intra-condition element tests*, perform simple comparisons of memory element fields to constant values, and simple comparisons of element fields to other fields within the same working memory element. $O(1)$ tests include *equality*, *inequality*, and basic *numerical order comparisons*. Controlled productions can use additional $O(n)$ tests such as *variable-length string order comparisons*. With all of the former tests being constant-time-bounded, and with a compile-time constant specification of the number of tested fields (the program source), all automatic intra-condition element test sequences are constant-time-bounded. Please consult our earlier papers for illustrations of the details of this matching process.[8,9]

However, the tests of 'newly-arrived' and 'look-out' contain no intra-condition element tests. Instead, they are *inter-condition element tests*, representing *joins* of two or more working memory elements. The Rete algorithm performs the intra-condition element tests for a working memory element before attempting to join it to other elements matched by other condition elements. In the case of 'look-out', no intra-condition constraints appear for sensors, visited, or inspect elements. The result is that the matcher will perform the join tests, comparing the ^*x* and ^*y* location fields, for each possible sensors–visited pair. In this program there is normally only one sensors element, but as a sensors element is made or updated, the join tests of 'look-out' (and all controlled productions that join sensors and visited elements) are applied between the sensors element and *all* visited elements in working memory. After some maze exploration there will be many visited elements subject to these tests. The absence of any compile-time limit to the number of memory elements tested by a join through the abutment of two condition elements is the fundamental source of time indeterminacy in Rete matching.[16]

## 4.3. Reactive Movement in the Automatic Partition

Automation partition matching trades expressive power for run-time efficiency and reduced computational complexity.[17] By compiler fiat, at most one working memory element can match an automatic condition element. Each successfully matched working memory element discards any prior match. In Rete terms, each condition element in an automatic production contributes at most one memory element to a join. Such a join reduces to a constant-length sequence of simple $O(1)$ tests. Prohibiting memory growth eliminates the time indeterminacy of variable-sized joins.

Listing 2 shows three automatic productions from the maze program. The first, '*panic-left-up*' detects a human to the left. It also determines that there is an avenue up from its current location that is further from a wall than the competing down avenue. Once fired, 'panic-left-up', removes the sensors element so that no other production can react to it. It then makes a *move* element for upward movement, which in turn triggers the second production '*automove*'.

With only one condition element, 'panic-left-up' matching consumes no join time. All tests are intra-element tests. Note that the tests of this production are extremely specialized. Most automatic productions have specialized intra-element tests because these tests must safeguard desired matches from being overwritten. Remember that a new match eliminates any previous match to a condition element. By the time matching gets to inter-element join tests, the contributing memory elements are unique. The intra-element tests select each condition element's unique memory element for join matching.

Leading intra-element test sequences common to more than one condition element execute only once for a single working memory element. Only when intra-condition element test sequences diverge are distinct match tests compiled. The result is that automatic intra-condition element tests are compiled into a decision tree, with a single place register at each leaf storing a reference to the matching working memory element. For instance, 'panic-left-up' and the third production of Listing 2, '*panic-left-right*', share the initial test '*sensors ^left-sense human*'. When the HUMAN appears to the PROGRAM's left sensors, this test executes only once, with the testing of the two

```
(p panic-left-up 125; prefer right angle turns from human
    {(sensors ^left-sense human
        ^up-distance {⟨escape⟩ > 1} ^down-distance ≤ ⟨escape⟩)
      ⟨sense⟩}
    →
    (remove ⟨sense⟩)
    (make move ^direction up ^urgency 125)
)
(p automove 127
    {(move ^urgency > 0 ^direction {⟨way⟩ ⟨⟩ nil}) ⟨moving⟩}
    }(lastmove) ⟨former⟩}
    →
    (modify ⟨moving⟩ ^direction nil ^urgency 0)
    (modify ⟨former⟩ ^direction ⟨way⟩)
    ; each ''call move'' generates a new ''sensors'' element
    (call move ⟨way⟩)
)
(p panic-left-right 124
    {(sensors ^left-sense human ^right-distance > 1) ⟨sense⟩}
    →
    (remove ⟨sense⟩)
    (make move ^direction right ^urgency 125)
)
```

Listing 2. Three automatic productions for emergency reactions.

productions diverging after that point. Both productions may trigger, but when the first to execute removes the sensors element, the alternative production will no longer trigger.

Production 'automove' joins two working memory elements. There are no inter-condition element restrictions, so the most recent move request with an urgency $> 0$ combines with the most recent '*lastmove*' record to trigger the automatic move. 'Automove' nullifies the move element, updates 'lastmove', and calls the C language move driver. A controlled production with this left-hand side could match multiple move request/lastmove record joins. Since 'automove' is an automatic production, it can only match the most recent elements satisfying its tests. It responds to the immediate sensory and control information in constant time.

### 4.4. Garbage Collection at the Controlled-Automatic Interface

Controlled productions that search and learn can generate redundant and outdated working memory elements that constitute garbage. Also, automatic productions can generate sensory and movement messages that are buffered in the CP. Outdated messages in these buffers constitute garbage as well. The classical approach to garbage collection in LISP systems is to bring the system to a halt when storage capacity is exhausted, and recover all reclaimable memory during this halt interval.[18] Clearly such an approach is not suited to a reactive, time-constrained system. *Incremental garbage collectors* (sometimes called *real-time* collectors) avoid halting for storage reclamation by distributing reclamation activities in small, constant-time-bound pieces across all calls for storage allocation.[18–20] The problem with such systems is that they exact a small penalty from all processes, both those with and those without $O(1)$ execution requirements, for storage reclamation activities.

PRIOPS performs garbage collection by using mechanisms built into controlled matching and by using explicit controlled reclamation productions at the controlled-automatic interface—priority 0 productions. The PRIOPS reclamation strategy avoids penalizing automatic processing. A ready list of initialized working memory elements is available for automatic productions that send messages into controlled buffers. During automatic execution productions remove initialized elements from the ready list and add message elements to controlled buffers in $O(1)$ time. When automatic execution completes, the controlled matcher replenishes this ready list to prepare for the next burst of automatic activity. The explicit garbage collection productions recover buffered memory elements that, through testing of contents and time stamps, are found to be redundant or outdated. Replenishing the ready list places an average real-time requirement on controlled storage management, since the ready list must contain sufficient elements to satisfy the most demanding burst of automatic activity. The size of the ready list is coded directly into the PRIOPS program. Dynamic adjustment of ready list size is an area for future work.

Listing 3 shows an explicit garbage collection production. '*Collect-old-move*' recovers an older move element after a newer one is posted. Remember that an automatic production such as 'automove' from Listing 2 will trigger only on the most recently matched move element, so this garbage collection is necessary only for the CP. Standard OPS5 and controlled PRIOPS conflict resolution strategy results in an execution for 'collect-old-move' that binds the most recent move element to the first condition element, and the older move element to the ⟨older⟩ second condition element, which 'collect-old-move' removes from working memory. This collection occurs after all automatic use of working memory elements, including the most recent move, is done.

### 4.5. Learning and Learned Productions

Learning rules build automatic productions for escape in subsequent traversals of the current maze. Learning rules execute only when the PROGRAM exits from the maze. They examine visited records in working memory and write production definitions to a file for later compilation. Their priority allows garbage collection productions to work before commencing learning.

The maze program learns an escape route by using a primitive form of production *chunking*. Chunking uses knowledge acquired during a problem solving episode to build specialized productions that embody that knowledge, thereby avoiding comparable searches in the future. In the SOAR production system, chunking is an inherent component of the architecture.[21] SOAR uses both domain knowledge and generic weak search methods to search problem spaces, and automatically builds chunk productions that avoid repeated searches.[22,23] The PRIOPS maze program uses maze-specific productions to build its chunks.

```
(p collect-old-move 0      ; 2 moves shown, 1 outdated
    (move ^direction ⟨way⟩)
    {(move ^direction ⟨⟩ ⟨way⟩) ⟨older⟩}
    →
    (remove ⟨older⟩)
)
```

Listing 3. A priority 0, controlled garbage collection production.

Learned productions trigger on the present location of the PROGRAM. Only when the HUMAN blocks the escape route will these productions fail to trigger in a learned maze. At other times they pre-empt all other matching and actions in the production system. These productions are of course not present for a novel maze.

Listing 4 shows learning production '*learn-pass-up*', followed by the learned escape production '*auto-24-1-up*'.

Maze learning proceeds after a successful escape by performing a depth-first search from the EXIT along paths traversed by the PROGRAM. A *learn* memory element directs the search similarly to the inspect elements for initial maze exploration from Listing 1. The left-hand side of 'learn-pass-up' joins a learn and visited record to build a link from the visited element's location to a location already examined in the learning search. For this production, the original escape route included an 'up' move from the visited location to an adjoining location. Join tests match the ^*x* and ^*y* fields of the joined memory elements. The '^*visits* < *10000*' test prunes locations that are part of dead-end paths. Dead-end detection code marks visited records with a '^visits' value of 10000 during the original maze search.

The '*write*' actions on the right-hand side of 'learn-pass-up' generate production text such as that of 'auto-24-1-up' in Listing 4. 'Learn-pass-up' builds the location into this learned automatic production, making it extremely specific. At priority 127, its matching pre-empts all other matching and, when matching succeeds, any other queued processing remains queued while the right-hand side of 'auto-24-1-up' executes. When 'auto-24-1-up' moves the PROGRAM to an adjacent location that triggers another priority 127 learned production, all lower priority processing continues to wait. 'Auto-24-1-up' shares its initial '^*up-sense*' test with all other '*auto-X-Y-up*' learned productions. In addition, this production shares the '^up-sense' <> '*human ^x 24*' test sequence with all other 'auto-24-Y-up' productions. Recent work on chunking in SOAR has concentrated on trading generality for matching speed by generating efficient *unique-attribute chunks* instead of generalized *multi-attribute chunks* that create large join cross-products.[24] PRIOPS automatic productions take this approach to an extreme, trading generality for both speed and *speed predictability* by compiling $O(1)$ *unique-event* chunks. The next section demonstrates performance gains achieved by learning automatic reactions.

```
(p learn-pass-up -2; translate declarative memory into auto production
    {(learn ^status learning ^direction up
        ^fromx <endx> ^fromy <endy>) <passed>}
    {(visited ^visits < 10000 ^x <endx> ^y <endy>) <memory>}
    ; spot was visited
    →
    ; first write the learned production
    (write learnfile ''(p auto-'' <endx> ''-'' <endy> ''-up 127\n'')
    (write learnfile ''{(sensors ^up-sense <> human ^x''
        <endx> ''^y'' <endy>'') <sensing>}\n'')
    (write learnfile ''{(lastmove <oldmove>}\n'')
    (write learnfile ''->\n'')
    (write learnfile ''(remove <sensing>)\n'')
    (write learnfile ''(modify <oldmove> ^direction up)\n'')
    (write learnfile ''(call move up)\n)\n\n'')
    ; learned production written, now make this the new dest.
    (remove <memory>); not needed any longer
    (modify <passed> ^status done)
    (bind <up> (compute <endy> - 1))
    (bind <down> (compute <endy> + 1))
    (bind <left> (compute <endx> - 1))
    (bind <right> (compute <endx> + 1))
    (make learn ^status learning ^fromx <endx> ^fromy <up>
        ^direction down)
    (make learn ^status learning ^fromx <endx> ^fromy <down>
        ^direction up)
    (make learn ^status learning ^fromx <left> ^fromy <endy>
        ^direction right)
    (make learn ^status learning ^fromx <right> ^fromy <endy>
        ^direction left)
)
(p auto-24-1-up 127
    {(sensors ^up-sense <> human ^x 24 ^y 1) <sensing>}
    {(lastmove) <oldmove>}
    →
    (remove <sensing>)
    (modify <oldmove> ^direction up)
    (call move up)
)
```

Listing 4. Maze escape learning and a learned escape automatic production.

## 4.6. Maze Statistics

We ran the PRIOPS maze program on an AT&T PC-6300, which contains an 8 MHz 8086 processor and an 8087 math coprocessor. PRIOPS was compiled using Microsoft® C 5.1 with the "/Oti/Gs /AL /FPi" compile switches for optimization, memory management, and floating-point library selection; the maze application itself uses no floating point processing. The current PRIOPS compiler generates intermediate code for both Rete matching and right-hand side execution. A planned modification to PRIOPS will support generation of C source code for compilation to native run-time code. PRIOPS comprises about 12,000 lines of C code.

An additional 800 lines of C code support the maze environment, and the maze's PROGRAM itself is coded in 940 lines of PRIOPS productions. With reference to Fig. 3, there are 2 initialization, 9 garbage collection, 2 declarative memory maintenance, 31 controlled maze search, 1 controlled move, and 14 learning productions. There are 24 HUMAN avoidance, 5 EXIT approach, and 1 automatic move productions. Learning acquires 116 automatic productions of the type in Listing 4 for the maze of Fig. 2.

With no interference from the HUMAN, the PROGRAM takes 909 seconds and 566 moves (1.6 seconds/move) to discover a 104-step path to the EXIT for the maze of Fig. 2. Post-exit learning uses an additional 172 seconds.

Learning automatic behavior improves performance dramatically. Automatic escape productions reach the EXIT in 34 seconds and 104 moves (0.33 seconds/move). Then the PROGRAM sits at the EXIT for 21 seconds running matching for deferred production tests. Listings 1 and 4 help illustrate the source of this delay. Note that the two controlled productions of Listing 1 (and many other controlled productions as well) trigger on sensors elements. Now examine 'auto-24-1-up' in Listing 4; it, too, matches sensors elements. During learned-production escape from the maze, priority 127 matching of productions such as 'auto-24-1-up' defers any controlled matching required for sensors elements. Only when the PROGRAM reaches the EXIT, and no automatic productions are firing pre-emptively, can deferred controlled matching execute. This deferred matching for productions such as 'newly-arrived' causes the 21-second delay. Optimal coding of controlled productions would eliminate this delay, but the point here is to illustrate the effect of priority-based matching deferral in PRIOPS.

If we change the priority of learned productions like 'auto-24-1-up' to 0 , thereby placing them into the CP, the escape statistics change. Now learned escape, acting in the CP, takes 64 seconds and 104 moves (0.62 seconds per move), and 2 seconds for termination. There is no deferred matching, since all controlled matching completes before CP conflict resolution. It is also noteworthy that the total time for automatic escape is 11 seconds less than the total time for controlled escape. How does automatic matching achieve this speedup? By combining assertions and retractions of working memory elements where possible. Since automatic matching allows only one memory element-to-condition element match per distinct condition element, only the most recent memory element assertion or retraction is queued at each automatic matching step. Suppose memory element $A$ has matched condition element $X$, then a more recently asserted memory element $B$ also matches $X$. The match scheduling algorithm will abort the match of $A$ in joins of $X$. Condition element $X$ can only match the single most recently asserted memory element that satisfies its tests, in this example element $B$. Only $B$ participates in subsequent joins. The AP insistence on bounded resources forces it to reuse memory, thus avoiding some search as well as garbage collection. Controlled matching cannot use this enhancement, since multiple memory elements may match a single condition element at a given time. Therefore the

PRIOPS AP provides not only $O(1)$ matching with pre-emptive priorities, but also provides opportunities for additional speed enhancements beyond the capabilities of standard Rete matching.

## 5. CONCLUSIONS

Although we have tested PRIOPS using only simple experimental problems to date, we feel confident that it will scale to meet the needs of genuine knowledge-based embedded applications. The synthesis of $O(1)$ pre-emptive match processing and the production system notation provides the ability to specify important environmental conditions and timely reactions at a more appropriate level of abstraction for knowledge-based problems than is provided by traditional embedded software techniques. The fact that humans use a comparable two-tiered approach to timely interaction with physical environments indicates that the PRIOPS fundamental approach is correct. Research in learning, both in human automatic process acquisition and production system learning mechanisms such as chunking, offers promise of methods for machine construction of appropriate automatic productions.

Future work on PRIOPS will include research on dynamic learning. The maze learning discussed here relies on hand coding of application-specific, *ad hoc* learning productions. Human automatic behavior acquisition relies almost entirely on practice. Learning should involve incremental refinement of controlled processing into automatic productions. Other planned work includes construction of tools for analysis of automatic partition data flow and more complete examination of activities belonging to the controlled-automatic interface.

## REFERENCES

1. N. Wirth, "Toward a discipline of real-time programming", *Commun. ACM* **20**, 8 (1977) 577–583.
2. I. Jacobson, "Language support for changeable large real time systems", *OOPSLA '86 Conf. Proc.*, Ed. N. Meyrowitz, ACM, 1986, pp. 377–384.
3. T. J. Laffey, P. A. Cox, J. L. Schmidt, S. M. Kao and J. Y. Read, "Real-time knowledge-based systems", *AI Magazine* **9**, 1 (Spring, 1988) 27–45.
4. T. A. Cooper and N. Wogrin, *Rule-based Programming with OPS5*, Morgan Kaufmann, 1988.
5. C. L. Forgy, *OPS5 User's Manual*, Memo CMU-CS-81-135, Carnegie-Mellon University, July, 1981.
6. C. L. Forgy, "On the Efficient Implementation of Production Systems", Doctoral thesis, Department of Computer Science, Carnegie-Mellon University, January, 1979.
7. C. L. Forgy, "Rete: A fast algorithm for the many pattern/many object pattern match problem", *Artif. Intell.* **19** (1982) 17–37.
8. D. E. Parson and G. D. Blank, "Constant-time pattern matching for real-time production systems", *Proc. Applications of Artificial Intelligence VII*, Vol. 1095, Part 2, Ed. M. Trivedi, Society of Photo-Optical Instrumentation Engineers, 1989, pp. 971–982.
9. D. E. Parson and G. D. Blank, "Automatic versus controlled processing: An architecture for real-time production systems", to appear in *Int. J. Expert Syst.: Research and Applications* **2**, 3/4 (1989) 397–422.

10. W. Schneider and A. D. Fisk, ''Attention theory and mechanisms for skilled performance'', in *Memory and Control of Action*, Ed. R. A. Magill, North-Holland, 1983, pp. 119–143.
11. W. Schneider and R. M. Shiffrin, ''Controlled and automatic human information processing: I. Detection, search, and attention'', *Psychol. Rev.* **84**, 1 (1977) 1–66.
12. R. M. Shiffrin and W. Schneider, ''Controlled and automatic human information processing: II. Perceptual learning, automatic attending, and a general theory'', *Psychol. Rev.* **84**, 2 (1977) 127–190.
13. G. Agha, ''Global synchrony and asynchrony'', Section 2.2, *Actors–A Model of Concurrent Computation in Distributed Systems*, MIT Press, 1986, pp. 9–11.
14. A. Gupta, *Parallelism in Production Systems*, Morgan Kaufmann, 1987.
15. M. Tambe, D. Kalp, A. Gupta, C. Forgy, B. Milnes and A. Newell, ''SOAR/PSM-E: Investigating match parallelism in a learning production system'', *ACM SIGPLAN Notices* **23**, 9 (1988) 146–160.
16. V. Haley, ''Real-time for Rete'', *Proc. ROBEXS '87: The Third Annual Workshop on Robotics and Expert Systems*, Research Triangle Park, NC; Instrument Society of America, 1987.
17. H. J. Levesque and R. J. Brachman, ''A fundamental tradeoff in knowledge representation and reasoning (revised version)'', in *Readings in Knowledge Representation*, Ed. R. J. Brachman and H. J. Levesque, Morgan Kaufmann, 1985, pp. 42–70.
18. R. P. Gabriel, ''Memory management in LISP'', *AI Expert* **2**, 2 (February, 1987) 32–38.
19. H. Lieberman and C. Hewitt, ''A real-time garbage collector based on the lifetimes of objects'', *Commun. ACM* **26**, 6 (1983) 419–429.
20. D. Ungar and F. Jackson, ''Tenuring policies for generation-based storage reclamation'', *OOPSLA '88 Conf. Proc.*, Ed. N. Meyrowitz, ACM, 1988, pp. 1–17.
21. J. E. Laird, P. S. Rosenbloom and A. Newell, ''Chunking in SOAR: The anatomy of a general learning mechanism'', Memo CMU-CS-85-154, Carnegie-Mellon University, September, 1985.
22. J. E. Laird and A. Newell, ''A universal weak method'', Memo CMU-CS-83-141, Carnegie-Mellon University, June, 1983.
23. J. E. Laird, A. Newell and P. S. Rosenbloom, ''Soar: An architecture for general intelligence'', Report No. STAN-CS-86-1140, Stanford University, December, 1986.
24. M. Tambe and P. Rosenbloom, ''Eliminating expensive chunks by restricting expressiveness'', *Proc. Eleventh Int. Joint Conf. Artificial Intelligence*, Vol. 1, August 1989, pp. 731–737.

**Dale E. Parson** is a Ph.D. candidate in computer science at Lehigh University, and a software engineer with AT&T Bell Laboratories. His research interests include embedded processing, learning, and industrial application of real-time inference. His current work involves the design and implementation of design capture software for a computer-aided VLSI design system. He received the M.S. degree in computer science from Lehigh University in 1986.

**Glenn David Blank** is an Assistant Professor in the Computer Science and Electrical Engineering Department at Lehigh University. His research interests include intelligent control, knowledge-based systems, cogitive science, and natural language processing. A theme of his work is to achieve real-time behavior in intelligent systems by exploiting constraints found in human cognitive processing. He received the Ph.D. in cognitive science from the University of Wisconsin, Madison, in 1984. He is a member of AAAI, ACL, IEEE, and ACM.